MW00815272

Visual Antietam Vol. 2: Ezra Carman's Antietam Through Maps and Pictures: The West Woods To Bloody Lane

Ezra A. Carman

Edited and Illustrated by

Brad Butkovich

Copyright © 2019 Historic Imagination LLC

www.historicimagination.com

All rights reserved.

ISBN-13: 978-1-7325976-1-7

Dedication

This book is dedicated to my mother. A kind and loving mother and grandmother, she has always been there for myself, my siblings, her grandchildren, and great-grandchildren. She selflessly sacrificed everything to raise the four of us. Thank you Mom, for everything.

CONTENTS

Introduction

Ezra A. Carman is regarded as the father of Antietam historiography. Colonel of the 13th New Jersey Infantry during the battle, he devoted a large portion of his later life to documenting the battle and preserving the battlefield. He "served as a trustee on the Antietam National Cemetery Association Board from 1866 to 1877 and as an 'historical expert' and member of the War Department's Antietam Board for Antietam National Battlefield Site from 1895 to 1897." He spent the better part of this period of his life writing a comprehensive manuscript detailing the Maryland Campaign, to include the battles at South Mountain before the battle, and the fight at Shepherdstown afterwards. He also spent a significant amount of effort to build an accurate order of battle, along with the strength of the armies engaged. The result was a detailed and meticulously researched account of the actions in Maryland and Virginia during that fateful September 1862. Adding to his work, he created a series of maps showing the movement and flow of the battle over the course of the day. He even published a revision several years after publication based upon the feedback and critique from fellow veterans. His work has served as the foundation for much of the following history of the battle. Though written more than a century ago, it holds up to modern scrutiny quite well. As historian Thomas G. Clemens wrote, "while a few inconsistencies and analytical judgments can be questioned, the remarkable point is how often Carman got it right."

I first became acquainted with the manuscript when it was included in the 1999 release of the computer game *Sid Meier's Antietam!*. I was fascinated by the detail presented in the document, but soon set it aside as I read other accounts, most notably John M. Priest's *Antietam: The Soldier's Battle* and Stephen W. Sears' *Landscape Turned Red: The Battle of Antietam*. However, it wasn't until farther along in the digital age, when I discovered and downloaded the Carman/Cope maps in high resolution from the Library of Congress, that I was able to fully appreciate Carman's work.

My Civil War interests have always centered on maps and visual context. My website www.civilwarvirtualtours.com details several battles with maps, videos, and photos. For my previous battle studies on Pickett's Mill and Allatoona Pass I created all the maps myself. After a discussion with friends, I decided that instead of researching and writing my own text, I would use Carman's manuscript instead. In my opinion, it is still the most detailed and readable study of the battle currently available. Thus was the genesis for this three volume set.

The *Visual Antietam* series is intended for both readers who visit the battlefield, and those, perhaps overseas, who will never have the chance to see it. On every opposite page of the Carman text is an image to help the reader visualize the battlefield. The maps detail the movement of the men and units far more often than most other works. There are pictures of the landscape, both period and modern, to help the reader understand the terrain and "lay of the land." And finally, where appropriate are pictures, not just of the generals, but also of the common soldiers and line officers that fought on the battlefield that day. Given the graphics heavy nature of the work, a single volume would have been too large. The series is divided into three volumes. Those wishing to visit the battlefield with the books can do so with individual volumes in a convenient carry size.

This series is not envisioned to be a detailed, heavily annotated study of the campaign or battle. The full, proper title of Carman's manuscript is *The Maryland Campaign of September 1862*. However, since I am focusing on only the battle itself, I have altered the title. Campaign chapters and those that do not relate directly to the battle have been omitted. There are few footnotes in the text. My purpose was to bring his book, and more specifically the battle, to life with an emphasis on visual context. For those wishing to read comprehensive versions of the Carman manuscript, digging into his source material and methods, I highly recommend Thomas Clemens' *The Maryland Campaign of September 1862. Volume II: Antietam* (and Volumes I and III of course) and Joseph Pierro's *The Maryland Campaign of September 1862: Ezra A. Carman's Definitive Study of the Union and Confederate Armies at Antietam*. Both are thoroughly researched and noted.

Very few editing changes were made to the manuscript. Some changes are for readability, some to bring the text up to modern standards. These include standardizing times by adding colons between the hour and minutes instead of periods, adding commas consistently to numbers between the thousands and hundreds, indenting large quotes, and changing book titles to italics. As stated, footnotes are minimal. I only used them to highlight important changes in the text, such as misspellings, as well as sections where Carman added large clippings from the *Official Records of the Rebellion*. Otherwise, Carman's idiosyncrasies have been left alone, such as using recrossed instead of re-crossed. Or Louisianians instead of Louisianans.

Volume 2

The Visual Antietam series is divided into three volumes. *Visual Antietam Vol. 1: Ezra Carman's Antietam Through Maps and Pictures: Dawn to Dunker Church* opens the battle on the evening of September 16th, and continues through the opening fighting in the infamous Cornfield and East Woods, ending with the Confederates ultimately being expelled from both. Volume 2 continues the narrative by focusing on the struggle for the West Woods and the Sunken Road. *Visual Antietam Vol. 3: Ezra Carman's Antietam Through Maps and Pictures: The Middle Bridge to Hill's Counterattack* brings an end to the trilogy by focusing on the fighting around the Middle Bridge, Burnside's Bridge, and Ambrose P. Hill's counterattack.

Most of the pictures in this work were taken as close as possible to the hour they occurred in 1862, even taking modern daylight savings time into account. For Volume 2, this is not as much of an issue, as much of the fighting took place in late morning and early afternoon, providing plenty of good lighting.

I hope the reader will enjoy the numerous maps and photos throughout the book, and that it will pull the descriptive text together to provide a better understanding of the battle fought in the woods and fields along the Hagerstown Turnpike.

Carman's manuscript spans the entire Maryland Campaign. The Battle of Antietam falls in the middle. This is reflected in the unusual chapter numbering in this book. It contains chapters 17-19 of his larger work.

Acknowledgments

Several people contributed to the making of this volume, and I wish to extend my heartfelt thanks and acknowledgement for their efforts.

I have known David Powell for a number of years now through our shared interest in the Battle of Chickamauga and all things in the Western Theater. He has been giving tours of the battlefield for decades now, and I've been lucky to have been to many of them. He has also authored what I think is the definitive study on Chickamauga, both in his multi-volume study and his map book. I am honored that he agreed to write the Foreword for this second volume of my *Visual Antietam* series.

Scott Felsen has been tramping around Civil War battlefields with me for a couple of years now. His enthusiasm and great stories make for excellent company! An experienced professional photographer and videographer, he agreed to travel with me to Antietam and gave me excellent tips on snapping the pictures for this trilogy, plus the use of far better cameras than I own. Several of the images are credited to him.

I have only recently made the acquaintance of Stephen Recker, author of *Rare Images of Antietam: And the Photographers Who Took Them*. Yet he has allowed me to use one of the earliest images of the Sunken Road from his collection for this book, and has agreed to write the Foreword for Volume 3. I very much look forward to working more with him in the future.

I also wish to again thank my proofreaders Andy Papen, Patrick McCormick, and Scott Felsen for reading over the manuscript and pointing out all those little details and layout errors that escape the eye when you've stared at the same words for months at a time. Their help was invaluable.

Foreword

If there is one overriding request that any Civil War author receives about his published work, that request has to be: "More maps, please." No matter how aptly a written description we provide, nothing explains things better than a well-crafted map. Certainly historians who write tactical or operational monographs hear this request most often of all, since we attempt via text to render explicable what are often highly-confusing and complex troop maneuvers. To further complicate matters, the words of the veterans we rely on to help tell those tales are also often confusing or even contradictory. It should be no surprise, then, that works of tactical military writing lean heavily on maps of all sorts.

I am certainly no different. Nothing piques my interest like the phrase "troop movement map." It promises me a new way to understand a battle, fight, or skirmish. However, talented writers are not also (usually, anyway) talented cartographers. By necessity, most authors need collaborators in their mapmaking endeavors. This need for collaboration, along with its associated costs, is why most histories never have as many maps as authors or readers desire. Fortunately, increasing digitalization has given us an increase in maps for some works, but there is still a long way to go. When I do encounter a project that gives equal weight to both the text and graphics, I welcome it.

Both Brad and I share one additional interest, which only enhances our inner cartophile: The hobby of wargaming. Wargaming, whether done with cardboard counters on paper game-boards or with miniature figures on 3-D terrain models, requires accurate maps. And given the nature of gaming, when played they are dynamic, not static. The various unit pieces move across the map via regulated time intervals. As the game progresses, turn-by-turn, the players are presented with an animated storyboard of sorts, charting the course of the unfolding action in the particular scenario being recreated. Players become accustomed to thinking of battles in terms of both maps and movement, representing engagements in a very visual medium.

Of course, games diverge from history because the players make different choices and decisions than did their historical counterparts. Most games are not meant to recreate history absolutely. But that doesn't mean that an especially historically minded player can't simply use the medium of the game to recreate the actual history to the best of his ability. I have done so myself, tracking historical troop movements in fifteen- or thirty-minute intervals, with the aim of better understanding the flow of an action. Moreover, as an author, I discovered that wargames also helped me in another way: to think of a situation globally, and to consider the actions of all the forces on a battlefield, whether they were active or not at any given moment in time.

It is also only natural, when describing a specific action or battle, to focus on the action. That is, after all, where the drama is. This is true for the men involved, as well: the more active a unit in combat, the more likely to find multiple primary sources describing the event in question. Nothing sparks a spate of memoirs like a highly contested event, as any perusal of primary sources like the *National Tribune* or the *Confederate Veteran* magazine will quickly demonstrate.

But sometimes the unit that does not become involved is equally vital to understanding an engagement. This is where good maps excel. Maps force the viewer to think of all the forces on a field of battle, not just those that became caught up in the fighting. I learned this lesson when I undertook my own mapping project, *The Maps of Chickamauga*, published in 2009. Mapping that field forced me to devote equal consideration to those troops who did not move or were relegated to a tactical backwater. Sometimes those forces were deliberately in reserve, or simply assigned to what turned out to be a quiet sector of the line. Or, more dramatically, sometimes commands just failed to act on their orders.

Two quick examples drawn from the war's most famous battle might help explain. On July 1, a great many accounts survive from the two divisions - those of Generals Heth and Pender - of Confederate Lieutenant General A. P. Hill's Corps, which detail their heavy combat of that Wednesday afternoon in Pennsylvania. Thanks to the exhaustive work of many historians in unearthing those accounts, any student of July 1st can track individual regiments – sometimes even companies – across the field. But we know far less about what Hill's last division under Richard Anderson did that day, for in fact it did very little beyond march onto the field and go into reserve that afternoon as directed by General Lee. It is one thing to read about Lee's decision not to commit Anderson's powerful command to battle on July 1, just as the Union line fell back to Cemetery Hill. It is another to see that massive block of troops on Herr Ridge, inactive, while the fight raged, in map after map of the battle. Graphically,

Anderson's presence, hovering over the unfolding action, repeatedly focuses reader attention on their presence; that enhanced attention leads any student to want to know more.

Similarly, merely reading about Confederate General Ambrose Wright's solitary assault against Cemetery Ridge on the evening of July 2 at Gettysburg could leave the reader wondering what Wright's Georgians were attempting to accomplish. However, a map of that same event will inevitably draw any reader's eye to the brigades of Carnot Posey and William Mahone, next in line to the north; and immediately raise the question of why they did not advance alongside Wright's Georgians?

Which brings us to the current project. Ezra Carman, the Civil War officer and subsequent historian of the battle of Antietam whose narrative is presented within, was a talented historian. And like many historians, when it came to mapping the battle, he needed a collaborator. His partner in the venture was a professional of the first water: Lieutenant Colonel Emmor B. Cope, the U.S. Army Engineer tasked with surveying the battlefield. Cope meticulously surveyed the entire field, going so far as to identify the different types of fences and crops in the fields, to produce an unrivaled graphic portrayal of the terrain in question. Onto this canvas, Carman could then interpret the mountain of source material he gathered from participants to place unit after unit on the field in an organized timeline. Together, Carman's and Cope's fourteen maps trace the course of the fighting on America's "Bloodiest Day" from start to finish. They are an indispensable complement to Carman's massive, richly detailed manuscript (1,800 pages) on the battle.

The sheer size of both Carman's manuscript and the maps, however, make them difficult to use, especially simultaneously, and especially out on the field. Fortunately, Carman's opus has now been published in a couple of editions, making his text much more accessible. Especially useful is Thomas Clemens's three-volume annotation of Carman's work, extensively footnoted, which introduces more than a century of modern scholarship on Antietam and provides commentary on Carman's interpretations. The maps, however, are a different story. As originally published at 72x45 centimeters, or roughly 28x17 inches, each of the maps is very large. This size was deemed necessary to capture all the detail and nuance of each phase of the fight. However, using these maps on the field as-is makes for an awkward experience, requiring folding and re-folding as one moves around the terrain to re-center the map on the scene in question. Conversely, reducing their size to make them fit a less unwieldy format (even an oversized volume) renders those same details and nuances difficult to read.

Brad Butkovich's work circumvents these problems by creating thirty-two new original maps for Volume 2 alone, more than double the number of Carman-Cope maps, to track the battle's progression. Beginning with the Carman-Cope maps as a base, Butkovich then pulled additional information from a host of sources to produce a modern cartographic interpretation of the engagement. By cropping and inserting these new maps into Carman's text at the appropriate locations, Butkovich thereby preserved the clarity of the original cartography and the benefits of new scholarship while marrying each map segment to Carman's detailed description of the action, all at an eminently readable and useful size. The result is a smoothly unfolding visual and narrative flow, presented page-by-page. As a result, despite a surfeit of other writing on Antietam – including other map studies – This work makes a very real contribution to the scholarship of the battle.

David Powell
Author of *The Maps of Chickamauga*

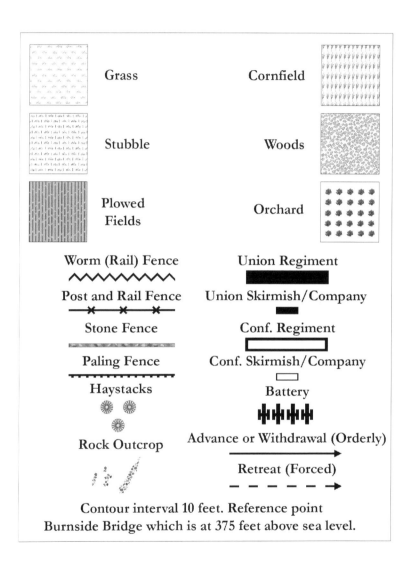

Grass

Cornfield

Stubble

Woods

Plowed Fields

Orchard

Worm (Rail) Fence

Union Regiment

Post and Rail Fence

Union Skirmish/Company

Stone Fence

Conf. Regiment

Paling Fence

Conf. Skirmish/Company

Haystacks

Battery

Rock Outcrop

Advance or Withdrawal (Orderly)

Retreat (Forced)

Contour interval 10 feet. Reference point
Burnside Bridge which is at 375 feet above sea level.

Chapter 17

The West Woods and the Dunker Church (9 a.m. to 11 a.m.)

The battle begun at Daybreak had been engaged with great determination and monstrous losses. It was nearing 9 o'clock and, with the advance and success of the Twelfth Corps and the retreat of the Confederates into the West Woods and in the direction of Sharpsburg, there was a grateful lull in the sanguinary contest, broken only by an occasional musket shot and then by the guns of Monroe's Battery, which opened fire from the plateau opposite the Dunker[1] Church, which fire was replied to by a battery of S. D. Lee's, in open ground south of the woods and west of the Hagerstown road.

The struggle that followed around the Dunker Church and in the West Woods was participated in by Greene's Division and three regiments—125th Pennsylvania, 2nd Massachusetts, 13th New Jersey—of Williams' Division, Twelfth Corps and Sedgwick's Division, Second Corps, on the one side; on the other side by Early's Brigade, the remnant of Jackson's Division; George T. Anderson's Brigade of D. R. Jones' Division; three brigades—Kershaw, Semmes, and Barksdale—of McLaws' Division, and

---

[1] Carman uses the alternate spelling Dunkard throughout the manuscript instead of Dunker. Dunkard now reflects a more conservative sect split from the church post-war. I have kept the more accurate lineage spelling of Dunker.

1

Walker's Division of two brigades. The Union force numbered about 7,500 men; the Confederate force about 8,200. This does not include the artillery on either side.

The Second Corps was a veteran organization and had seen much hard service. Palfrey says it "contained some poor but many excellent soldiers. The hard fate which its Second Division met in this battle (Antietam) may be an excuse for stating that up to May 10, 1864, the corps never lost a gun nor a color, and that it was then and had long been the only corps in the army which could make that proud claim." Walker says the corps represented in an unparalleled degree the history of the war in the East.

> That corps which in fair fight with Lee's great army, had captured forty-four Confederate flags ere it lost a color of its own, that corps which, under the command of Sumner, Couch, Warren, Hancock, and Humphreys—illustrious roll!—left nearly 40,000 men killed and wounded upon the battle-fields of Virginia, Maryland, and Pennsylvania; that corps among whose generals of division were numbered Sedgwick, Richardson, Howard, French, Barlow, Birney, Miles, Mott, Gibbon, Webb, and Alexander Hays; the corps which crossed the Chickahominy to the rescue of the beaten left at Fair Oaks; which made the great assault at Marye's Heights; on which fell the fury of Longstreet's charge at Gettysburg; which was the rear guard, October 14th, at Auburn and Bristoe; which stormed the salient at Spotsylvania, and at Farmville fought the last infantry battle of the war against the Army of Northern Virginia.

On the evening of September 16th, when McClellan directed Sumner to send the Twelfth Corps across the Antietam that night, Sumner correctly requested that the Second Corps should go, also, but McClellan would not consent; he gave orders to hold the corps in readiness to march an hour before daybreak, to support Hooker, but not to move until further orders. In anticipation of going that night Sumner had already sent some of his batteries across the Antietam. Sumner's men had all breakfasted before daybreak, filled their canteens and rolled their blankets; they were ready to march but no orders came, and a little after 6 o'clock Sumner, with his son, Captain S. S. Sumner, of his staff, went to headquarters, but a few yards distant, for orders and personal instructions. McClellan had not yet awakened from sleep and none of his staff seemed disposed to disturb him, though the roar of the battle was sounding in their ears. Sumner waited, walking to and fro on the veranda of the Pry house, or sitting on the steps, the roar of battle increasing and the detonation of the heavy guns shaking the panes and shivering the sash of the windows, which let into McClellan's room the full sunlight, but McClellan did not make his appearance.

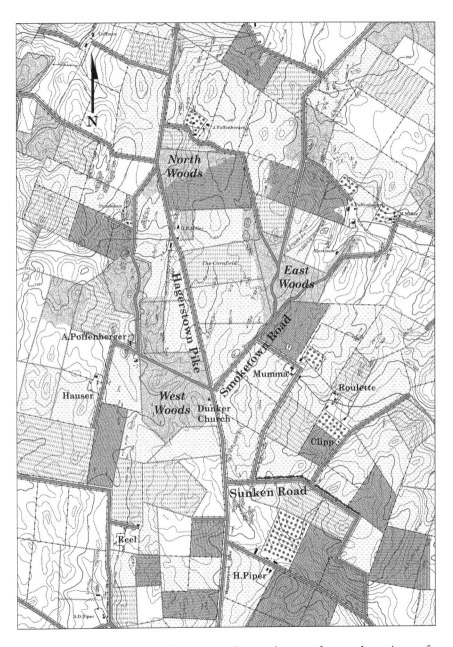

Map of important terrain features on the northern and central portions of the battlefield.

Members of the staff were watching Hooker's struggle, which was in full view, yet McClellan could not be seen and one of his staff members remarked that Hooker's fight was only a rearguard affair, as "Uncle Bobby Lee" was too much of a soldier to fight in that position with a river at his back. And the opinion was expressed to McClellan, also, that morning, whether he shared it or not we do not know.

Finally, at 7:20 a.m., after waiting more than an hour, Sumner received his orders to cross the Antietam with two divisions, Richardson to follow when relieved by Morell's' Division of the Fifth Corps. He put Sedgwick in motion immediately, French following, went down the hill in rear of McClellan's headquarters and crossed the Antietam at Pry's Ford, where Doubleday had crossed the evening before, and when across ascended a gentle slope for about a quarter of a mile, halted and formed his lines. He then moved in three parallel lines, brigade front, nearly due west, came to the field south of the East Woods, flanked to the right and, entering the woods, marched northward, then faced to the left, thus forming a column of three deployed brigades, Gorman's in front, next Dana's, then Howard's The column was now facing west, parallel to the Hagerstown road, 550 yards distant, and separated from it by the "Bloody Cornfield" over which the tide of battle had ebbed and flowed since daybreak, and, notwithstanding the struggle in it, Palfrey says "the corn was very high and very strong." There was a short halt while the east fence of the cornfield was being thrown down, and the men had time to see that "the ground beneath those great, fair Maryland oaks was strewn with the killed and wounded of the earlier battle." It was 9 o'clock when Sumner formed Sedgwick's Division for the attack in the East Woods; it was at the same time that the 125th Pennsylvania, of the Twelfth Corps, crossed the Hagerstown road and entered the West Woods at the Dunker Church.

Upon hearing of Sumner's approach General Williams, commanding Twelfth Corps, had sent a staff officer to apprise him of his position and the situation of affairs, and, when he came into the woods, Williams rode up from the left, from near Mumma's, gave him the position and condition of his men, and made some precautionary suggestions as to the line of advance and care of his flanks, which were not well received. Sumner had already been informed by Ricketts that Hooker's corps had been dispersed and could not rally 300 men, and he seems to have come to the conclusion that the Twelfth Corps was in not much better condition.

Nor did he stop to satisfy himself on that point or to make a reconnaissance,

> or for anything more than a quick study of the field over which the Twelfth Corps had attacked. The enemy had been pushed back and a counter-attack might be expected at any moment. As the early success

4

Brigadier General Alpheus S. Williams
Library of Congress

which had attended Union arms on that part of the field had just been gained by the Twelfth Corps, it was obvious that this success should be followed up before the enemy could recover from its effects and resume the offensive. His resolution had to be taken, and was taken, on the instant. The emergency of the occasion would not permit him to await the arrival of French's Division, which he expected to appear at any moment, for he had given the most positive orders to that officer to put and keep the head of his column abreast the division of Sedgwick, more than this he had sent several staff officers to reiterate the orders and had reasonable grounds for the belief that they had been obeyed.

On the contrary Walker intimates that Sumner neglected to give such orders to French: "so proud was he of his gallant troops, so full of fight, so occupied with the thought of engaging the enemy, that he did not even see to it that French was brought up within supporting distance, but allowed him, for want of proper direction, to diverge widely to the left." Be it as it may, Sumner did not wait. He felt so strong in these three brigades of Sedgwick's Division that he could not imagine anything stopping them, and determined to crush the Confederate left with one terrific blow, then swing his column around with a grand, bold half-wheel to the left, and sweep down the Confederate line, driving it before him through Sharpsburg, and heaping it up in disaster before Burnside, who, crossing the lower bridge, will complete the victory.

While Sumner is forming his column of attack and removing the fences, we note the condition of affairs around the church, where first the contest is to be waged, and the preparations being made by the Confederates to regain the ground lost by them, or at least to hold the Dunker Church and West Woods.

We left Monroe's Rhode Island battery in position on the plateau opposite the Dunker Church. Monroe says:

> A battery of the enemy here opened upon me, but no attention was paid to it, and the fire was perfectly ineffective; but the battery with one section opened upon a body of the enemy (Colquitt's men), who were seen retreating at the left of their front, and about 125 yards distant, throwing them into great confusion. The other four guns opened with canister and case upon a large force advancing through the woods in front, which were very open, and, with the assistance of the other section, which had accomplished its object by a few shots, and the First New Hampshire Battery, checked the enemy, and he retired out of sight. While engaged in forcing back the enemy in the wood, a body of sharpshooters had, unobserved, crept along under a

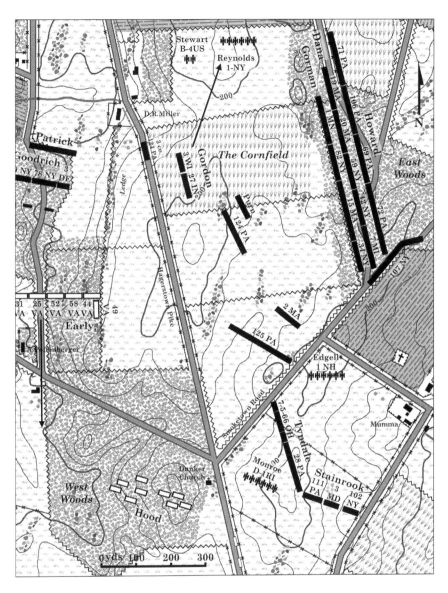

Situation after the Twelfth Corps had cleared the Cornfield and East Woods of Confederates. Sedgwick's division forms in the East Woods for the attack toward the West Woods. Portions of Gordon's brigade move out of the way, but other Twelfth Corps units do not. Greene's division holds the reverse slope of the plateau fronting the West Woods. Hood's battle weary division barely holds the East Woods, while Early's Brigade moves south to confront the growing danger posed by Greene and the 125th Pennsylvania.

little ridge that ran diagonally to the front of the Rhode Island battery and opened a most (unnerving?) fire upon it, killing and disabling many horses and men. As quick as possible, a section was directed to open upon them with canister, which, though it caused them no injury, they lying down under the ridge, kept them almost silent, they firing but an occasional shot, but without effect. While this section was keeping the sharpshooters silent, the other four guns, with the guns of Lieutenant Edgell, opened upon the battery that was still firing, and soon silenced it. I then ordered my battery to limber to the rear. The sharpshooters took advantage of the opportunity thus afforded, and opened most briskly, severely wounding a number of men and killing and disabling a large number of horses.

Perceiving the dangerous situation he was in and the great difficulty he would have in withdrawing his guns under this fire, Monroe sent a request to Greene to keep the sharpshooters down, so that he could get the guns away, but the answer came that he could not, for want of ammunition. The cannoneers were rapidly leaving their posts on account of wounds, and the drivers were constantly employed in relieving disabled horses. When the order "Limber to the rear" was given, it was executed almost in the twinkling of any eye, but the enemy behind the ridge, in the road south of the church, protected by fence rails thrown up and depressions in the ground, had them at their mercy, and right well did they improve the opportunity by showing the temper of it. They rose up in an unbroken line and poured a storm of lead into them. Five guns were gotten off with few losses, but the one remaining was less fortunate. As the horses made the turn to bring the limber to the trail of the gun, they were quickly shot down. Before a disabled horse could be disengaged from the team another would fall. Monroe was now short-handed for men, and Lieutenant Fiske rode off for some, soon returning with 15 or 20 infantrymen, who ran the piece to the rear, amid the cheers of friend and foe. Four guns went back to near the corner of the East Woods. The right section went north to the cornfield and took position near the Hagerstown road and nearly opposite the Miller straw stacks, where it remained until its ammunition was exhausted, when it retired to the position from which it had advanced earlier in the day.

Meanwhile, Battery A, First Rhode Island, Captain John A. Tompkins[2], had come up. This excellent battery was attached to Sedgwick's Division and had crossed the Antietam by the upper bridge, on the evening of the 16th, and parked on the Hoffman farm. At 8 a.m. of the 17th, Tompkins was ordered to go to the front and report to Hooker. He passed M. Miller's

---

[2] Carman misspells his name as Thompkins throughout the text. I have used the correct spelling as confirmed in his report in the Official Records.

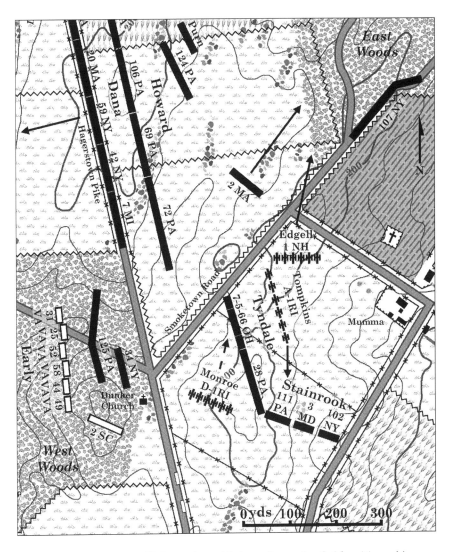

Monroe's and Edgell's batteries withdraw from the field as Tompkins arrives. At the same time, Sedgwick's division is advancing to the north, and Early is engaging the 125th Pennsylvania in the West Woods.

house, followed the road to and through the East Woods, and was ordered by Hooker to go into position on the plateau opposite the church. He made a circuit of the burning buildings at Mumma's, passing to their left, and went at a gallop down the lane beyond and came up as Monroe was retiring. He went into battery a little farther south from Monroe's position and more under cover from the fire of the sharpshooters, who had so annoyed Monroe, his right gun near where Monroe's left had been and the others on ground descending to the left, all pointing south or nearly so. As soon as the six guns came into position, Tompkins opened fire upon a battery directly in his front across the Hagerstown road, and south of the West Woods, and upon D. H. Hill's infantry in the Sunken Road, and, at the time, the 125th Pennsylvania and 34th New York were being driven out of the woods at the Dunker Church.

Very soon after the 125th Pennsylvania had assisted Monroe's Battery to cross the Smoketown road, and while lying down in the field, about 350 yards from the Hagerstown road, awaiting orders, Captain E. L. Witman of Crawford's staff rode up with Crawford's order to advance into the West Woods and hold them at all hazards. Why such an order was given to this one regiment, when the entire line was awaiting Sumner's preparations, is not known; it was directed by neither Sumner nor Williams, but it was instantly obeyed. The men sprang to their feet and went forward, double quick, driving before them a few Texans and Georgians, crossed the Hagerstown road at 9 o'clock and halted in the edge of the West Woods, just north of the Dunker Church. There was very little opposition to this advance, the Confederates, who were on the road in the immediate front, disappearing in the woods beyond the church, some of them to the south, below the church, where, as we have seen, they remained to the great annoyance of Monroe's Battery.

When Hood fell back to the Dunker Church it was with the intention of collecting and reforming every thing that had gone back and contest further Union advance, and to that end Jackson, Hood, and others made great efforts; with the exception of Hood's men but a few could be held. Colonel Wofford says: "After some time the enemy commenced advancing in full force. Seeing the hopelessness and folly of making a stand with our shattered brigade and a remnant from the other commands, the men being greatly exhausted and many of them out of ammunition, I determined to fall back to a fence in our rear, where we met the long looked for reinforcements, and at the same time received an order from General Hood to fall back farther to the rear to rest and collect our men." Hood's men were retreating from the woods as the 125th Pennsylvania entered them at the church.

When the 125th Pennsylvania had crossed the Hagerstown road Captain John McKeage was ordered to deploy his company as skirmishers and

Looking southwest from S. D. Lee's former position, and the area where Monroe's battery deployed. The Hagerstown Pike runs through the middle of the view, and the high ground behind is where Lee took his new position after falling back. *Miller's Photographic History.*

advance cautiously to a ridge in front, and company B was formed, facing south, about 20 yards north of the church, its left opposite the northwest corner of it. The regiment then advanced about 20 yards and halted. As soon as Colonel Higgins entered the woods he saw that he was without support in rear and on his right; he was aware that an enemy was on his right front, and gave his horse to one of his officers, with instructions to ride back to Crawford, inform him of the situation, and ask for support, as, without it, he would be unable to hold his position, and that the enemy would certainly flank him and cut him off, as he was far in advance of the corps. The regiment then advanced and halted on the crest of a ridge about 120 yards from the road, its left west of and about 20 yards to the right of the church, its right beyond a ravine, which, about 200 yards north of the church, crosses the Hagerstown road and runs west through the woods. The line was nearly parallel to the Hagerstown road. Captain McKeage, who had halted his skirmishers on the ridge, was now ordered to advance and see what was in front. With little or no opposition the skirmishers went to within 20 yards of the west edge of the West Woods, where fire was opened upon them by the 49th Virginia of Early's Brigade, from a ravine on the right, and Early, gaining the open ground in their front, advanced firing, the Pennsylvanians falling back, firing. While at the front they saw not only Early's men, but some troops—George T. Anderson's—advancing on their left from the direction of Sharpsburg, and from them, also, they received fire, which was returned.

Leaving the 125th Pennsylvania for a moment we return to Early, whom we left in the north part of the middle body of the West Woods, confronting Patrick and Goodrich, keeping his eye on the three companies of the 124th Pennsylvania, on the Hagerstown road, and anxious about the presence of Monroe's Battery, Greene's Division and the 125th Pennsylvania on his right rear. He considered his condition as extremely critical, but recognized the great importance of holding his ground; "for had the enemy gotten possession of this woods, the heights immediately in rear, which commanded the rear of the whole line, would have fallen into his hands." He determined to wait for the reinforcements promised by Jackson, hoping that they would arrive in time to meet the 125th Pennsylvania, before it entered the woods, and threw his right flank back quietly under cover of the woods, and parallel to the Hagerstown road, so as not to have his rear exposed in the event of being discovered, still keeping an anxious eye on Greene's Division, which he had seen disappear on the plateau opposite the church, and very soon saw the 125th Pennsylvania move into the woods at the church. He looked to the rear for reinforcements, but could not see them coming. He saw himself cut off from the main body of the army on the right and a force threatening his left. There was no time to be lost, and he immediately ordered his brigade to move by the right flank,

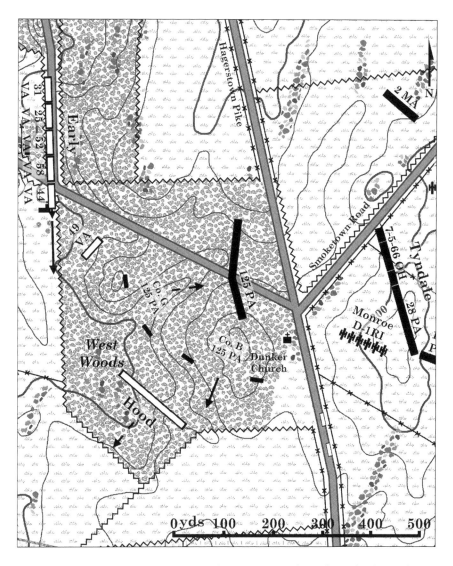

The 125th Pennsylvania arrives in the West Woods and sends skirmishers
to the western edge. They push the remnants of Hood's Division out of the
woods to the southwest, but are greeted by Early's Brigade to the west.
Early sends the 49th Virginia ahead, and its fire forces the Pennsylvania
skirmishers there to retire.

parallel to the Hagerstown road, and directed Colonel Grigsby, who commanded what was left of Jackson's Division, about 200 men, to move back in line, so as to present front to Patrick and Goodrich. Early moved back along the rear of the ridge, concealed from view, and in the belief that his presence was not suspected. Passing from behind the ridge he came in full view of the skirmishers of the 125th Pennsylvania, and made his presence known by directing the 49th Virginia, his leading regiment, to open fire upon them. They fell back and Early continued to move by the flank until his entire line was exposed. Just at this time he observed the promised reinforcements coming up, at the southern corner of the woods, and ordered his brigade to face to the front and open fire.

The reinforcements that Early saw coming up was Colonel George T. Anderson's Brigade of D. R. Jones Division closely followed by three brigades of McLaws' Division. Early in the morning Anderson was lying on Cemetery Hill in support of the Washington Artillery. He was ordered by General Lee to the left to support General Hood, and, without a guide or directions to find him, moved off, directing his course by the sound of the musketry, and succeeded in finding Hood, who pointed out the position he wished him to occupy. When found Hood's men were retreating from the West Woods and the position he ordered Anderson to take was the southwest face of the woods. When within 200 yards of the woods Anderson was fired upon by the skirmishers of the 125th Pennsylvania, upon which he ordered his brigade sharpshooters forward, the Pennsylvanians, struck at the same time by Early, fell back, and Anderson advanced to the fence, bounding the southwest face of the woods, which was torn down and piled for breastworks, behind which the men laid down. Just after Anderson reached the fence, Kershaw's Brigade marched up in his rear. So far we have brought Early and Anderson to this part of the field and while they are driving in the skirmishers of the 125th Pennsylvania, we accompany McLaws and Walker.

From his position on Cemetery Hill, General Lee had watched the severe struggle on his left and observed Burnside on his right. Early in the morning he had sent Walker's Division to guard the Antietam at Snavely's Ford, but perceiving that the weight of McClellan's attack was on the left, knowing Sumner was in motion to augment it, and fully convinced he had nothing to fear from Burnside, he concluded to throw Walker's and McLaws' divisions to meet it, yet, not sure of holding the ground around the Dunker Church, fearing in fact that he would lose it, before they could reach it, he determined to take up a second line, on the ridge nearer Sharpsburg, and walked from Cemetery Hill in that direction, at the same time ordering some batteries to the indicated position, behind which he proposed collecting his infantry, some of which was then being rallied, those who had been in action. In a field on the outskirts of the town, Lee

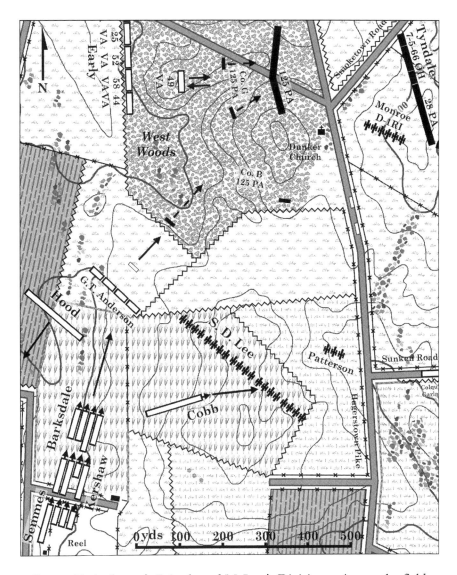

George T. Anderson's Brigade and McLaw's Division arrive on the field. Anderson sends sharpshooters ahead to clear the Pennsylvanian skirmishers from the wood's edge. McLaw's Division closes up behind Anderson, but Cobb's Brigade is mistakenly sent too far to the right.

met Captain Thomas H. Carter, who was retiring his battery from Rodes' position in the Sunken Road. Carter says: "He seemed to fear that the whole left wing, then hard pressed and losing ground, would be turned, and that the enemy would gain possession of the range of hills some three quarters of a mile to the left of Sharpsburg. He ordered me to this ground with all the artillery that could be collected, to prevent this movement. Having communicated with Major Pierson several batteries were gathered together on this part of the field. General Lee soon arrived there in person."

After giving some directions Lee was put on his horse and an orderly led it up the road toward the Dunker Church, soon meeting Colonel S. D. Lee, who, at the earnest solicitation of Hood, was on his way to Cemetery Hill to inform him of the critical state of affairs. Colonel Lee says:

> At the time Jackson and Hood were driven back, and were with difficulty holding the ground near the Dunker Church, Hood came up to my battalion of artillery, which had been engaged during the entire morning and was pretty well wrecked having lost 35 (over 75) men and 60 horses, and ordered me to turn my artillery over to the next officer in command and to go personally to find General R. E. Lee and tell him the condition of affairs, and to say to him that unless reinforcements were sent at once the day was lost. I protested against leaving my artillery in its wrecked condition. He insisted, however, and I went. I soon met General Lee on horseback with one orderly, moving at a walk towards that part of the field and about half way between Sharpsburg and the Dunker Church. I reported the condition of affairs on the left, and delivered General Hood's message. General Lee quietly said 'Don't be excited about it Colonel, go tell General Hood to hold his ground, reinforcements are now rapidly approaching between Sharpsburg and the ford; tell him that I am now coming to his support.' I said 'General, your presence will do good, but nothing but infantry can save the day on the left.' I started to return and had not gone over a hundred yards, when Lee called me and pointed to McLaws' Division, then in sight and approaching at a double-quick.

Some Confederate writers have severely criticized McLaws for not arriving on the field on the 16th, immediately following Jackson, and for not reinforcing Jackson on the left, earlier on the morning of the 17th, which, if done, they contend, would have defeated McClellan's army. The criticism is an unjust one. It must be remembered that, though not marching as many miles as Jackson, since the morning of the 10th, McLaws had been engaged in more arduous service and had done more fighting. He had been detained in Pleasant Valley until the morning of the 16th, and,

Colonel Stephen D. Lee
Library of Congress

when he crossed the Potomac that morning and marched to Halltown, was without provisions, and, as Jackson's men had already appropriated the stores captured at Harper's Ferry, he was obliged to hunt up provisions. His command was very much fatigued. A large number of his men had no rations, and those who had had had not had time or opportunity to cook them. All had been without sleep during the night previous, except while waiting for the wagon-trains to pass over the pontoon bridge at Harper's Ferry. His success in procuring provisions was very meager, he got but one issue only. After vain effort to get supplies at Charlestown, some three miles distant, he returned to his command at 3 p.m. of the 16th, marched from Halltown, followed the route taken by Jackson and Walker, and halted only when it was too dark to see the road, within two miles of Shepherdstown. When receiving urgent orders from Lee to hasten forward, he again took up the march at midnight, many of the regiments still without provisions. He crossed the Potomac before daylight, it was so dark he used torches, and, before sunrise of the 17th, the head of his column reached the vicinity of Lee's headquarters, near Sharpsburg.

At this early hour he did not hear the sound of a gun, nor were there any noticeable indications that a battle had been fought, nor that one was imminent. He rode into town looking for General Lee, but no one could give him any information. He rode back to halt his command and "look around" to find someone who could tell him where to go and met Longstreet and staff coming from the rear. Longstreet directed him to send R. H. Anderson's Division down the road to the hill beyond the town, where it would receive orders. Longstreet having informed him where he could find General Lee, in a small grove, he reported to him for orders. Lee was dressing for the day, and said, as McLaws dismounted from his horse, at the front of his tent, "Well general I am glad to see you, and have to thank you for what you have done, but we have I believe a hard day's work before us, and you must rest your men. Do not let them come quite this far as the shells of the enemy fall about here, and halt them about a quarter of a mile back in the road and I will send for you when I want you." When told that but a few moments before he had received an order from Jackson to go to the right, Lee replied: "Never mind that order but do as I told you and consider yourself as specially under my orders."

McLaws rode back and halted his division, hastened R. H. Anderson, who was in his rear, sent word along the lines for the men to rest, and not to stray as they might soon be needed, dismounted, turned his horse loose, and in a very few minutes was asleep in the tall grass, as were most of his men.

McLaws' Division was composed of the four brigades of Generals J. B. Kershaw, Howell Cobb (commanded by Lieutenant Colonel C. C. Sanders), Paul J. Semmes, and William Barksdale, and the batteries of Captains J .P.

Major General Lafayette McLaws
Library of Congress

W. Read, M. C. Macon, E. S. McCarthy, and H. H. Carlton. It was a veteran division, and a good one, and had seen much hard service. Kershaw had 936 officers and men, Cobb 398, Semmes 709, and Barksdale 891, an aggregate in the division of 2,934 officers and men, including the three batteries that became engaged. McLaws accounts for the small number carried into action by "the straggling of men wearied beyond endurance and of those without shoes." Notwithstanding that he lost over 1,100 men on the 17th, his absentees, who joined before the morning of the 18th, made his force nearly as large as it was on the morning of the 17th.

Somewhat more than an hour after McLaws had laid down and fallen asleep Major Walter H. Taylor of General Lee's staff awakened him, with the information that as he had not been able to find him, concealed by the tall grass, his adjutant-general had been ordered to go forward with the division. McLaws rode at once to the head of the column, leaving Lee's headquarters and Sharpsburg to the right, struck the road leading from Sharpsburg to New Industry, on the Potomac, which was followed a short distance, stopped to pile knapsacks, then approached the southwest part of the West Woods. On the march were met the broken commands of Ewell and Hood retiring from the woods, with their tales of terrible fighting and great slaughter. Wounded men were being carried on stretchers to the rear, or being assisted by the stout arms of their comrades, guns were being hauled off by hand, the horses being killed or disabled; batteries that had saved their horses were dashing to the rear, and stragglers, without muskets, filled the fields. Manly's North Carolina Battery and Macon's Richmond (Fayette) Artillery, were ordered to prominent positions near Reel's house, which they held during the day, without becoming engaged, and McLaws went forward with his four brigades and three remaining batteries.

An officer of General D. H. Hill's staff pointed to the position which the division was expected to occupy. McLaws was ignorant of the ground and of the location of other troops, and at his request, Hood, who was near, riding by himself, indicated the direction to advance, and he quickly resolved upon the formation of his line, which was that Cobb's Brigade should move off to the right and advance north into the West Woods, Kershaw on Cobb's left, then Barksdale, with Semmes on the left of the line. McLaws, who had ridden ahead, realized the critical condition of affairs. Troops were seen retreating from the woods, but 300 yards distant, very rapidly, and he saw that the 125th Pennsylvania was occupying them. He was anxious to cross the open space between himself and the woods before the latter were fully occupied by the enemy and ordered an advance before his line had entirely formed. Meanwhile a brigade was slipping from his hands. Cobb's Brigade which had been ordered to the right, to enter the woods from the south, marched so far to the right, under a misapprehension of orders, that it became entirely detached from the

View of plowed field where R. H. Anderson's Division deployed and John G. Walker's Division advanced toward the enemy. Looking north from modern Mondell Road. *Author's collection.*

division, and formed on the left of Rodes' Brigade, which was in the Sunken Road, thus reducing McLaws to the three brigades of Kershaw, Barksdale and Semmes; Kershaw on the right and the first engaged. As McLaws' line was then formed, or would have been formed, had all the brigades taken position before the advance was ordered, it faced northeast, Kershaw on the right, about 150 yards from the southwest face of the woods, in rear of George T. Anderson, Semmes on the left, in the direction of the Hauser house, and Barksdale in the center.

Jackson now came up and ordered McLaws to send a brigade to support Stuart. Kershaw was directed to form line while advancing and told that he must get to the woods before the enemy had full possession, and to do this must not wait for his full brigade to come up in line, but double quick his leading regiment, getting it in line as it went forward.

The 2nd South Carolina was the leading regiment of Kershaw's Brigade. It was commanded by Colonel John D. Kennedy and numbered 253 officers and men. Kershaw made a brief speech of encouragement and ordered it forward to clear the woods and retake a battery, beyond the church, which it was reported had been abandoned. It moved double quick by the right flank, passed to the right of George T. Anderson's recumbent men and up along the south edge of the woods, and began to climb the fence to enter the woods, at a point about 200 yards southwest of the church, when it was fired upon by the retiring skirmishers of the 125th Pennsylvania, and Colonel Kennedy was wounded, Major Franklin Gaillard succeeding to the command. Beyond the wounding of Colonel Kennedy the regiment suffered very slightly, being on lower ground the fire of the 125th Pennsylvania went over it.

The Pennsylvanians were retiring before Early's advance. It had not been Early's attention [sic] to advance after his first fire and the Pennsylvania skirmishers began to fall back, as he had observed some of the long expected reinforcements preparing to advance into the woods from the direction of his right, and was afraid of exposing his men to their fire, and that the two movements would throw both attacking parties in confusion, as they would have been at right angles. In addition another column was seen approaching his flank. He says: "The enemy in front, however, commenced giving way, and the brigade, which I have always found difficult to restrain, commenced pursuing." This pursuit began as Kershaw was ordering the 2nd South Carolina forward, and, leaving that regiment where it was fired upon, and where, Kershaw says, it became "entangled in a rail fence," we follow Early's advance.

When the Pennsylvania skirmishers, after firing at Early and the 2nd South Carolina, rallied upon their regiment it opened fire; Monroe's Battery threw shrapnel, and Early's men were checked and thrown into some confusion; some men in front were killed and wounded by their comrades

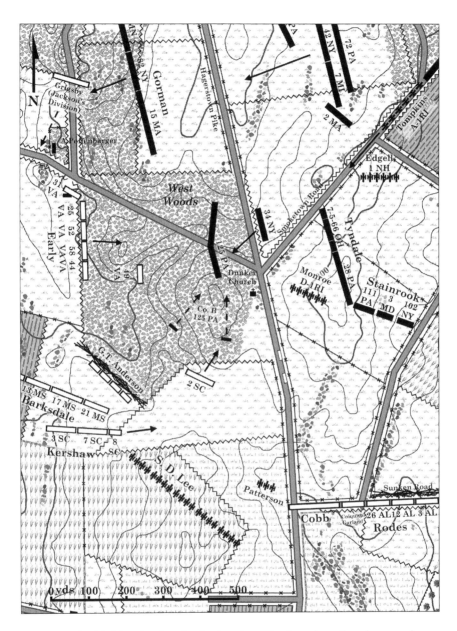

McLaw's Division begins deploying, but Kershaw is ordered to send a regiment to take possession of the woods before the Pennsylvanians can consolidate their position. The 2nd South Carolina and Early's Brigade move up to engage the 125th Pennsylvania. The 34th New York arrives behind the Pennsylvanians, having drifted too far to the left.

in rear, Colonel Smith, 49th Virginia, was severely wounded, but continued on the field, and Lieutenant Colonel J. C. Gibson was disabled by a wound in the leg. Early's men were old soldiers and well disciplined; they quickly recovered from the confusion into which they had been thrown and returned the fire of the 125th Pennsylvania with great effect. Early led the 49th Virginia in two charges up the hill and then fell back to the bottom, it is said, to confuse the aim of Monroe's gunners. These movements had the effect of breaking the alignment of the brigade and again throw it into confusion, to which there was now added the appearance of Sedgwick's Division on his left, to which we return.

The fences skirting the cornfield had been thrown down; Williams ordered the regiments of his division to fall back out of the way, an order only partially obeyed, some remaining to be passed over, and at 9:10 a.m. Sumner ordered Sedgwick's Division forward. We quote Walker:

> It was a beautiful sight, those three lines of battle, as they emerged from the first belt of woods, passed through the cornfield, ripe almost to harvest—and, moving steadily westward, crossed the Hagerstown pike. But, surely, they are not going to attack the enemy in that order! Other dispositions doubtless are to be made. The three lines are scarce seventy yards from front to rear. Two hundred men moving by the flank, in single file, would extend from the head of the column to its rear. Should those troops advance in this order, all three lines will be almost equally under fire at once, and their losses must be enormously increased. And where are the brigades that are to support them on the right and left, and protect the flanks of this perilously dense column? French is out of reach. The shattered brigades of the Twelfth Corps are holding stiffly on to their ground, under cover, but are hardly in numbers or condition to undertake the offensive; and certainly, without a distinct effort to bring them forward, they will not be on hand if Sumner's column, in its forward rush, shall be assailed in flank. Richardson indeed could be up in forty minutes; and half that time would serve to draw French in toward Sedgwick's left. But Sumner does not wait...All his life in the cavalry, he has the instincts of a cavalry commander...The order is still forward. Leaving the "Dunker Church" on their left and rear, Sedgwick's Division, in close array, in three lines by brigades,...crossed the Hagerstown pike.

In this advance the left regiment of Gorman's Brigade, the 34th New York, moved straight for the Dunker Church, its left clinging closely to the Smoketown road, but, when nearing the Hagerstown road, orders were given to the brigade to oblique to the right, which orders were obeyed by three regiments, but the orders did not reach the 34th New York, which

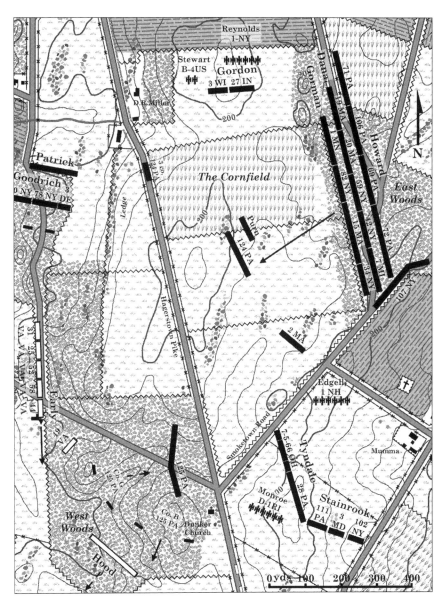

Sedgwick's division begins marching toward the West Woods. Several
Twelfth Corps units are still in their path.

went straight ahead, crossed the road just north of the church and came up in the rear of the 125th Pennsylvania, then engaged, the other regiments of Gorman's Brigade crossing the road 250 yards and more to the right.

It would be a simple matter to say that Sedgwick's Division of 5,000 men marched into an ambush, was attacked in front and on the flank by the brigades of Early, Semmes, Barksdale and G. T. Anderson, the 2nd and 3rd South Carolina, and about 200 men of Jackson's Division, in all about 4,036 men, with some help from Stuart's artillery, and, as the historian of the Second Corps says, were "at the mercy of their enemy, crushed by the fearful blow," and "driven out in disorder," with "terrific slaughter," having "two thousand of them disabled in a moment," and "all the successes of the morning lost." This would be a brief and very accurate statement of what occurred, but we shall enter into some details of how all of this occurred, so far as the meager, confused and contradictory character of the official reports may enable us, with such assistance as is given in the most excellent histories of Palfrey and Walker, both gallant officers of Sedgwick's Division. Palfrey says:

> Sedgwick's Division...swept steadily forward. Their march was rapid, and nearly directly west. There was very little distance between the lines. The recollections of the survivors range from forty feet to thirty paces. Not a regiment was in column—there was absolutely no preparation for facing to the right or left in case either of their exposed flanks should be attacked. The total disregard of all ordinary military precautions in swift and solitary advance was so manifest that it was observed and criticized as the devoted band moved on. A single regiment in column on both flanks of the rear brigade might have been worth hundreds of men a few minutes later, might indeed have changed the result of the battle. As the column pressed forward into the open space between the pike and the West Woods, its left just reaching the Dunker Church, it came under sharp artillery fire, and met with some loss. The lines were so near together that the projectile which went over the heads of the first line was likely its billet in the second or third. The swift shot were plainly seen as they came flying toward us. They came from Stuart's unseen guns, planted beyond the woods on or near the high ground which the Federal troops ought to have occupied. As the division entered the West Woods, it passed out of fire, and it moved safely through them to their western edge. There was a fence, and, bordering it on the outside, a common wood road. The brigade of General Gorman, followed that by Dana, climbed this fence, and then their lines were halted. For some cause unknown, the left of the two brigades almost touched, while the line of Gorman's Brigade diverged from the line of Dana's, so that there was a long

Major General John Sedgwick
Library of Congress.

interval from the right of the former to the right of the latter. It is doubtful whether the third line even entered the West Woods. If they did, they did not stay there long. There was a little, and only a little, musketry firing while the troops were in this position, but the Confederate guns to the right of Sedgwick's position were active and efficient, firing now canister.

Walker substantially follows Palfrey. He says:

Even when the leading brigade emerged from the farther side of the grove no enemy is seen in front. Only Stuart's horse batteries, from some high rocky ground on the right, search the woods, as they had the cornfield, with shell and solid shot. What means this unopposed progress? Is it well or ill, that this ground should not be disputed? Does it signify success or danger? It means that the Confederates have refused their left, and that Sedgwick is now pressing, in column, with his flank absolutely unprotected, past the real front of the enemy and is aiming at that portion of their line which is drawn back. It is at once a position of power and danger. If he will let Gorman go on until he strikes something, but hold Dana until the ground is cleared front for a left half wheel, to bring him facing south, and at the same time throw Howard's Brigade into column of regiments, to be moved steadily west to support Gorman or south to support Dana, the second division will at least have a chance—a small chance to achieve a victory against the superior forces which Lee is gathering against it, but large chance to make a strong resistance, to give a blow for every blow it must take, and, at the worst to fall back without disorder. But neither the chance of victory nor the chance of safety is to be taken. Without fronting so much as a regiment south, without increasing the intervals between the crowded brigades, two of which almost touch each other on the dangerously exposed left, Sumner, riding with the field officers of the leading brigade, drives his column straight westward to find the enemy. As the leading brigade emerges from the grove last mentioned, fire is opened upon it from a line extended along the crest of a slight ridge in front, upon which stands a farm house, barn and stacks of corn, which from the left and rear of this line one of Stuart's batteries plays upon Gorman's front. Our men drop like autumn leaves, but the regiments stand up to their work, without a quiver, the colors are advanced and the battle begun with good set purpose.

In the advance of Gorman's Brigade the 1st Minnesota was on the right, 82nd New York second in line, and the 15th Massachusetts on the left of

Major General Edwin V. Sumner
Library of Congress.

the 82nd New York. The 34th New York, on the extreme left, becoming detached, fought, as we shall see, at the Dunker Church. In its advance through the cornfield the 1st Minnesota passed over the 27th Indiana, then over the three companies of the 124th Pennsylvania, lying in the Hagerstown road, and onto the narrow plateau a few yards south of Miller's barn. Sumner was riding with Colonel Sully and perceiving that the regiment, 1st Minnesota, had not removed the hood from its colors, exclaimed: "In God's name what are your men fighting for? Unfurl those colors." The regiment now descended the plateau to lower ground and the West Woods, swept across the front of Goodrich's Brigade, almost touching it, and pushed through the woods to a rail fence bordering them on the west, and halted at the fence, beyond which was a cornfield on ground gradually rising to the crest of the Hauser ridge, on which was a small piece of woods concealing the 13th Virginia, which was supporting Pelham's Battery.

The Minnesota regiment was a little over 500 yards west of the Hagerstown road. There was no opposition when the fence was reached and no enemy in sight; immediately on coming to a halt the skirmishers of the 13th Virginia opened fire from the cornfield, but were driven back to the woods about 220 yards distant, soon after which Pelham's Battery opened fire. The 82nd New York, advancing on the left of the 1st Minnesota, gained the outer edge of the woods, its two right companies formed behind the fence, the rest of the regiment in open ground, faced more to the south, with the cornfield in front and connected with the right of the 15th Massachusetts. The Massachusetts regiment, as it approached the Hagerstown road, began obliquing to the right, crossed the road and open field beyond, descended the wooded slope and came directly in front of the A. Poffenberger building, was closing up to the 82nd New York, and as it gained the summit of a slight elevation, its left became hotly engaged with Jackson's Division, some of whose men were at the foot of the rise of the ridge near Hauser's, but many of them covered by the barn, stacks and rock ledges, not over 25 yards beyond the wood road bordering the west edge of the woods. Raine's Battery, on the ridge, 500 yards distant, added its fire to that of Jackson's men, and was silenced by the sharpshooters, but would not stay silenced. The two right companies of the regiment crossed the wood road and took cover of a rock ledge in open ground, the remainder of the regiment in the edge of the woods, the left extending in the direction of the Dunker Church, and about 500 yards distant from it. The center and left were opposite the Poffenberger house and barn, the left being on the slope of the wooded ridge and about 70 yards from the wood road. The company of sharpshooters on the left were advanced to the wood road and barn.

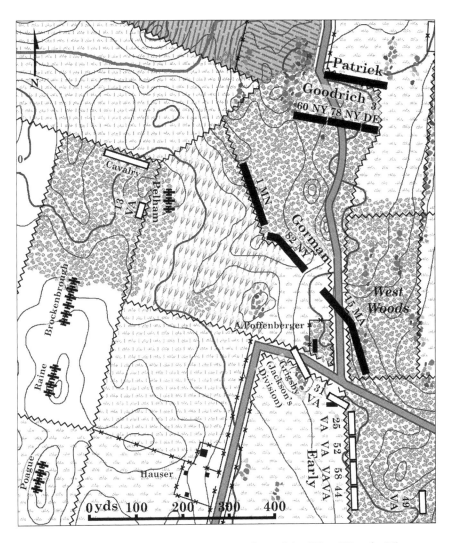

Gorman's brigade arrives at the western edge of the West Woods. They are confronted and stopped by the remnants of Jackson's Division and several batteries.

Dana's Brigade followed Gorman's. From right to left it was thus formed: 19th and 20th Massachusetts, 59th New York, 42nd New York, and 7th Michigan. Dana had been ordered to keep his line about 75 yards in rear of Gorman. On emerging from the East Woods he saw part of Williams' Division lying on the ground in front, which he took to be Gorman's line, upon which he halted and ordered his men down, but they were hardly down, when he received an order to move on, double quick, and enter the woods in front. The outline of the woods was irregular, presenting a salient point, where the woods came to the road 300 yards north of the church, where his left regiment, the 7th Michigan, entered, and hardly had it entered than when it became engaged with an enemy on its flank. Dana immediately ordered the 42nd New York to change front to support the Michigan men in resisting the flank attack, and the three right regiments were permitted to move on, enter the middle woods and halt very close to Gorman's line, then engaged.

Howard's Brigade was close upon Dana's. Its line was formed with the 71st Pennsylvania on the right, 106th right center, 69th left center, and 72nd on the left. Howard reports that after passing out of the East Woods, by Sumner's order he detached the 71st Pennsylvania, to the support of Mansfield's Corps, and halted his brigade, but Colonel Wistar has no recollection of having received such an order or of halting his regiment. "At this point," says Howard "the musketry fire began to tell on us, and I received an order from General Sedgwick to move up my entire line." Howard says he delayed his line for the detached regiment to come up, and then crossed the Hagerstown road. The brigade was under severe artillery fire and struck the road obliquely, the right first reaching it and climbing the high rail fence on either side, then pushing on into the woods, the left of the line extending toward the church, the three right regiments continuing across the open field and beyond and into the woods in rear of Dana's right, where they came under fire of shell and solid shot. Howard says: "Just after passing the turnpike I noticed confusion on the left and quite a large body of men falling back.... I pushed the third line on a little farther, and into the woods beyond the turnpike, preserving the distance about first indicated.... The second and third line, as far as I could observe from my position near the center of the line, were lying down as ordered." Howard rode with the 106th Pennsylvania, second regiment in line. Colonel Owen of the 69th, next on the left, reports that as the brigade reached the top of the hill, where the open field and woods join, he noticed many of the regiments to the left of the division falling back in great confusion, and immediately suggested the propriety of moving the brigade obliquely to the left. Orders having been received, however, to dress to the right, the brigade entered the woods in good order, and was dressed by the right of

Brigadier General Oliver O. Howard
Photographed as a Major General
Library of Congress.

Dana's Brigade. This, however was not done by the entire brigade; the left regiment was being swept from the field.

At the time Sumner was in the rear of the first line; Sedgwick was not seen and Howard did not act as the occasion required. Had he taken the responsibility of changing front to the left with his three regiments, when he saw this attack upon his flank, either by throwing forward his right or retiring his left, or both, and forming line perpendicular to the Hagerstown road, on high and very favorable ground, he would have formed a rallying point upon which other regiments could have formed, and McLaws, in all probability would have been checked, for we cannot doubt that the men, who, in July following, held the "Bloody Angle" at Gettysburg, against Pickett's charge, would have shown the same spirit here as they did on that occasion; but, disregarding the attack on the left, he thought it more important to carry out an unimportant direction to dress on the line of Dana's Brigade, and went on into the woods and ordered his men to lay down.

Thus, while the left of Dana's and Howard's brigades were crumbling away, the right and center of the two brigades advanced and entered the middle body of the West Woods and came up in rear of Gorman's line, then heavily engaged. This body of woods is 150 yards in depth, east to west, and in that space were crowded, "jammed" one might say, the three lines, on a sloping hill-side, exposed to artillery and musketry fire, and the rear lines unable to fire a shot, unless over the heads of comrades in front.

We return to the 125th Pennsylvania at the Dunker Church and the Union regiments involved in its defeat and expulsion. The 34th New York, as we have seen, was advancing on the left of Gorman's Brigade; as it approached the Hagerstown road it double quicked, crossed the road and came up in rear of the left wing of the 125th Pennsylvania, its left going about 30 yards beyond the church. Perceiving that there was no support on his left, Colonel Suiter, commanding the regiment, sent an officer to see what there was in that direction, and saw the 2nd South Carolina moving up the hill toward the church. The left of the 34th New York was refused and faced southwest, the right wing, in rear of the left of the 125th Pennsylvania, faced nearly west. Almost as soon as the 34th New York came up, the 7th Michigan of Dana's Brigade, entered the woods to the right. This regiment was the left of its brigade and advanced into the woods about 60 yards, until nearly reaching the right of the 125th, when it halted for alignment. It was but two minutes when Confederate colors and troops were seen advancing up the ravine, in the old wood road on its left, but fire was not opened as the men had been cautioned that a Union skirmish line was in front on that flank, and almost immediately two volleys in quick succession were poured into the right of the 125th Pennsylvania and left of the 7th Michigan, which broke the former and laid low one half of the left

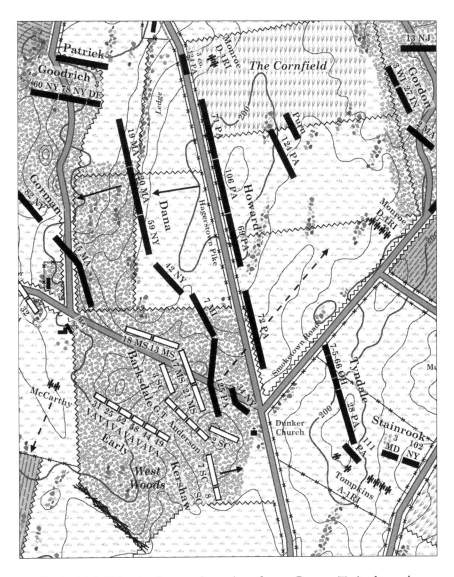

Barksdale's Brigade charges through and past George T. Anderson's Brigade and places a withering fire on the 125th Pennsylvania. The 2nd South Carolina does the same from the south. The Pennsylvanians are pushed back out of the woods. The 42nd New York and 7th Michigan from Dana's brigade shift south to try and fill the gap between the Pennsylvanians and the 15th Massachusetts.

wing of the latter. At the same time the entire front of the 125th Pennsylvania and 34th New York became involved. All these attacks were made by Barksdale's Brigade, a part of Early's and the 2nd South Carolina of Kershaw's, and George T. Anderson was advancing to the fray.

The 2nd South Carolina had been pushed into the woods to check the advance of the 125th Pennsylvania and troops supposed to be following it, until McLaws could form his command. This was soon accomplished and McLaws gave the signal, by waving his handkerchief, for the movement to be made; Barksdale's Brigade entered the woods on their left edge to support the left of the 2nd South Carolina; the 3rd South Carolina entered the woods in rear of Barksdale's left; charged down from near Hauser's on the front of the 15th Massachusetts and 82nd New York; Kershaw led the 7th and 8th South Carolina over George T. Anderson's men to support and form on the right of the 2nd South Carolina, and Anderson followed and joined in the attack. These movements were made in the order stated, in quick succession, all report becoming quickly engaged, and all claim to have driven the enemy before them.

It will conduce to a clearer understanding of the somewhat complicated and confused movements of the attacking troops if we first consider the advance of Semmes' Brigade, on the front of the 15th Massachusetts and 82nd New York, closely and severely engaging those regiments, while others were working on the flank and rear of the entire division. Semmes' Brigade, as it came on the field, was ordered by McLaws to move forward in line to the support of Stuart's cavalry and artillery, on the extreme left. The brigade was then on the high ground near the Hauser house, numbered 709 officers and men, and from right to left was thus formed: 32nd Virginia, 10th Georgia, 15th Virginia, and 53rd Georgia. Semmes says: "Immediately the order was given 'by company into line' followed by "Forward into line' both of which movements were executed in the presence of the enemy, under a fire occasioning severe loss in killed and wounded." It advanced steadily 200 yards, the left passing through the Hauser apple orchard, under a severe fire from the 15th Massachusetts and 82nd New York, when orders were given to commence firing, as Semmes says, at long range for most of the arms in his brigade, for the purpose of encouraging the men and disconcerting the enemy, and the effect was visible in the diminished number of killed and wounded. Crossing the fence which ran nearly north and south, just east of the Hauser house, the brigade, under a murderous fire, charged across a stubble field, men falling at every step, and was brought to a halt, the right at a rocky knoll very near the A. Poffenberger barn, which gave some protection from the galling fire of the 15th Massachusetts, on the hill-side, 130 yards distant, and the skirmishers at the barn and in the old wood road. The center and left of the brigade were under partial cover of the many projecting rock ledges. The

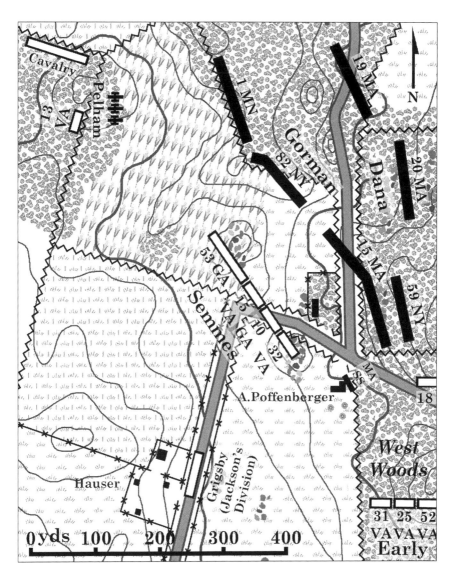

Semmes' Brigade and several Confederate batteries engage Gorman in a withering firefight.

conflict here was at close quarters and very severe, the entire brigade suffering from the fire of the 15th Massachusetts, 130 to 190 yards in front, and an enfilading fire from the right. In advancing to this position and holding it a very few minutes, nearly one half of the brigade were killed and wounded, the loss being particularly severe in the 10th Georgia and 15th Virginia, each losing more than one half their number. Three of the four regimental commanders were wounded.

The loss inflicted by Semmes upon the 15th Massachusetts and the two lines in its rear was severe, and to this was added the fire of several pieces of artillery that were run up on the Hauser ridge and poured an incessant stream of canister and shrapnel along the entire front of the three right regiments of Gorman's Brigade and upon the exposed and defenseless lines in the rear. Two guns of the First Company Richmond Howitzers, under Lieutenant R. M. Anderson, moved on Semmes' right, but the open, exposed field was no place for artillery, it could not live under the fire which swept it, and, under orders, Anderson withdrew his guns to the high ground in rear, south of Hauser's.

Barksdale was nearing the woods when Semmes began his advance. He halted at a fence a short time until he saw that Semmes was under way across the field, when he went over the fence south of the barn, and, entering the woods, immediately came under fire. At this time Early was making a vigorous attack on the 125th Pennsylvania, advancing and falling back, and again advancing, then lying down. The left regiments were in some confusion, when Captain Lilley, 25th Virginia, observing a line coming up, called to his own men to hold on a little longer, as help was coming, and in a moment Barksdale came up on the left and joined the attack. Two of his regiments advanced up the ravine straight for the right of the 125th Pennsylvania, quickly followed by an advance covering its entire front, all firing with the precision of veterans at green troops. After firing six to eight rounds, the right of the 125th Pennsylvania gave way in disorder, carrying with it a few of the 34th New York, and it was just before this that the 7th Michigan closed up on the right of the 125th Pennsylvania and had its left wing almost swept away by the terrific fire that had broken the Pennsylvanians. The left of the Pennsylvania regiment, having the moral support of the 34th New York, in its rear, remained a little longer—but not much longer—for as the right gave way the 2nd South Carolina appeared on its left. This regiment soon freed itself from the entanglement of the rail fence, and entering the south face of the woods came into line, as it advanced, to the cover of some wood piles, about 120 yards to the left of the 125th Pennsylvania, upon which it opened a very effective fire—"the most deadly fire," writes one of its officers, "the regiment ever delivered" full upon the exposed flank of the 125th Pennsylvania and the oblique front of the 34th New York. The effect of this fire was that the Pennsylvanians

The Mary Locher cabin, leased by Alfred Poffenberger at the time of the battle. The knoll to the left foreground is where Grigsby and the remnants of Jackson's Division briefly held out against Sedgwick's advance, and where the right of Semmes' line, the 32nd Virginia, was anchored during their firefight with Gorman. Photo taken in the 1930s. *Library of Congress.*

gave way and retreated, leaving the 34th New York exposed in front and on both flanks. The 2nd South Carolina started in pursuit of the Pennsylvanians, but a well directed volley of the 34th New York drove it back. A member of the Carolina regiment says: "The first Union line was very quickly driven, but an oblique line (34th New York) apparently older soldiers, was not so easily moved and checked us." The check was of very brief duration. Early had fallen back to change front and check Sedgwick, who was seen marching past his left, but Barksdale was still advancing and George T. Anderson was moving on its front. As soon as the 7th and 8th South Carolina passed over his brigade, while it was lying down at the southwest face of the woods, Anderson started by the left flank, double quick, along the fence, passed to the right of the 3rd South Carolina, which was swinging to the left, and went up the ridge as the 125th Pennsylvania was retreating. He was soon on the left of the 2nd South Carolina, though not connecting with it. He poured in two or three volleys, the 2nd South Carolina did the same, and the 34th New York was driven out of the woods, as the 72nd Pennsylvania of Howard's Brigade entered the woods near the church.

Howard's line advanced from the East Woods in some disorder. As it approached the Hagerstown road the right of the brigade began obliquing to the right, while part of the left wing, which had been halted, when attracted by the contest around the church, began to oblique in that direction. Part of the 69th regiment followed the 106th, and part overlapped the 72nd, but was soon moved to the right, and, under a fire that struck down many, the 72nd reached the road, somewhat broken by the rush of the 125th Pennsylvania through it. It was aligned by dressing to the right, and then advanced about ten yards into the woods. Its left, which was near the church, could not fire because some of the 34th New York were in front, but the right wing was uncovered and began firing. The 34th New York was almost instantly driven out and the 2nd South Carolina, Anderson's Brigade and part of Barksdale's opened full upon the 72nd Pennsylvania, which was ordered by Sumner to retire by the right flank. It had fired but a few rounds, some men had not fired a shot, and the regiment retreated to the right and rear, under a heavy fire, which inflicted much loss. It went back in some disorder, stampeded five of the seven companies of the 124th Pennsylvania and carried them back to the East Woods.

The 125th Pennsylvania had been in the woods not to exceed 30 minutes and the 34th New York and 72nd Pennsylvania less than half of that time; in that short time and in their retreat their losses were severe; the former had over 140 killed and wounded, the 34th New York 33 killed and 111 wounded, 46 per cent of the number engaged, and the 72nd Pennsylvania lost over 200 killed and wounded. In falling back all went over the ground

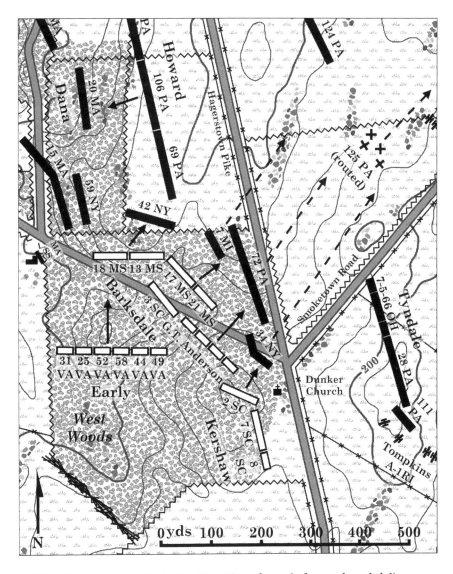

The Confederate units in the West Woods push forward, and deliver a devastating fire upon the remaining Union regiments. The Union left flank in the West Woods collapses and streams out of the woods into the open fields beyond. Howard's brigade continues marching westward until it comes up directly behind Dana.

of their advance and rallied in rear of some batteries that had been put in position near the East Woods.

Early, Barksdale, and Anderson claim to have driven the three regiments from the woods; one does not note the presence of the other or that anyone was assisting. Early says: "The enemy in front commenced giving way, and the brigade, which I have always found difficult to restrain, commenced pursuing, driving the enemy in front entirely out of the woods." Barksdale says: "In a few moments I engaged them, and, after firing several volleys into their ranks, drove them through the woods and into an open field beyond." Anderson makes the brief report that he "engaged the enemy and drove them for about a half mile, my men and officers behaving in the most gallant manner." He did not pursue beyond the ground held by the 125th Pennsylvania, where he halted, about midway between the church and the open field northwest of the Hagerstown road.

It was while engaged with the 125th Pennsylvania that both Early and Barksdale saw Sedgwick's line crossing the open plateau on their left. Early says he could not stop his men, who were in pursuit, and he advanced until his left flank and rear "became exposed to a fire from the column on the left (Gorman) which had advanced past my position. I also discovered another body of the enemy [Dana], moving across the plateau on my left flank, in double-quick time, to the same position, and I succeeded in arresting my command and ordered it to retire, so that I might change front and advance upon this force." At this time the left of Early's Brigade was in some confusion and he was on the right with the 49th Virginia; and the change of front was not effected with the precision one would expect from reading his official report.

Barksdale, when he discovered the enemy moving past his left, did not find it necessary to fall back to change front, he simply ordered his left wing—13th and 18th Mississippi—to wheel to the left and attack, while the 17th and 21st, after assisting in driving out the 125th Pennsylvania, 34th New York and 72nd Pennsylvania, turned upon the 7th Michigan and 42nd New York. At this moment the 3rd South Carolina came to Barksdale's support. It entered the woods just to the right of the wood road that led past the church, and advanced under a severe fire, drawn by Barksdale's Brigade that had preceded it. When it had passed some distance through the woods, in the direction of the church, to form on the left of the 2nd South Carolina, Sedgwick's lines were seen passing its left, upon which it changed direction to the left and came up in rear of the 17th Mississippi, and Anderson, as we have seen, came up and filled the gap between it and the 2nd South Carolina.

It will be remembered that when the Mississippians struck and routed the right of the 125th Pennsylvania, they also struck down nearly half of the 7th Michigan. The 7th fell back a few feet and making a partial change of front

The West Woods. During the battle, the trees were mature and there was little undergrowth except in the ravine. *Author's collection.*

returned the fire and while so engaged the 72nd Pennsylvania came up on its left, but a little to the rear and began firing. The contest was very short and both regiments badly shattered fell back. The remnant of the 7th Michigan retreated across the road, one half of the regiment lay dead or wounded in the woods or on the road, and a rally was made on the colors in the open ground south of Miller's cornfield, and his line formed, facing nearly south, quite a number of the 72nd Pennsylvania and some of the 69th rallying upon it, as also, some of the 42nd New York.

The fate of the 42nd New York was similar to that of the 72nd Pennsylvania and 7th Michigan. When the 7th Michigan was first, Dana ordered the 42nd New York, which was next in line from the left to change front. As it advanced promptly on open ground to gain distance, it received a volley from the ravine, inside the woods, which swept away every fifth man from the ranks, before it had formed in a new position. It had closed up on the colors and advanced obliquely toward the woods and another volley again thinned its ranks and the line began to waver, but soon steadied and reached the edge of the woods about 50 yards beyond the 7th Michigan, and was about to enter them, when it received such murderous volleys from Barksdale's men and the 3rd South Carolina that it retreated over the open field and across the Hagerstown road, with a loss of 181 officers and men, 52 per cent of the number in action. Early in the engagement Dana was painfully wounded, but remained with his two regiments until they were driven from the field. He pays them this tribute: "Although the shattered remnants of them were forced by overwhelming numbers and a cross fire to retreat in disorder, I bear them witness that it was after nearly half the officers and men were placed 'hors de combat.'"

Barksdale's Brigade suffered very severely in the brief encounter, but, with the 3rd South Carolina, pursued to and beyond the fences both at the north and east edges of the woods and powered their fire at the retreating regiments in the open fields beyond, the open fields over which the three Union lines had marched to the middle woods and where they were now exposed to a fire from the rear. Barksdale says: "The 17th and 21st pursued the enemy across the open field, when perceiving a very strong force moving to the right and attempting to flank them, and all of our own forces having retired from that part of the field, they fell back, under protection of a stone fence, in good order." The stone fence to which Barksdale fell back was beyond the southwest corner of the West Woods.

G. T. Anderson, who had come up and filled the interval between the 2nd and 3rd South Carolina, did not join Barksdale in the pursuit; there was no enemy in his own front after he had assisted in driving the 34th New York and 72nd Pennsylvania from the woods, and while he was at another part of the line a mounted officer dashed up to the brigade with a report that Kershaw, on the right, had been repulsed and the brigade was likely to

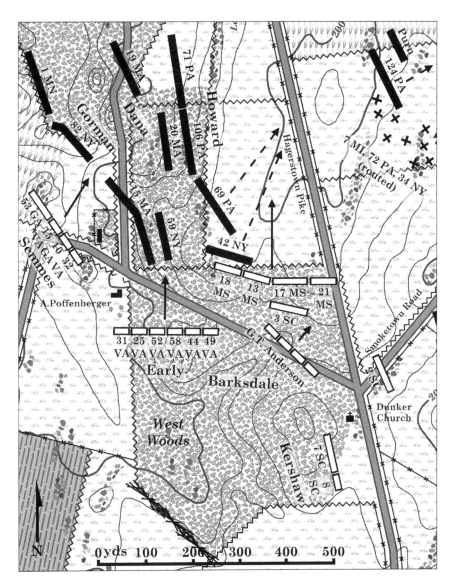

Barksdale's Brigade pushes the 42nd New York and 69th Pennsylvania out of the way and continues into the fields north of the woods. Semmes advances against Gorman, and Early follows up against Gorman's left flank.

be cut off and ordered a retreat. Some confusion ensued, but Anderson coming up reformed his line and moved to the right and rear, to the fence he had crossed in entering the woods, from which position he was soon ordered to the assistance of D. H. Hill at the Sunken road.

Before this movement of Anderson's, and simultaneously with the pursuit made by the 17th and 21st Mississippi, the 13th and 18th Mississippi, and 3rd South Carolina pushed northward along the edge of the wood and over the open field west of the Hagerstown road and directly in rear of Sedgwick's three lines; Semmes was still contending with the front and left of Gorman's line, and Early was forming to attack the flank of the 15th Massachusetts. About the same time, Kershaw was advancing to the attack on Greene's Division opposite the church.

While all this was transpiring at and near the Dunker Church, Sumner was riding in the rear of Gorman's right encouraging it to a fresh advance. As he rode up to Colonel Kimball of the 15th Massachusetts, he said: "Colonel, how goes the battle?" to which Kimball replied: "We are holding our ground and slowly gaining, but losing heavily as you can see." At this moment both Colonel Kimball and Major Philbrick discovered that the enemy had turned the left flank and was moving steadily upon the rear of the division and called Sumner's attention to it. He could not believe it, but when satisfied that it was so, exclaimed: "My God, we must get out of this," and rode to the rear to change the position of the other brigades to meet the enemy. From where Sumner left the 15th Massachusetts, it was but a few yards to where Howard had halted his men and ordered them to lie down, and it was soon after this that Sumner, appearing on the left at the line, his white locks stirred by the breeze, rode toward the right of the line, giving orders, which, at first, as understood by the men, were for a charge, and, in response, the men rose up and gave him a cheer and began to fix bayonets, but now Sumner was heard to say: "Back boys, for God's sake move back; you are in a bad fix." Howard, who was at the right of his line, says Sumner came riding rapidly, with hat off and his arms stretched out, motioning violently, while giving some unintelligible command, and that the noise of musketry and artillery was so great that he judged more by the gestures of the general as to the dispositions he wished him to make than by the orders that reached his ears. He judged that his left had been turned, and immediately gave the necessary orders to protect his flank, by changing front to the left with his brigade. "I think, even then," says Howard, "I could have executed such an order with troops which, like my old brigade, had been sometime commanded by myself, and thoroughly drilled; but here, quicker than I can write the words, the men faced about and took the back track in some disorder." In his official report Howard says: "the troops were hastily faced about, and moved toward the rear and right in considerable confusion."

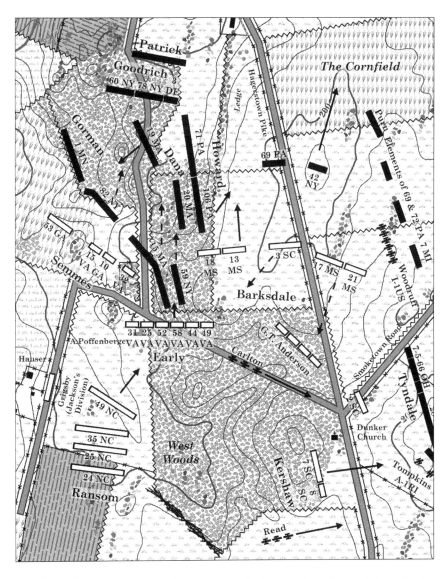

Barksdale's Bridge splits as it moves north. The 17th and 21st Mississippi, along with the 3rd South Carolina of Kershaw's Brigade, are pushed back by artillery and rallying infantry in the open field south of the Cornfield. The 13th and 18th Mississippi continue north, pushing back Howard's brigade. Finding Confederates behind them and Semmes in front, Gorman's regiments retreat. Ransom's Brigade of Walker's Division arrives and moves to take position along the west edge of the West Woods.

The 72nd Pennsylvania had been crushed at the first onset, the 69th went off in better order, and 106th, according to accounts given by some of its survivors, started to fall back by the right flank, "which soon became a hasty, disorganized and disgusting retreat." The historian of the 106th makes a better showing:

> Arriving at the fence running at right angles to the Hagerstown road across the open field north of the Dunker Church, an effort was made to rally and check the advance of the now elated enemy, who were emerging from the woods in large numbers...the colors were planted on the fence.... Colonel Moorehead, though injured by the fall of his horse, remained on the field, at once took advantage of this opportunity, and, assisted by Major Stover, ordered the men to stand by their colors, and stand they did. Detachments of other regiments joining them, they opened fire, pouring volley after volley in quick succession into the advancing enemy, who thinking they had struck our second line, checked their advance, and finally fell back under cover of the woods.

A portion of the regiment fell back to some hay stacks, where it was joined by the 15th Massachusetts.

In coming into position the 71st Pennsylvania became somewhat out of touch with the 106th its left, and it was not until the first two lines had given way, in the vain effort to change front, that it became engaged, and it suffered more from the fire on its left and rear than from that on its front. On ascending a projecting mass of rocks to get a clearer understanding of affairs, Colonel Wistar perceived that the entire left was in full retreat, being already some distance to the rear, closely followed by the Confederates. The regiment seemed to be practically alone, was suffering severely, and in immediate danger of being enveloped and captured. It was quickly formed into column of companies, to better effect a retreat through the Confederates, then in rear, but somewhat disordered by their own pursuit. In this movement Wistar was wounded and captured, the regiment escaping in fairly good order.

Howard says his brigade was first to retreat and Palfrey writes: "The third line, the Philadelphia Brigade, so called, was the first to go." Under the circumstances this would be very natural, and we cannot see that any particular stigma attaches to the men, however harshly we may criticize the superior officers, but the statement of Palfrey has been disputed and warmly resented.

When Dana endeavored to change front with the 7th Michigan and 42nd New York, he permitted the 59th New York, 20th and 19th Massachusetts to go forward and halt in rear of Gorman, and very soon the 59th New

Colonel Turner G. Morehead of the 106th Pennsylvania sitting on a rock outcropping on the battlefield. *Library of Congress.*

York closed upon and began firing through the left wing of the 15th Massachusetts, upon the enemy in front. By this fire many of the Massachusetts men were killed and wounded, and the most strenuous exertions were of no avail either in stopping this murderous fire, or in causing the second line to advance to the front. At this juncture Sumner rode up and his attention being called to this terrible mistake, he rode to the right of the 59th New York and ordered it to cease firing and retire which it did in considerable confusion. Survivors of the regiment say they fired but seven or eight rounds, were subjected to a cross fire and Sumner "cussed them out by the right flank," and that they went out in much confusion and did not stop until they reached the Nicodemus house, when an officer directed them to the right, as the Confederate artillery was sweeping the ground directly to the north, and a section of Cooper's Battery, supported by Hofmann's[3] Brigade, was taking position near the toll-gate, beyond Nicodemus'. As the regiment went out, some of the men saw a regiment, moving by companies in echelon and delivering a fire which checked the enemy. This was probably the 71st Pennsylvania or the 19th Massachusetts.

The 20th Massachusetts was on the right of the 59th New York; stood some time under a very severe fire, when orders were given to face to the rear and fire. Palfrey, who was an officer of this regiment, and wounded in the woods, says "The only fire delivered by the 20th Massachusetts of the second line was delivered faced by the rear rank. In less time than it takes to tell it, the ground was strewn with the bodies of the dead and wounded, while the unwounded were moving off rapidly to the north." The regiment quickly broke, some parts of it went through the 19th Massachusetts, after that regiment had made a stand beyond the woods, and formed in its rear.

The 19th Massachusetts was the right of Dana's line. It suffered severely as it entered the woods under a fire of musketry, canister and shell, which it could not return, as the first line was in its front; Colonel Hinks was wounded, a great number of officers and men were struck down, and a part of the 82nd New York retreated in disorder through it. As soon as its front was partially changed the regiment advanced a short distance and opened fire, but had delivered a few rounds only, when a fire came upon its left and rear, upon which it delivered a volley by the rear rank, then, changing front, moved out of the woods with the 1st Minnesota of Gorman's Brigade.

The 82nd New York of Gorman's Brigade, when in line, was in a very exposed position and suffered severely from the fire of Raine's Battery in its front. Part of the regiment fell back through the 19th Massachusetts, but the greater part of it remained until the left and center of the two brigades in rear had gone, the regiment on its left was moving, when it was ordered

---

[3] Carman misspells his name Hoffman throughout the text. The correct spelling is Hofmann, as evidenced by his signed reports in the *Official Records*.

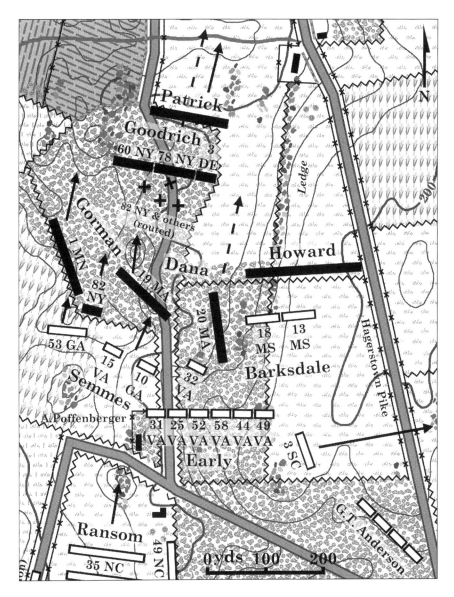

Howard's brigade forms a hasty line that stops Barksdale's advance. Semmes' advance combined with Barksdale appearing behind them prompt Dana and Gorman's remaining regiments to retreat. Routed soldiers push through Goodrich's brigade and they join the rout. Patrick falls back in an orderly manner.

back to the outer edge of the woods, and formed on the right of the 1st Minnesota.

After Gorman had expended 40 to 50 rounds of ammunition it became evident that the enemy was moving in large force on the left, when the firing became terrific and in five minutes after the regiments around the church had been driven out, the enemy's fire came pouring hotly on his left and rear. Being in front, without orders of any kind from any one, and finding that the rear lines were changing position and had already moved from their original places, he gave an order, which reached no one but Colonel Sully, to move quietly and quickly by the right flank. Gorman says in his report:

> Shortly before this I heard Major General Sumner directing the third line to face about, in order to repel the enemy, which had broken our left, supposing the design to be to take up a better position than the one just previously occupied, I having informed the general that my left must be supported or I could not hold the position. The attack of the enemy on the flank was so sudden and in such overwhelming force that I had no time to lose, for my command could have been completely enveloped and probably captured, as the enemy was moving not only upon my left flank but also forcing a column toward my right, the two rear lines having both been moved from their position before either of my three right regiments changed theirs.

As soon as Colonel Sully received Gorman's orders to leave the woods and hold the enemy in check, while the rest were retiring and to cover their withdrawal, he about faced the 1st Minnesota and moved back at a double quick, under a shower of canister from a Confederate battery. As the regiment went back it was in such manner that its left fell onto the right of the 19th Massachusetts, of the second line, which, also, was falling back and changing front, and the two swung backward to a rock-ledge about 100 yards north of the woods, and formed line nearly perpendicular to the Hagerstown road, a part of the 82nd New York joined the right of the 1st Minnesota, and for a time, the pursuit of the enemy was checked, though with some loss.

We left the 15th Massachusetts at the moment Sumner rode to Howard. The firing had been incessant upon it for twenty minutes, but it stood resolutely to its work, the men falling rapidly from the fire in its front, but now a still more deadly fire came upon its left and rear from Early and Barksdale, and perceiving that the second and third lines had gone, Kimball ordered the regiment to move off by the right flank. It retired in fairly good order, some 225 yards to the right and rear, faced about, and came under a severe artillery fire by which Captain Clark S. Simmonds and others were

The 15th Massachusetts's view of the battlefield taken at their monument near the center of the regiment's position. The area would have still been wooded, and the modern road a farm path. The Mary Locher/Alfred Poffenberger cabin is just across the road in the trees. *Author's collection.*

killed and some wounded. It remained in this position a few minutes and then retired to the North Woods. In its brief encounter the loss of the regiment was 318 killed, wounded, and missing, the greatest loss sustained by any regiment on the field, and 52 1/2 per cent of those taken into action.

Not all the regiments of the second and third lines, which were broken by the attack on their flank and rear, fell back without halt or offering some resistance to the advancing enemy. We have already noted that the 106th Pennsylvania displayed its colors on the fence running from the northeast corner of the middle body of woods to the Hagerstown road and opened fire by which it is claimed pursuit was checked, and the same was done by parts of the 71st Pennsylvania and 20th Massachusetts, also by the 15th Massachusetts, as it was leaving position. All this had an effect, but the pursuit by the 3rd South Carolina and Barksdale's 13th and 18th Mississippi was checked, in the open field between the woods and the road, and about 225 yards from the south edge of the field when it began, by the appearance of infantry and artillery upon the right flank of the pursuing force.

The 3rd South Carolina was on the right of Barksdale and of the pursuing line; after it had advanced 225 yards and come under fire of the 106th Pennsylvania, at the fences, Colonel Nance, its commander, discovered a Union force on his right, men of the 7th Michigan, 72nd Pennsylvania, Purnell Legion and others, who had rallied east of the road, and his advancing line was enfiladed by an artillery fire, all of which caused him to halt, change front to the right and rear and throw his line into a slight hollow in the southern part of the field, parallel to and 165 yards from the Hagerstown road.

The artillery fire came from Woodruff's Battery (I, 1st U. S.). Woodruff crossed the Antietam late on the 16th and parked near Hoffman's. Early on the 17th he followed the route taken by Tompkins Rhode Island battery and halted behind the East Woods. Major Clarke, chief of Sumner's artillery, rode up, said that Sedgwick was having a hard time and ordered the battery forward. It went through the East Woods at a gallop and over the fields straight for the Hagerstown road, through a stream of fugitives. One of its officers, preceding the guns, cleared the ground and the battery dashed up, went into position about 150 yards from the road and 350 yards north of the church and opened its six guns with canister upon the 3rd South Carolina, which caused it to change front, fall back and seek cover, and the same artillery fire ranged through Barksdale's ranks.

Woodruff was closely followed by Cothran's Battery (M, 1st New York) of the Twelfth Corps. Before Sumner's arrival this battery had been ordered by Hooker to the front. It was then in the field near D. R. Miller's and in rear of where Gordon's Brigade and Ransom's Battery had been engaged. It went down through the East Woods to the Smoketown road, where Cothran had been told he would be met by a staff officer to assign him a

View of the West Woods from Monroe and Cothran's positions near the edge of the East Woods. *Author's collection.*

position. Meanwhile Sedgwick's Division had come up and gone forward. After a brief wait the battery went down the Smoketown road to the corner of the woods and turned into the field, on the right, as the 125th Pennsylvania and 34th New York fell back. There was no staff officer or other to give orders, Cothran saw Woodruff engaged in front with infantry and, without awaiting or seeking orders, went forward and into position on Woodruff's right and opened with canister and spherical case, not only upon the 3rd South Carolina and Barksdale's men, but upon the woods around the church.

Barksdale's 13th and 18th Mississippi advanced along the edge and in the woods on the left of the 3rd South Carolina. At first, notes the historian of Kershaw's brigade, they were staggered by the resistance of Dana's left, but recovering, moved up the slope, partly in open field and part among the straggling oaks, "while the shell and canister thinned their ranks to such an extent, that when the infantry was met, their galling fire forced them to retire in great disorder." Barksdale reports that his pursuit was for a considerable distance over ground covered with the dead and wounded of the enemy, but he did not deem it prudent to advance farther without support, and ordered the two regiments to fall back to the woods in front of his first position. McLaws says: "The ground over which the Mississippi Brigade (General Barksdale) advanced, and to his right, was thickly strewn with the dead and wounded of the enemy, far exceeding our own, and their dead was much more numerous than their wounded. The close proximity of the combatants to each other may account for the disproportion." Barksdale's loss was 33 per cent, killed and wounded. Barksdale's two regiments and the 3rd South Carolina were checked and repulsed about 225 yards from the south edge of the field, over which they charged when Dana's left gave way. On the left Early went no farther, but halted at his first position, under cover of the rocky ledges in the woods, and farther pursuit was left to Semmes and the artillery under Stuart.

While the rear and flanks of Sedgwick's three lines were being pressed and crushed by the 3rd South Carolina, Barksdale and Early, Semmes, as we have seen, was heavily engaged in their front. When the line began to waver he poured in heavy volleys and advanced in a northeast direction, his right over the ground held by the right of the 15th and 20th Massachusetts, and 71st Pennsylvania, his left through the most northern body of the West Woods. He had already lost heavily in his engagement with Gorman's front, and the more than 700 officers and men, who had entered the fight, had dwindled to less than 500. His advance was not in connected line, there being wide intervals between some of the regiments, and these became much scattered in the pursuit, some parts of them flying ahead of the others. Semmes reports that he drove the enemy "from position to position, through woods and field, expending not less than 40 rounds of

Semmes' and Barksdale's view from the northern edge of the West Woods. The David R. Miller house is to the right. The Miller barn is just off camera to the right. Patrick's brigade rested and deployed in this area before retiring. *Author's collection.*

ammunition and went farther to the front than the troops on the right by about 300 yards, and was for a time exposed to a terrible front and enfilading fire, inflicting great loss." It was this advance of Semmes that forced the front or turned the right flank of all the detachments that had united in checking the advance of Barksdale and the 3rd South Carolina, and that finally expelled Goodrich and Patrick from the north body of the West Woods.

It will be remembered that when Sedgwick's Division entered the West Woods the right of Gorman's Brigade swept past the front of Goodrich's Brigade, Twelfth Corps, which was closely supported by Patrick's Brigade, First Corps. As Sedgwick's fugitives went to the rear they rushed through and over the three small regiments of Goodrich, carrying them with them. Everything was in wild disorder. Patrick at once again threw his three small regiments under cover of the rock ledge, beyond the woods and perpendicular to the road, partially to rally the retreating troops and partially to hold on with his few remaining cartridges until order could be restored and assistance come forward. The 21st New York, Colonel W. F. Rogers, on the right. Rogers says no heed was paid to his effort, officers and men alike striving to reach the rear: "It was a complete rout, and they passed on out of sight." In front of the greater part of the line the pursued and the pursuers were so close that Patrick's men could not fire.

In Semmes' advance the 32nd Virginia was on the right of the brigade. It charged over the ground held by the right of the 15th Massachusetts and, after a check of a few minutes, until the 10th Georgia came up on its left, pushed entirely through the woods, passing some of Barksdale's men, but seeing none of Early's, and came into the open ground where Patrick was seen rallying his brigade and endeavoring to stem the tide of fugitives going to the rear.

The 10th Georgia and 15th Virginia advanced on the left of the 32nd Virginia and halted ten or fifteen minutes in the wood road, beyond where the right of the 15th Massachusetts had been. At the end of this halt they again advanced through a skirt of woods to the fences bounding the woods on the northeast; the Georgians in this advance claim to have "driven the enemy with heavy slaughter" and the Virginians captured many Pennsylvanians of Howard's Brigade. The two regiments halted near the fence when they saw Patrick in front.

Patrick was a tenacious and resourceful fighter and undoubtedly would have checked the farther advance of Semmes' three regiments, now reduced to less than 250 men, especially as the 1st Minnesota, 19th Massachusetts, and part of the 82nd New York had now rallied to his right, had the right not been turned by the 53rd Georgia, Stuart's artillery and its infantry support, the 13th Virginia of Early's Brigade. The 53rd Georgia was the left of Semmes' Brigade, and the largest regiment in it, having double the

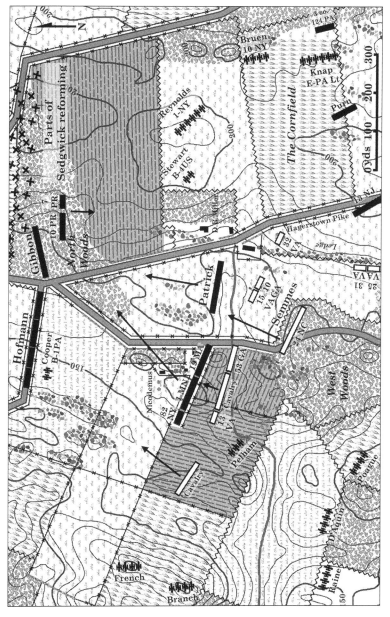

The Confederates' final push north of the West Woods. Several Union regiments make a stand at the Nicodemus farm. Patrick's brigade retires from the hollow west of the Miller farm.

number of any other regiment. In its advance it struck the 82nd New York, 1st Minnesota, and 19th Massachusetts, as they were retiring and changing front, and followed them nearly to the north edge of the woods, when, perceiving the line they had formed, under partial cover, it halted. Stuart, with artillery and the 13th Virginia, was advancing on its left.

There was not much opportunity for Stuart to use his cavalry, much of it had been detached to gather the infantry stragglers and the small body of Fitz Hugh Lee's Brigade left to him was supporting artillery, which, on the left, had been placed under Stuart's direction. Stuart was very active with his artillery. He had been given a very important position to hold—the high ground that lay between the left of the infantry and the river, and that, once occupied by the Union troops, would render the Confederate left untenable. He occupied it to good purpose aggressively. With the many batteries assigned him he had kept up a constant and very annoying fire and with such effect as led to the belief that a continuous line extended from the Dunker Church to very near the Potomac, a belief that had its effect upon the Union movements early in the day. When Sedgwick's Division approached he checked its advance at the west edge of the woods with some of this artillery and the 13th Virginia infantry, aided by the few men of Jackson's Division, and gave time for McLaws to come up, make his dispositions and attack. When Sedgwick's lines began to break, Poague's, Raine's, Brockenbrough's and D'Aquin's batteries started northerly along the Hauser ridge and kept up an advancing fire from all favoring points, all the time under a severe fire from the Union guns, but all the time advancing and firing. As these batteries continued moving to the left the guns were mixed up, D'Aquin's being generally in the lead. Some were halted in the Nicodemus cornfield, the highest point on the ridge, and opened fire upon the 59th New York, 15th Massachusetts and detachments of other regiments that had halted near the Nicodemus place, but one battery, supported by the 13th Virginia, moving between the woods and the cornfield, came to a knoll on the flank of the 1st Minnesota and about 260 yards from it, where it had an enfilading fire upon its line. At the same time the 13th Virginia was seen working past the right of the line, threatening its rear, and an order was given for the entire line to fall back. In falling back the 1st Minnesota and 82nd New York passed over the field in rear, in line with and almost in contact with the 13th Virginia on its right, facing about to repulse the 53rd Georgia, which was now following them; and the 1st Minnesota, rushing through the Nicodemus farm yard, under a shower of canister, "tumbled over the stone fence, and, in less than thirty seconds, formed on the colors in the Nicodemus lane, every man in his place"; the fragment of the 82nd New York with them, and immediately moved to the corner of that part of the North Woods extending west of the Hagerstown road. The 19th Massachusetts fell back on the left of the 1st Minnesota, and

Looking south from Hofmann and Cooper's position along the road leading from the Hagerstown Pike. *Author's collection.*

both faced about to check the further Confederate advance, as a section of Cooper's Battery came up and went into position a short distance out in the open field on the right.

Cooper's section was supported by Hofmann's Brigade. When McLaws made his attack this section under Lieutenant Fullerton, was in the field to the right and front of Hofmann's Brigade, that lay along the Hagerstown road, in support to the artillery on the high plateau north of J. Poffenberger's. When it was seen that Sedgwick's men were falling back Hofmann moved to the right and front with his entire brigade and the section of artillery, and took position with his artillery, and took position with his infantry behind the stone fences of the road leading west from the toll-gate on the Hagerstown road, and the two rifled guns were run forward into the open field beyond, between the road and the Nicodemus place, and on the right of the 1st Minnesota. The enemy's battery was now quickly silenced and, for about 20 minutes, both the Minnesota and Massachusetts men exchanged fire with the sharpshooters of the 13th Virginia, supporting the Confederate battery, and silenced them. This was the limit of the Confederate pursuit; it was checked, reports Stuart, "by the enemy's reserve artillery coming into action."

Meanwhile Patrick had fallen back. When he saw the line on his right falling back and the colors of the 53rd Georgia passing his right and others advancing in his front, he ordered his regiments to retire by the right flank. Colonel Rogers, commanding the 21st New York, on the right, says: "The enemy's skirmishers continued warily to advance. There seemed to be no force to oppose them. My men had by this time exhausted their ammunition. I soon received orders to move to the rear and at once commenced to retire. This seemed to give greater encouragement to the advancing skirmishers, who quickly followed, firing as they advanced, causing many casualties, during our retreat." Patrick reports that the brigade "was withdrawn in an unbroken line," and Colonel H. C. Hoffman, 23rd New York, reports that his regiment retired in such perfect order as to attract General Howard's attention, who was vainly endeavoring to rally his men, a short distance in rear and who, pointing to the New York men, said: "Men this the way to leave a field. That regiment acts like soldiers. Do as they do, men, and we shall drive them back again in ten minutes." Patrick marched up the Hagerstown road to the North Woods and joined Gibbon's Brigade, which was deployed through the woods to arrest further retreat.

In an article in the *National Tribune*, Howard writes: "When we reached the open space (where Patrick rallied) Sumner and every officer of nerve made extraordinary efforts to rally the men and make head against the advancing enemy, but that was impossible until we had traversed the open space, for now we had the enemy's artillery and infantry both pursuing and flanking our broken brigades by rapid and deadly volleys."

The David R. Miller farm looking south along the Hagerstown Pike. Patrick and Semmes' brigades fought in this area. *Indiana at Antietam.*

The retreat was arrested and the greater part of the division rallied at the North Woods. When the 7th Pennsylvania Reserves retired from the contest with a part of Hood's Division, it went up the Hagerstown road and well into the North Woods, where it was joined by the 10th Reserves, which, a few minutes before the advance of McLaws, had been withdrawn from its position near the West Woods, on Patrick's right. As Sedgwick's stragglers began to come back, Major C. A. Lyman, 7th Reserves, deployed both regiments and endeavored to stop them. While so employed Sumner rode up, inquired who they were, and ordered the two regiments forward. Promptly and prettily they advanced to the south edge of the woods and halted, where they came under an enfilading fire by which Captain James L. Colwell, of the 7th Reserves was killed and many wounded. The cool presence of these two small regiments was of great effect and upon them Howard rallied a part of his brigade and the division retreated no farther, but took position in and about the woods.

Walker, in his *History of the Second Army Corps* says:

> It is easy to criticize Sumner's dispositions at Antietam—the dangerous massing of Sedgwick's brigades, the exposure of the flank of the charging column, the failure of the commander to supervise and direct, from some central point, all the operations of the corps; yet no one who saw him there, hat in hand, his white hair streaming in the wind, riding abreast of the field officers of the foremost line, close up against the rocky ledges bursting with the deadly flames of Jackson's volleys, could ever fail thereafter to understand the furious thrust with which a column of the Second Corps always struck the enemy, or the splendid intrepidity with which its brigade and division commanders were wont to ride through the thickest of the fight as callously as on parade.

All this is conceded, yet the fact remains that these splendid troops of the Second Corps were much disorganized and many of them sadly demoralized when they fell back, and, unfortunately, that partial demoralization extended to their commanders. We again quote Walker:

> If it is not a profanation to say such a thing about Edwin V. Sumner, he had lost courage; not the courage which would have borne him up a ravine swept by canister at the head of the old First Dragoons, but the courage which, in the crush and clamor of action, amid disaster and repulse, enables the commander to cooly calculate the chances of success or failure. He was heartbroken at the terrible fate of the splendid division on which he had so much relied, which he had

Richard F. Bernard Co. A, 13th Virginia Infantry
Library of Congress

deemed invincible, and his proximity to the disaster had been so close as to convey a shock from which he had not recovered.

Nor had he recovered from this shock an hour or more later when Franklin came up.

As soon as Semmes' men saw that Patrick was retiring from his position behind the stone ledge they rushed forward, cheering and firing. The 32nd Virginia, on the right advanced to the stacks south of Miller's barn, where it was halted until supports could be brought up. It was reduced to less than 80 men, and these took cover behind the stacks. The 10th Georgia and 15th Virginia, passing the left of the 32nd Virginia and the barn, halted in rear of the rock ledge from which Patrick had withdrawn, where they engaged some Union troops that were under cover of the stone fences of the Hagerstown road. Men of both regiments crossed the road to the D. R. Miller house, where they found a number of Union men, wounded and unwounded, some of whom were captured and sent to the rear. These movements followed those of the 53rd Georgia, which had been checked on the open ground to the front and left of the position taken by the 10th Georgia and 15th Virginia. Semmes was now about 450 yards in advance of the point where Barksdale had been repulsed and Early had halted.

When Stuart had driven the 1st Minnesota and 19th Massachusetts from the field he came riding out of the woods to the 32nd Virginia and inquired for Semmes. Just then a Union battery across the Hagerstown road opened upon the barn, stacks, and infantry in sight, and Stuart told Semmes that the battery must be taken, to which Semmes replied that his men had been very severely engaged and were about out of ammunition, and that Barksdale was in the woods to the rear and not engaged, upon which Stuart dashed off after Barksdale.

The artillery fire that opened on Semmes came from a section of Campbell's Battery, under Lieutenant Stewart, that had such a serious and thrilling experience near the same stacks very early in the morning, and some of whose dead still lay near them. When Sedgwick's men passed to the rear, through the woods, closely pursued by the enemy, this section was in position very near where Stewart had his section in Miller's field at the beginning of the fight, and Reynolds' New York battery was on its left. Both were under a heavy fire from two Confederate batteries beyond the woods, which had their exact range. Stewart was unable to get his own range on account of the smoke of the musketry, so limbered to the rear and came up on Reynolds' left, when one of his men called attention to a body of Confederate infantry in front, apparently on the Hagerstown road, and the left or most advanced part of the line, the 53rd Georgia, appeared to be falling back. Stewart loaded his guns with canister, waited until he saw four stands of colors in their front and began firing. It was at this time that

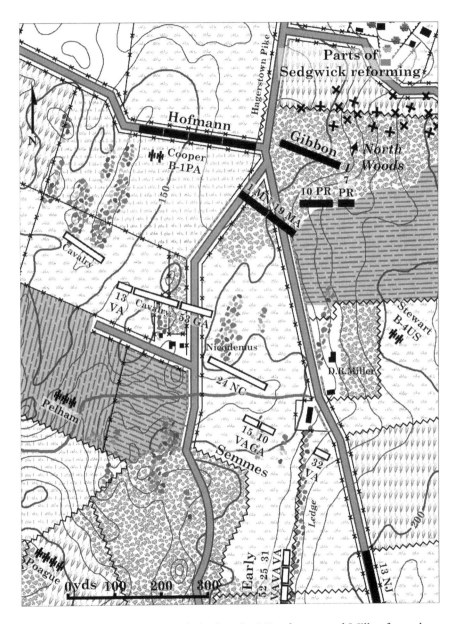

The Confederate advance is halted at the Nicodemus and Miller farms by units from the First Corps, the remnants of Sedgwick's division, and artillery on the field east of Miller's.

Stuart came up and advised Semmes to capture the battery. Semmes remained but a short time after Stuart dashed off for Barksdale; no troops came to his support or to capture the battery, whose canister was very annoying, enfilading a part of his line, and he ordered his regiment back into the woods, Stewart following them with canister until they were out of sight. They went back in good order to the position from which they had started, collected and buried their dead and cared for the wounded. The loss of the brigade was severe; 314 killed, wounded, and missing, being 44 per cent of those engaged; of which the 53rd Georgia left 30 per cent; the 32nd Virginia, 45 per cent; the 10th Georgia 57 per cent; and the 15th Virginia, 55 per cent. Three of the four regimental commanders were wounded, and many of the best line officers killed and wounded.

It is difficult to determine the part taken by Early in the pursuit through the West Woods. He made a very elaborate and graphic report of the battle, covering four and a half solid pages of the official records, in which he shows all his earlier movements on the field; his great anxiety for reinforcements, and the advance made upon the 125th Pennsylvania, and then spares but five lines to a statement of his change of front and the expulsion of Sedgwick from the woods. He says: "Just as I reformed my line Semmes', Anderson's and part of Barksdale's brigades of McLaws' Division came up, and the whole, including Grigsby's command, advanced upon this body of the enemy, driving it with great slaughter entirely from and beyond the woods, and leaving us in possession of my former position." His "former position" was perpendicular to the Hagerstown road and 130 yards south of the north edge of the middle body of the woods. Some officers of the brigade state their impression that a part of the line went clear out of the woods and half way to the Miller stacks, but instantly fell back to the woods. There is no question as to Early's engagement on the flank of the 15th Massachusetts and his advance over the ground held by it and the 20th Massachusetts, to the position held by him earlier in the day, but he appears to have followed Semmes' right and Barksdale's left over this ground, and not in front line and clearly engaged. This also appears from the record of losses. Semmes' in the short time he was engaged lost 44 per cent of his men. Barksdale lost 33 per cent, while Early, who had been much longer engaged, suffered a loss of but 16 per cent, the greater part of which was in his engagement with the 125th Pennsylvania. Semmes makes no mention of any troops preceding him and reported to McLaws that he was not supported by and did not see Early's Brigade.

General Early, after acknowledging the assistance rendered him by Semmes, Anderson, Barksdale and Grigsby, says: "Major General Stuart, with the pieces of artillery under his command, contributed largely to the repulse of the enemy and pursued them for some distance with his artillery and the 13th Virginia, under command of Captain F. V. Winston." Stuart

Brigadier General Jubal A. Early
Library of Congress.

says the enemy broke in confusion and were pursued for half a mile along the road. Evidently he did not see Early but "recognized in the pursuit part of Barksdale's and part of Semmes' brigades, and I also got hold of one regiment of Ransom's Brigade which I posted in an advantageous position on the extreme left flank after the pursuit had been checked by the enemy's reserve artillery coming into action. Having informed General Jackson of what had transpired I was directed by him to hold this advanced position and that he would send all the infantry he could get to follow up the success. I executed this order, keeping the cavalry well out to the left, and awaiting the arrival of re-inforcements."

Other affairs were taking place in and about the West Woods while Sedgwick's men were being driven through them, and after they had been driven from them. It was but a short time after the 3rd South Carolina had taken cover in the hollow parallel to the Hagerstown road, when Colonel Nance saw Kershaw's Brigade, about 380 yards to his right, advance "most beautifully" through the woods and up the slope beyond—the slope to the plateau opposite the Dunker Church—and he thought he saw Greene's Division break. His regiment belonged to Kershaw's Brigade, had become detached from it, in advancing to the attack on Sedgwick's flank, and he thought now to join it in pursuit of a routed enemy, upon which he crossed the Hagerstown road, and "passed to the summit of a hill in a freshly plowed field," 60 yards beyond the road, and to his surprise found Union troops under cover of the hill or ridge and opened fire upon them. These troops were the Purnell Legion; two companies of the 124th Pennsylvania, and a few men of Howard's Brigade, remaining near Woodruff's Battery. These opened fire upon the South Carolinians as soon as they made their appearance on the high ground, Woodruff turned his guns on them, and they were driven back to the road, where they remained but a moment, as Woodruff's canister was too much for them, and then fell back to the ravine from which they had advanced. Colonel Nance reports that "under the heavy fire of artillery and the press of fresh troops our line on my right (Kershaw) that just before advanced in such admirable style, fell back so far that I retired to the road I had just crossed. There I halted and fired for a time, until a further retirement required me to fall back to the hollow in which I had before changed my front. There I remained until the movements of the enemy and the absence of proper supports determined me to retire into the woods." These were the woods surrounding the Dunker Church and south of it, and finding no friends in them Nance led his regiment where he had first formed line, and took position behind a rail fence running parallel to the woods.

About this time Walker's Division came upon the field and entered the West Woods. This division, as we have seen, remained near Lee's headquarters, until 3 a.m. of the 17th, when it moved to the extreme right,

The plateau east of the West Woods. S. D. Lee's artillery battalion occupied this position during the early morning fighting. Greene's Federal division used a reverse slope defense on the other side of the hill to the right of the photo. The West Woods is to the left. *Library of Congress.*

to guard the Snavely and Myers' Fords, where it remained until nearly or quite 9 a.m., when an order from General Lee directed it to hasten to the left. It moved left in front, Ransom's Brigade leading, marching rapidly, left Sharpsburg to the right, and, after passing Reel's house, Ransom formed line by inversion, bringing the 49th North Carolina on the right. The line formed under severe fire and in the presence of troops that had been driven back. As soon as formed the brigade was pushed rapidly forward, marching in columns of regiments, northerly, along and near the west edge of the West Woods, when orders were given to "form to the right and resist the enemy in the woods."

The 49th North Carolina, on the right, made a right wheel, which brought it up to the fence bordering the woods. The 35th North Carolina, marching straight on, as soon as it cleared the 49th, wheeled to the right, passing by on either side of the A. Poffenberger barn, and the 25th North Carolina, passing by the left of the 35th, made the same movement, and the three regiments pushed eastward, up the wooded slope, upon which had stood the 15th Massachusetts and lines in rear of it, and halted in the east edge of the woods overlooking the open field and the Hagerstown road, but the 24th North Carolina, on the extreme left, did not wheel to the right, when it had passed the 25th, but kept straight on, and joining some of the Confederates in pursuit, became engaged, lost heavily, went clear out of the woods, north, and was caught up by Stuart and put in position on the extreme left.

Ransom reports that upon reaching the woods he "immediately encountered the enemy in strong force, flushed with a temporary success. A tremendous fire was poured into them, and, without a halt, the woods were cleared and the crest near the enemy occupied….The ground was filled with the dead and wounded of both sides." What enemy Ransom encountered and drove from the woods is a mystery to us. As a matter of fact, Ransom came up just as McLaws had driven Sedgwick north, and then swept eastward into the woods, after McLaws had passed northward, and McLaws left no Union troops behind him, west of the Hagerstown road, save dead, wounded and prisoners.

In the line formed just inside the east edge of the woods the 49th North Carolina faced the southeast corner of the open field, its right in the southern body of the woods. On its left was the 35th North Carolina, and, on the left of the 35th was the 25th. All were protected by a ledge of rock which ran along their entire front. The brigade numbered 1,600 men, but, as the 24th had gone far to the left, Ransom had about 1,250 in line. After taking this position Ransom, "determined to charge across the field in front and to the [East] woods beyond which was held by the enemy, but he again approached in force, to within 100 yards, when he was met by the same crushing fire which had driven him first from the position." This force,

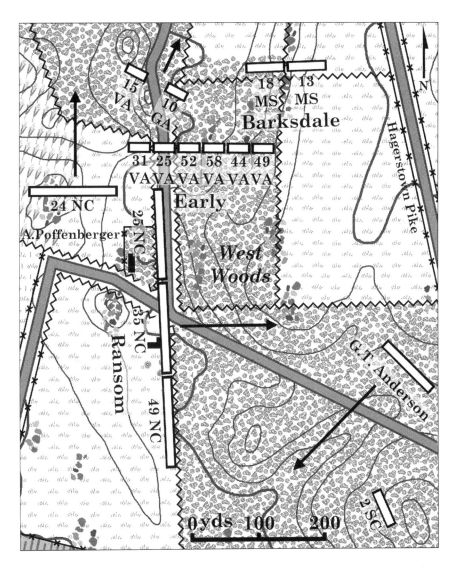

George T. Anderson's Brigade retreats from the edge of the West Woods.
Ransom advances into the woods. However, the 24th North Carolina
inadvertently continues north instead of forming on the rest of the brigade.

approaching Ransom and staying his projected advance, was two regiments—2nd Massachusetts and 13th New Jersey—of the Twelfth Corps.

When Sedgwick was being driven from the West Woods Sumner called upon the Twelfth Corps for help, the staff officer delivering the order to Williams, saying: "General Sumner directs you to send to the front all of your command immediately available." Williams had but few men available; Greene's Division was then engaged at the Dunker Church; Crawford's Brigade had become scattered and some of it roughly handled, and as Gordon held his brigade most convenient for a movement to the point indicated, he was ordered to advance at once. Gordon says:

> I was to move up towards the woods in front to support the troops there. The order, most urgent and imperative, furnished the only information I possessed that our forces had again entered the woods in our front. I deemed it of the utmost importance that my command should move forward with the least possible delay. I therefore in person gave the order to the regiments nearest me, without the formation of my entire brigade, intending to bring up other brigades to support or continue the line, as circumstances might require.

The regiments nearest Gordon were the 13th New Jersey and the 2nd Massachusetts that were in the East Woods. A staff officer rode up to the first and directed its colonel to go forward through the cornfield, across the Hagerstown road and into the West Woods, where he was to report to the first general officer he met, and he was informed that a part of the 124th Pennsylvania and other Union troops might be on the road near Miller's barn, and was twice cautioned not to fire upon troops in front as they were "our own men." The caution was communicated to the company officers and by them to their men. For the first time in their soldier experience the men loaded their muskets, and, the command being given, the regiment advanced in line of battle through the cornfield, becoming somewhat disordered as it neared the road, but it was ordered over the fence into the road, where it was thought reform. The right of the regiment was first to reach the fence, no men could be seen on the road, there were a few men off to the right and front, and nothing was visible to the immediate front, where there was ominous silence. Part of the regiment climbed the fence into the road and the rest were following when puffs of white smoke were seen at the rock ledge, 150 yards in front, and a hail of musketry went through the regiment, killing some and wounding many. It was a trying experience for a new regiment, the first time in action, and there was some confusion, but officers and men soon rallied; on the right Captain H. C. Irish crossed the second fence and called upon his men to follow, the

Colonel Ezra A. Carman
Colonel of the 13th New Jersey Infantry
Library of Congress.

gallant Irish fell dead a few yards beyond the fence, and the colonel, recognizing that a mistake had been made, ordered the men to form behind the first fence and hold the ground. This was soon found impossible, the men were being shot buy a foe they could not see, so perfectly did the ledge protect them; they scarcely knew how to load their muskets and were doing little or no execution; to hold them longer under fire would be murder and they were ordered back to the East Woods, retiring in good order, under the circumstances, and rallying on the spot from which they had advanced.

The 2nd Massachusetts advanced on the left of the 13th New Jersey, but, not in close connection with it, and a short distance in rear. It had a similar experience. Colonel Andrews reports:

> The regiment advanced in line, the 13th New Jersey on its right to a lane, fenced on both sides, which offered a partial cover, and which was about 100 yards from the wood held by the enemy. Here the regiment received a very heavy fire from a large body of the enemy posted in the woods. Our fire was opened in return; but the enemy having greatly the advantage, both in numbers and position, his fire became very destructive. Being unsupported it was impossible to advance and a useless sacrifice of life to keep my position. The regiment was accordingly marched back in perfect order to the position from which it had advanced.

The historian of the 2nd Massachusetts gives more particulars:

> While the 3rd Wisconsin and 27th Indiana, both of which had suffered severely, lay behind a slight ridge, and the 107th New York was some distance yet to the left, the 2nd Massachusetts and the 13th New Jersey moved up to the road, crossed the fence, and formed behind the second one. Captain Morse, with Company B, crossed the second fence. This was but a few rods above the church at the open ground. Sumner's corps was not visible. When soldiers appeared in the woods opposite, there was doubt who they were. 'Show your colors' said Colonel Andrews to the color bearer. Color Sergeant Lundy waved his flag. It was greeted by a shower of bullets. Fire was then opened and continued. But, as the smoke lifted, the small force found itself alone. On the left no troops were visible, on the right the left of the 13th New Jersey had given way. The enemy were sheltered in the woods and behind rocks, and were in great force. The flag staff was broken, the flag riddled, the socket shot away from the color bearer's belt. The brave Dwight was mortally wounded. A fourth of the men had fallen, and they were rapidly dropping. Suffering much more than the enemy could, and unsupported, the order was given, and the regiment fell

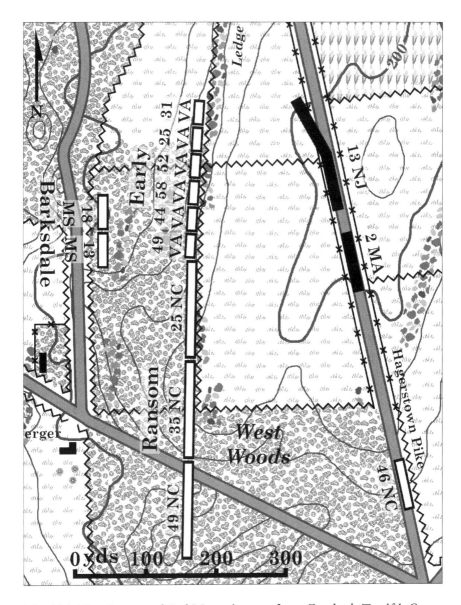

The 13th New Jersey and 2nd Massachusetts from Gordon's Twelfth Corps brigade advance from the East Woods and confront Ransom and Early when they reach the Hagerstown Pike.

back to the woods behind, thus uncovering the batteries. Cothran's and Woodruff's guns opened beautifully, and the advancing line of the enemy took shelter again.

The conduct of the two regiments was thus commended by General Gordon:

> The 2nd Massachusetts and 13th New Jersey pushed forward, with great alacrity, sufficiently far to find that the troops to be supported had retired, that a large force of the enemy lay concealed in the woods, while a not inconsiderable number showed themselves in the open field beyond. These regiments were received with a galling fire, which they sustained and returned for a brief period, then fell back upon their supports. So strong was the enemy, that an addition of any force I could command would only have caused further sacrifice, without gain.

As the two regiments went back the 3rd Wisconsin and 27th Indiana were met coming to their support. These, upon being informed of the condition of affairs, moved back and the four regiments took position in the edge of the East Woods in support to batteries. When the 2nd Massachusetts and 13th New Jersey were ordered to the front, the 107th New York, then in the southern part of the East Woods, was directed to close in to the right. While executing the movement a general officer rode up and ordered the regiment to move out into the field and support Cothran's Battery. This fine regiment moved with steadiness to the rear of the battery, just as the 2nd Massachusetts and 13th New Jersey were falling back, and maintained its ground for some hours and until relieved, although exposed to a front fire from the enemy and a fire over its head from batteries in the rear.

Besides the batteries of Woodruff and Cothran, there were others in front of the East Woods: Monroe's four guns at the southwest corner of the woods; Knap's at the southeast corner of the cornfield; Bruen's on Knap's right; in the field north of the corn were Reynolds' and Stewart's guns; and, under the impression that the West Woods concealed a large body of the enemy, on the point of advancing, these batteries opened a furious fire upon the woods. McLaws says: "There was an incessant storm of shot and shell, grape and canister, but the loss inflicted by the artillery was comparatively very small. Fortunately, the woods were on a side of a hill, the main slope of which was toward us, with numerous ledges of rock along it." Walker says "his brave men, lay upon the ground, taking advantage of such undulations and shallow ravines as gave promise of partial shelter, while this fearful storm raged a few feet above their heads,

The 2nd Massachusetts's view of Ransom's Brigade and the West Woods from the Hagerstown Pike. *Author's collection.*

tearing the trees asunder, lopping off huge branches, and filling the air with shrieks and explosions, realizing to the fullest the fearful sublimity of battle."

Meanwhile, there were stirring scenes, hard and brilliant fighting around the Dunker Church, where Greene's Division signally repulsed the right of McLaws' Division, supported by Manning's Brigade of Walker's Division, and, advancing across the Hagerstown road, secured a footing in the woods beyond and south of the church. It will be remembered that when Early, Barksdale and Anderson drove the 125th Pennsylvania, 34th New York and 72nd Pennsylvania from the woods at the church, they were assisted by the 2nd South Carolina, but this regiment did not change direction to the left and pursue Sedgwick's Division, nor did it halt and then fall back as did Anderson. After it fired its effective volley at the 34th New York and again at the 72nd Pennsylvania, a part of it passed north of the church and halting near the road fired at the retreating troops, but the greater part, passing south of the church, crossed the road, went by an abandoned caisson, and gained a prominent rock ledge, 110 yards east of the church and close to the Smoketown road, where it fired upon the retreating troops and upon Monroe's Battery, which, says a Confederate officer, "we thought was getting ready to fight or run away." Exultant at success and believing the Union line broken and driven entirely from this part of the field, Captain George B. Cuthbert, who was in that wing of the regiment, gave the order to form to the right, intending to advance a little farther to the higher ground on his right. Just as the movement began, and while most of the men were still facing north, Greene's men, some of whom had now replenished ammunition, rose up from behind the slight rise of ground which had concealed them and opened a fire that sent the surprised South Carolinians to the rear, across the road and about 150 yards beyond the church, where, under cover of the ridge, they rallied and moved to the right, out of the line of fire that the Union guns began pouring into the woods around the church. This lateral movement brought the regiment to within a few yards of the south edge of the woods, where it awaited the rest of the brigade.

It was about this time that Carlton's Georgia Battery of three guns came forward. When McLaws came up with his division this battery advanced along the Hauser ridge, and near Hauser's, Stuart rode up and asked for a battery which he proposed to push into the West Woods, to hold them until McLaws could get up and be deployed. McLaws objected, but Jackson ordered him to turn the battery over to Stuart. Carlton was ordered by Stuart to go through the woods to the Dunker Church and hold that position until Kershaw came up, even if he lost every man and gun of the battery. This was apparently before the 125th Pennsylvania had shown itself, and as he started to go Carlton heard the sound of firing in the

Area near the intersection of the Hagerstown Pike and Smoketown Road where the 2nd South Carolina fought. Looking east. *Author's collection.*

woods. He went down the Hauser lane, passing A. Poffenberger's, and thence by the cart road through the woods. As he came to the brow of the ridge, on which the 125th Pennsylvania had stood and from which it had just been driven, he came under the fire of Union artillery, 18 horses were almost instantly killed and he was obliged to put his guns in by hand, which was done near the northwest corner of the church. Stuart followed Carlton and as the two stood near the church they saw Greene's infantry and Tompkins' Battery, on the high ground to the right, and artillery in position and coming into position in the field to the left and front. The Union batteries in front opened on him; Tompkins after the repulse of Kershaw, turned two guns upon him, in less than twenty minutes every gun was disabled and he was ordered to the rear. More than half of his horses had been killed and infantry assisted to withdraw the guns. He went into position after the 125h Pennsylvania and 34th New York had been withdrawn from the woods; he withdrew immediately after Kershaw's repulse, which we now note.

Soon after the 2nd South Carolina had fallen back it saw advancing through the field on the south, a body of troops, supposed to be its own brigade, and the colors of the regiment were taken to the fence, unfurled and waved, to show that they were friends, and when they came up it was seen that they were the 8th South Carolina. This regiment had not closely followed the 2nd; it passed to the right of the route taken by it, and, under a severe fire of canister from Tompkins' guns, approached the road, and was so. . . (Here chapter ends in middle of sentence; as table of contents calls for 79 pages and this makes 74, apparently 5 pages are missing from the Library of Congress.)

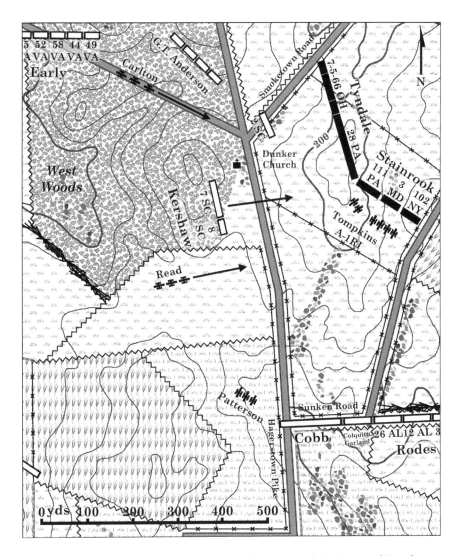

Kershaw's Brigade, supported by the batteries of Carlton and Read, advances from the West Woods toward the plateau east of the woods.

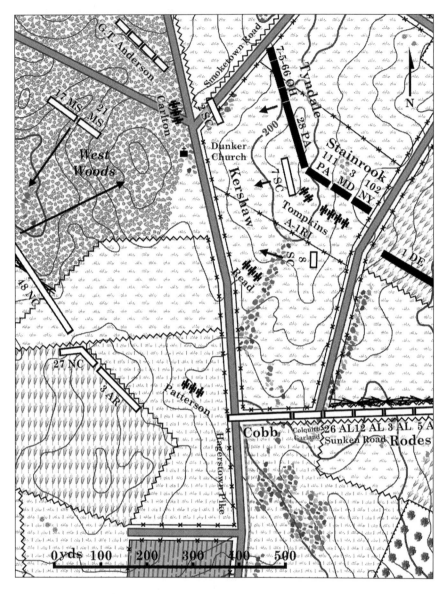

Kershaw's Brigade crests the plateau but is swept back by Greene's division. The 7th South Carolina forces Tompkins to abandon his right three cannon, and the 8th fires into the 1st Delaware as it approaches the Sunken Road. As the Confederates fall back, Greene's men advance to the top of the high ground.

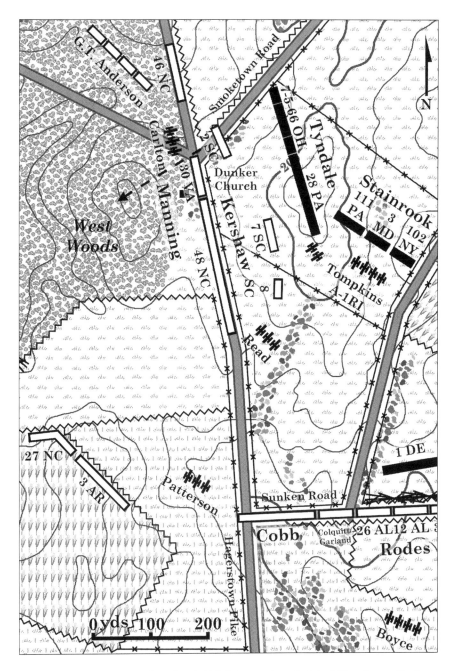

Manning's Brigade of Walker's Division arrives behind Kershaw. Both Confederate brigades engage Greene, but also have to contend with Union artillery fire from the northeast.

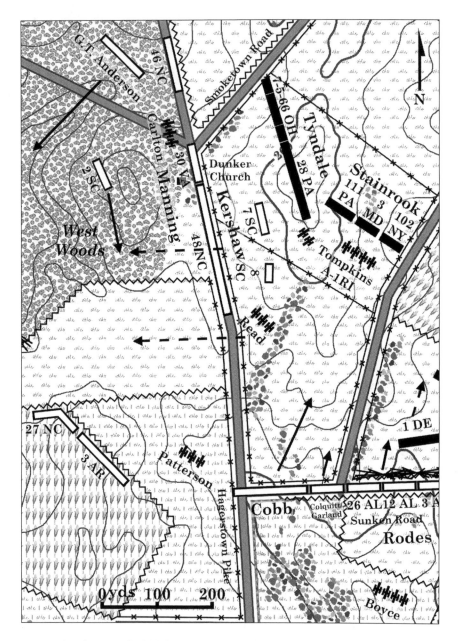

Kershaw's Brigade falls back into the West Woods, leaving Manning to fight Greene. Read retreats as well. The Confederates in the Sunken Road to the south advance.

Kershaw and George T. Anderson retire their brigades out of the West Woods. Carlton's battery retreats as well. Rodes' Brigade falls back, the remnants of Colquitt and Garland never advanced far to begin with, leaving Cobb temporarily exposed.

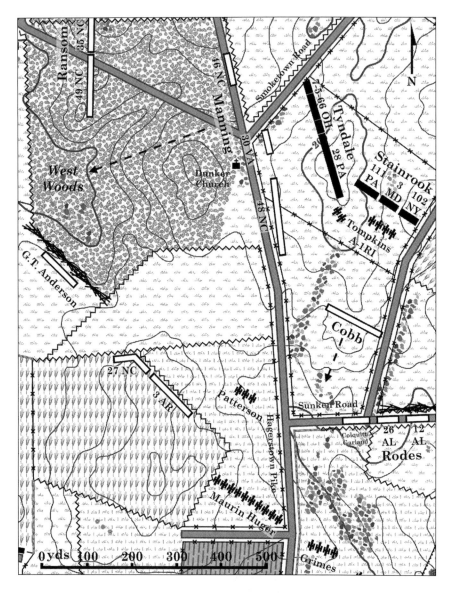

Slammed by artillery fire to the northeast near the East Woods and Greene to their front, Manning's Brigade falls back into the West Woods. Cobb's Brigade retreats to its former position in the Sunken Road.

Chapter 18

The Sunken Road
(9:30 a.m. to 1 p.m.)

While Sedgwick's Division was being driven through the West Woods a sanguinary struggle began for the possession of the Sunken Road, a struggle so bloody that since that day the road has been known as the "Bloody Lane." This lane or farm road, starting from the Hagerstown road about 600 yards south of the Dunker Church, runs in two courses, easterly and southeast, about 1,000 yards, then turns south and pursues a zig-zag course to the Sharpsburg and Keedysville road which it strikes midway between the crest of Cemetery hill and the Antietam. By rains and usage the roadway had been worn down to an ordinary depth of two or three feet, and in many places to a much greater depth, thus giving protection to troops lying in it. It was in the easterly stretch of this road that Colquitt's Brigade lay on the night of the 16th, Ripley's Brigade 600 yards in front, and, in its southeasterly course, on Colquitt's right, was Garland's Brigade, with Rodes' and George B. Anderson's on the right and rear, Rodes' on Garland's immediate right and at right angles facing the Antietam, with Anderson farther to the right also facing the Antietam. These five brigades constituted D. H. Hill's Division. While Ripley, Colquitt and Garland were engaged to the left and front with the First and Twelfth corps, Rodes was ordered to move to their assistance and Anderson was directed to close in to the left, and, soon thereafter, to form line on Rodes' right. Rodes reports that he received his orders about 9 o'clock, it was probably a half hour earlier, and he had hardly begun the movement before it was evident that the three brigades of the division engaged in front had met with a reverse, and that the best service he could render them and the field generally would be to form a line in rear and endeavor to rally them before attacking or being attacked. General Hill seems to have held the same view, for, at the moment Rodes came to this conclusion he received an order from Hill to halt and form line of battle in the Sunken Road. He had then passed the mouth of Roulette's lane, his left about 150 yards from the Hagerstown road. Rodes had five Alabama regiments. The 6th, Colonel John B. Gordon, was on the right, and to the left, in order named were the 5th, Major E. L. Hobson; 3rd, Colonel C. A. Battle; 12th, Captain Tucker, and 26th, Colonel E. A. O'Neal. The brigade numbered 850 officers and men.

In a short time small parties of Garland's and Colquitt's brigades, falling back in some disorder, were rallied and formed on his left, Rodes assuming command of them. Hill says he made an effort to rally all of Garland's and Colquitt's men at this point, but he was not successful, most of them passed on to Sharpsburg, but the 23rd North Carolina came off the field led by Lieutenant Colonel Johnston and took position in the road and some stragglers joined it. There were some men of the 13th North Carolina among those, characterized by Hill as stragglers, and Rodes says that a small portion of Colquitt's Brigade formed on his left. This part of his line received additional strength by the arrival of Cobb's Brigade of McLaws' Division, which took position in the Hagerstown road, at the mouth of the Sunken Road.

Carter's Virginia battery, which had been on Rodes' left, was sent to the rear when the brigade moved to the left, and when the new position was taken Patterson's Georgia battery of three guns occupied a knoll immediately in Rodes' front, about 250 yards, at the southwest corner of Mumma's cornfield, and was engaged in firing at Greene's Division, Twelfth Corps, then taking position at the Dunker Church, but Patterson's guns were quickly driven across the Hagerstown road; as we have seen by the fire of the 102nd New York, and they moved to the left.

George B. Anderson now came up and formed on Rodes' right. During the night of the 16th Anderson lay at the south end of the Sunken Road and astride the Sharpsburg and Keedysville road, his skirmishers thrown to the crest of the ridge, crossing the road, watching the middle bridge over the Antietam. Early in the morning there was a severe artillery duel between the batteries east of the Antietam and the Confederate batteries in Anderson's rear, on Cemetery ridge, and on his left, after which he moved up the ravine to his left, halted and formed line, and then moved up the same ravine to Piper's cornfield and again formed line facing the Antietam, as at his previous halt. Then moving into the Sunken Road he formed line on Rodes' right, in this order from left to right: the 2nd North Carolina, Colonel C. C. Tew, joined the right of the 6th Alabama, its second company from the right being directly opposite the entrance to Roulette's lane; on the

The Sunken Road looking west from near the intersection with the Roulette lane. There were little or no trees present during the battle, nor was the later James Ward cabin seen in the center. *Antietam: Report of the Ohio Antietam Battlefield Commission.*

right of the 2nd was the 14th North Carolina, Colonel R. T. Bennett, under good shelter from a front attack; on the right of the 14th, was the 4th North Carolina, Captain W. T. Marsh, and the 30th North Carolina, Colonel F. M. Parker was on the right of the 4th. This line, which was not a continuous one, was mostly under good cover. There were places where the road was crossed by rock ledges, and at these points there was great exposure and they were not occupied. Along this entire front of Anderson and Rodes was high ground overlooking the Sunken Road, broken only by a ravine through which ran Roulette's lane. Behind Anderson's entire line and extending to the left to the center of Rodes' Brigade was a field of dense corn. In many places in rear this ground was much higher than the Sunken Road and looked directly down into it. The road was a natural rifle pit. Anderson's Brigade numbered 1,174 officers and men and was of most excellent material; a southern writer has said of it:

> The fondness of this brigade for prayer meeting and Psalm singing united with an ever readiness to fight, reminds one of Cromwell's Ironsides. It fought well at Seven Pines, when one of its regiments, having carried in 678 officers and men, lost 54 per cent in killed and wounded. At Malvern Hill it suffered great loss. To see these poor devils, many of them almost barefooted and all of them half-starved, approach a field where a battle was raging was a pleasant sight. The crash of Napoleons, the roar of howitzers and crash of musketry always excited and exhilarated them, and as they swung into action they seemed supremely happy.

Immediately upon taking position General Anderson and Colonel Tew walked to the top of the hill in front and saw French's Division forming at the East Woods and, following the example of Rodes' men who had preceded them, the North Carolinians began to pile fence rails in their front. Rodes says: "A short time after my brigade assumed its new position and while the men were busy improving their position by piling rails along their front, the enemy deployed in our front in three beautiful lines, all vastly outnumbering ours, and commenced to advance steadily." D. H. Hill says the enemy "advanced in three parallel lines, with all the precision of a parade day." This enemy was French's Division of the Second Corps, and was composed of Generals Max Weber's and Nathan Kimball's brigades and three regiments of new troops, under command of Colonel Dwight Morris, 14th Connecticut. The three brigades were strangers to each other and had been thrown together as a division but the day before. French put his division in motion about 7:40 a.m., crossed the Antietam after Sedgwick and at first followed him closely, but gradually fell behind. The division marched with Max Weber on the left, Morris in the center, and Kimball on

Left hand stereo view of the earliest known photograph of the Sunken Road. Photograph taken by David Bachrach in late 1866 or early 1867. Published by William M. Chase. Taken from George B. Anderson's line looking past the Roulette lane. The curve is where Anderson's and Rodes' Brigades met. Note how sharp the walls of the road are, and how closely the fences are positioned compared to the park today. *Stephen Recker collection.*

the right. French says: "When my left flank had cleared the ford a mile, the division faced to the left, forming three lines of battle adjacent to and contiguous with Sedgwick's and immediately moved to the front."

French is in error in the statement that he formed his lines "adjacent to and contiguous with Sedgwick's." If such were the case he must have come up before Sedgwick's advance; and evidence is to the contrary, and to the effect that when Sedgwick advanced from the East Woods French had not come up. Upon the authority of Captain S. S. Sumner, son and staff officer of General Sumner, the statement was made by Lieutenant Colonel George B. Davis, U.S.A., in a paper read by him before the Military Historical Society of Massachusetts, April 6, 1897, that "the emergency would not permit him (Sumner) to await the arrival of French's Division," so Sedgwick was pushed forward without him, and that French had been given most positive orders to put and keep the head of his column abreast Sedgwick's Division and that these orders were reiterated by several staff officers. It is hard to question such authority, and it is passing strange how French formed his lines contiguous to Sedgwick and then failed to move with him if he had such imperative and reiterated orders. As a matter of fact Sedgwick's Division had advanced from the East Woods before the advance of French's three lines entered them, and there is no evidence that upon entering the woods he was met by Sumner's orders to follow Sedgwick, although it is highly probable such orders were given on the march from the Antietam.

French entered the East Woods about 9:15 a.m., halted and fronted to the left, looking southward. On his right front, 750 yards distant, he could see a Union battery in action, firing south, and behind it infantry in position, the left of the line resting on the Mumma lane, and he could see the Confederates in the Sunken Road. Walker says that French for "want of proper direction" was permitted to diverge widely to the left. In the absence of orders for "proper direction," or for a movement in any direction, he came to the quick and proper conclusion to advance and form on the left of the troops he saw in position—Greene's Division, which he supposed to be Sedgwick—and engage the Confederates in the Sunken Road, whose presence there threatened the left and rear of the Union line. To have done otherwise, under the circumstances, unless under specific orders, would have been highly reprehensible.

It required less than fifteen minutes to close up the columns and properly dress them. Then the brigades were ordered forward. Weber's in advance, followed by Morris' and Kimball's. Weber's Brigade was composed of the 1st Delaware, 4th New York, and 5th Maryland. They were old regiments, well drilled and disciplined, but never had been in battle. The brigade numbered 1,800 officers and men. The 1st Delaware was on the right, the 5th Maryland in the center, and the 4th New York on the left.

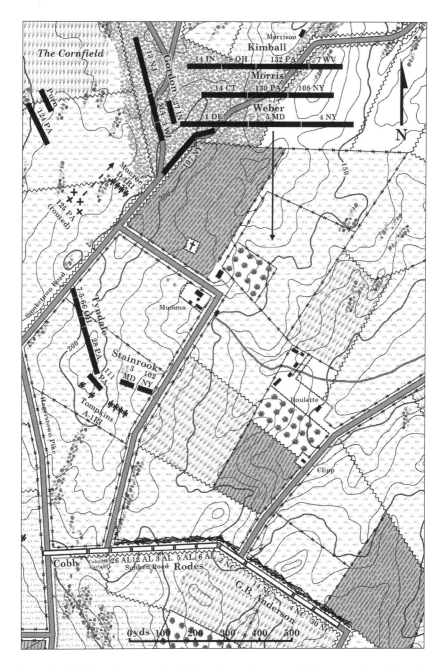

French's division faces to the left and marches south from the East Woods.
The brigades of George B. Anderson, Rodes, Cobb and the remnants of
Colquitt and Garland are waiting for them.

Weber ordered the colors of the 5th Maryland to be carried direct to the Roulette house, the regiments on the right and left dressing on the 5th Maryland, and the line, emerging from the East Woods, went forward, under the fire of a Confederate battery on the ridge south of Piper's house, and one west of the Hagerstown road, a fire which was very annoying, several shells falling into the ranks of the 1st Delaware. The color bearer of the 5th Maryland, who had been designated to give the direction, was a very heavy built German, over six feet in height and weighing nearly 300 pounds, very deliberate in movement, hence, by the right and left color bearers moving a little more briskly, the brigade, as it approached the Roulette place, assumed a concentric formation. The 1st Delaware disappeared in Mumma's cornfield, on the right of the Roulette house, the 4th New York was separated from the left of the 5th Maryland by Roulette's lane, which ran from the barn to the Sunken Road, and the 5th Maryland passed through the Roulette grounds and passing to the right of the dwelling entered the apple orchard, where the left of the regiment came under the fire of a small Confederate outpost in the Roulette lane, near the Clipp house. The regiment with the 4th New York drove back this advance party, a few men being killed and wounded on either side.

While driving back the Confederate outpost and brushing some skirmishers from the fences in front, the right of Weber's line was struck by the 8th South Carolina of Kershaw's Brigade, which had charged Tompkins' Rhode Island battery on the plateau opposite the Dunker Church. In the charge the 8th South Carolina passed the other regiments of its brigade and, as it mounted the crest overlooking Mumma's cornfield, saw troops moving through and beyond it and promptly halted and opened fire. It was a very small regiment of not over 40 muskets, but so sudden, unexpected, and well delivered was its fire that with the fire of the artillery, it caused momentary confusion. French says it was a "sudden and terrible fire." The Carolinians remained but two or three minutes upon Weber's flank and then fell back with their brigade which had been bloodily repulsed. At this time the 1st Delaware was in Mumma's cornfield, its right close to the fence of the lane, the 5th Maryland was in Roulette's orchard, its right connecting with the 1st Delaware, its left on Roulette's lane, and the 4th New York beyond the lane. Weber now ordered bayonets fixed and the brigade went forward on the run to the ridge overlooking the Sunken Road and from 50 to 80 yards of it. As it reached the crest of the ridge Rodes and Anderson's men poured in a cool, accurate fire which caused the whole line to recoil, but it quickly rallied and opened fire. On the right the 1st Delaware advanced so far that its left was but 50 yards from the Sunken Road, and the fire from the road and from a line on higher ground beyond it, was so severe that after a vain effort to advance, during which, Colonel Andrews says: "The second line [Morris], composed of new levies, instead

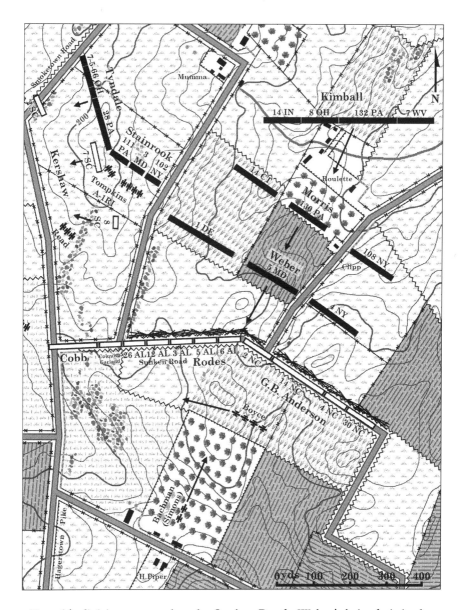

French's division approaches the Sunken Road. Weber's brigade is in the lead. The 8th South Carolina fires into the flank of the 1st Delaware, but the effect is momentary.

of supporting our advance, fired into our rear," the regiment having lost one fourth its men, and eight officers commanding companies killed or wounded, fell back through the 14th Connecticut and Mumma's cornfield to the grass field beyond. The color guard were all killed or wounded, and the colors left on the field with Lieutenant Colonel Oliver Hopkinson, severely wounded, who, afterwards brought them off. After the regiment had rallied in the field just beyond the corn, Major Thomas A. Smythe, Captain Richards, Lieutenants James P. Postles, Tanner and Nicholls, with about 75 to 90 men, went down the Mumma lane as far as the southwest corner of the cornfield, where, under shelter of rock ledges and the fencing, they remained skirmishing until about noon. Here Captain Richards was killed and from this advantageous position they repulsed several attempted advances of the enemy upon Tompkins' Battery which was close to their right and rear. On the left of the 1st Delaware, the 5th Maryland passed over the top of the ridge and was met by a murderous fire from the right of Rodes' Brigade and the 2nd North Carolina of Anderson, a fire so deadly that over one fourth of the regiment was struck down instantly, but the survivors lay down and returned the fire. In the charge the colors were carried about 30 feet to the front, and the men crawled forward and dressed on them, all the time maintaining a steady fire upon the enemy in the road at the foot of the hill about 50 yards distant. The 4th New York advanced on the left of Roulette's lane and as it reached the crest of the hill overlooking Anderson's men in the Sunken Road, about 50 yards distant, was met by a volley that laid low about 150 men, and the regiment recoiled, and lay down under cover of the crest. Exultant at their success portions of Anderson's Brigade rushed forward, but were quickly driven back. In this short contest of not over five minutes Weber lost one fourth of his brigade.

Rodes says the Union line came to the crest of the hill overlooking his position, and for five minutes bravely stood a telling fire at about 80 yards which his whole brigade delivered, and Colonel Bennett, 14th North Carolina, in whose immediate front the 4th New York advanced, says: "There advance was beautiful in the extreme and great regularity marked their columns and this precision of movement was preserved by the lines until a space not exceeding 50 yards separated the combatants. Then it was that a well directed fire sent them in disorder some 50 paces rearward."

Morris' Brigade of three new regiments followed Weber. When it advanced out of the woods, Weber's Brigade was about 300 yards ahead of it. The 14th Connecticut, on the right, passed through Mumma's orchard, nine companies passed to the right of Roulette's house and one to the left, and the entire regiment into Mumma's cornfield, the right reaching the Mumma's lane and the left close to the east edge of the cornfield. The 130th Pennsylvania, on the immediate left of the 14th Connecticut, advanced through Roulette's small cornfield, passed between the house and

View of the Sunken Road from the hill occupied by the 5th Maryland. The bend in the center marks the area where Rodes' and George B. Anderson's Brigades met. Colonel John B. Gordon's 6th Alabama fought just to the right of the bend. *Author's collection.*

the barn and then through Roulette's orchard with its left on the lane, while the 108th New York moved on the left of the lane, its right resting on it. The advance was made under severe artillery and musketry fire, the latter being directed at Weber, in advance, who was being followed at a distance not exceeding 200 yards. When the 14th Connecticut reached the south fence of the cornfield it came under the withering fire that was being poured on the 1st Delaware in its front, but the men climbed the fence and with much difficulty advanced from 50 to 65 yards over the grass field, when, unable to advance farther, it fell back to the cornfield. The 130th Pennsylvania advanced in line on the left of the 14th Connecticut, a part of it halted behind a stone fence, which was a continuation of the fence of Mumma's cornfield, some of the men advanced a few yards farther and many reached the line held by the 5th Maryland and remained upon it until relieved by the advance of Kimball's Brigade. On the left of Roulette's lane the 108th New York moved up to the line held by the 4th New York, its left extending beyond it, and received such a severe fire from Anderson's North Carolinians that it recoiled in disorder and lay down upon the northern slope of the ridge, and again portions of Anderson's command advanced beyond the Sunken Road and were quickly driven back.

It was about this time that Rodes, by Longstreet's direction, ordered an advance. A part of his line went forward and immediately came under such a severe fire that it was checked. Tompkins' guns from their fine position on the right and rear of the 14th Connecticut, opened with shell and case shot, and the line fell back in some disorder and was with difficulty rallied in the Sunken Road. Rodes says:

> Receiving an order from General Longstreet to do so, I endeavored to charge them with my brigade and that portion of Colquitt's which was on my immediate left. The charge failed, mainly because the 6th Alabama Regiment, not hearing the command, did not move forward with the others, and because Colquitt's men did not advance far enough. That part of the brigade which moved forward found themselves in an exposed position, and being outnumbered and unsustained, fell back before I could, by personal effort, which was duly made, get the 6th Alabama to move. Hastening back to the left, I arrived just in time to prevent the men from falling back to the rear of the road we had just occupied.

Rodes lost quite severely in this effort and among the killed was Captain Tucker, commanding 12th Alabama. Cobb's Brigade took part in this movement and on Rodes left. It will be remembered that when McLaws prepared for his attack upon Sedgwick, Cobb's Brigade moved too far to the right and brought up on the left of Rodes, where it was covered from

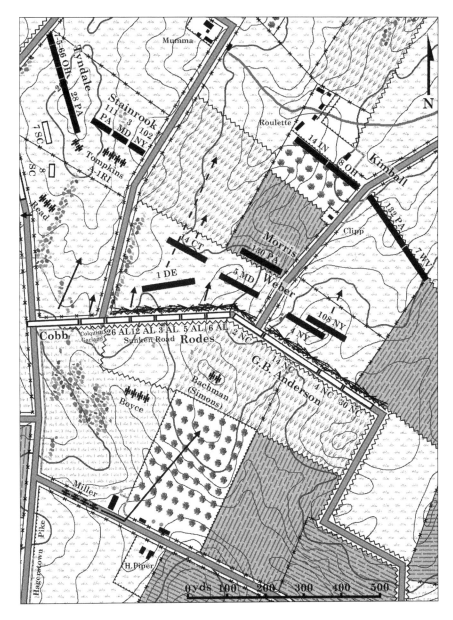

Morris' brigade closes on Weber in support. Many of his regiments intermingle with Weber's on the front line. The 1st Delaware is fired into by the 14th Connecticut behind it and retires. Rodes, Cobb, and Colquitt/Garland counterattack.

the Union musketry by a hill in front, but suffered from the heavy shelling of the batteries beyond the Antietam. For an hour the brigade was inactive, then Longstreet ordered it forward with Rodes and the men, "eager to meet the foe upon a more equal footing, gallantly pressed forward with a cheer, the top of the hill gained amid a galling and destructive shower of balls." There it remained until Colonel Sanders, seeing that Rodes had fallen back, leaving him without support, fell back to the cover of the fence from which it had charged. As Rodes was rallying the left of his brigade in the Sunken Road, a part of the 6th Alabama, under cover of the smoke, mad a rush for the colors of the 5th Maryland, and the colors and that part of the line near them fell back about 20 yards, when a rally was made and the Alabama men driven back to the road, the colors being advanced to their original position. In this affair Major Blumenberg, commanding 5th Maryland, was severely wounded.

The two brigades of Weber and Morris had made spirited efforts to drive the enemy but were brought to a stand; had lost heavily and, being new troops, had become confused and much broken; many of the men had gone to the rear, but enough of them remained on the firing line to resist the enemy, though without sufficient aggressive force to advance. While the two brigades were thus engaged with Rodes and Anderson, Captain S. S. Sumner of the corps staff, rode up to French with an order from General Sumner to push on and make a diversion in favor of Sedgwick, who was being severely handled by McLaws. This order came when Kimball, following Morris from the East Woods, had passed the Roulette buildings, and halted for alignment 350 yards in rear of Weber and Morris, the right wing—14th Indiana and 8th Ohio—midway in Roulette's apple orchard, the left wing—132nd New York and 7th West Virginia, beyond the Roulette lane. The 8th Ohio rested its left on the lane, on its right was the 14th Indiana; the 132nd Pennsylvania rested its right on the lane, on its left was the 7th West Virginia. The 132nd Pennsylvania was a new regiment; the others were veterans and had seen much service in Western Virginia and on the Peninsula. Kimball was a stiff and tenacious fighter; he had thwarted and defeated General Lee's efforts to force the Union position at Cheat Mountain, in September 1861, and defeated Stonewall Jackson at Kernstown, March 23 1862.

The Brigade had not been long halted when Sumner's order to press the enemy was received, and Kimball was directed to pass Weber and Morris, carry the crest of the ridge and drive the enemy from the Sunken Road with the bayonet. At this time the battle was raging 350 yards in front, and some officers and men of Kimball's Brigade were killed and wounded while yet in the orchard. The men were lying down, Kimball called them to attention, and as he went along the ranks said: "Boys we are going in now to lick the rebels, and we will stay with them, all day if necessary." Knapsacks were

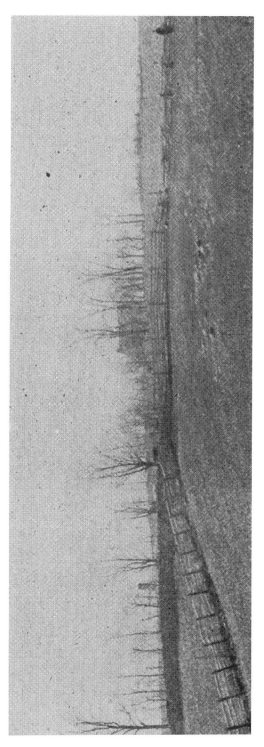

Southeastern corner of the Mumma cornfield looking south. The left flank of the 14th Connecticut was positioned here for much of its action. The monument to the 5th Maryland is visible on the elevation to the left, and the post war James Ward cabin along the road in the center. *History of the Fourteenth Regiment, Connecticut Vol. Infantry.*

taken off and piled under the apple trees, bayonets fixed, and the entire line, starting at a double-quick, moved steadily and magnificently forward over the open plain, under a heavy fire of shell and in the face of a sheet of musketry, which dropped men here and there; the right wing swept past the left of the 14th Connecticut and over that part of the 130th Pennsylvania on its left and, as it approached the 5th Maryland and some of the 130th Pennsylvania in front, cried, "get to the rear you fellows" and, with a roar and blaze, passed over the ridge to receive such a staggering fire from artillery on the right, and the musketry of Anderson and Rodes in front that it recoiled to the line held by the 5th Maryland, and the right wing of the 14th Indiana was closed in to the left, under cover of the ridge, to avoid the artillery fire, to which it was exposed, and in this position, both the 14th Indiana and 8th Ohio opened a steady fire which was continued until the Confederate were driven from the road or surrendered, and many of the 5th Maryland remained and fought with them. Kimball says:

> Directly in my front, in a narrow road running parallel with my line, and, being washed by water, forming a natural rifle-pit between my line and a large cornfield, I found the enemy in great force, as also in the cornfield in rear of the ditch. As my line advanced to the crest of the hill, a murderous fire was opened upon it from the entire force in front. My advance further was checked.

As soon as Kimball's men recovered from the staggering blow, under which they had recoiled, the color bearers of the 14th Indiana and 8th Ohio crawled along the ground and planted their colors defiantly on the very crest of the ridge, the full color guard rallying around them. On these the men formed and, lying face to the ground," began their work, firing at the heads and shoulders of such of the enemy as exposed themselves in the Sunken Road, and at others who were firing from the cornfield beyond, and in this manner says Kimball: "For three hours and thirty minutes the battle raged incessantly, without either party giving way." Kimball overestimates the time; he was in action a little over two hours.

With the advent of Kimball and his firm hold on the ridge the 5th Maryland, under direction of its company officers, began to withdraw by squads of a half dozen or more. There was some confusion in the withdrawal and in endeavoring to check it and get his brigade in order Max Weber was wounded and lost his leg. Some men of the 5th Maryland remained on Kimball's line, but the greater part of them were rallied at the Clipp house and near Roulette's barn, where they were joined by the 4th New York. A part of the 130th Pennsylvania fell back, but the greater part remained in rear of the 8th Ohio, and the 14th Connecticut maintained its position in the south part of Mumma's corn, its left 65 yards in rear of the

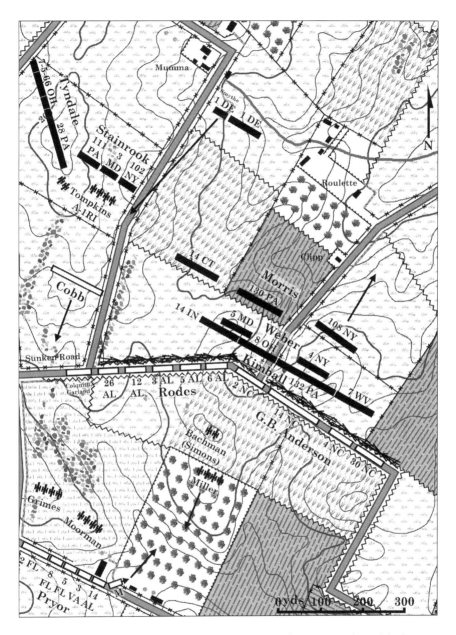

Kimball's brigade, having been ordered forward, intermingles with those left from Weber and Morris on the height above the Sunken Road. Cobb's Brigade falls back. The first brigades of Richard H. Anderson's Division begin to arrive at the H. Piper farm.

14th Indiana. On the right of the 14th Connecticut, on high ground, well protected by the fences of Mumma's lane and the outcropping rocks, was the detachment of the 1st Delaware, and 289 yards to the right and rear was Tompkins' Battery, which poured a constant fire of shell and case-shot upon the Confederates in the Sunken Road and in the cornfield beyond it.

In Kimball's advance the left company of the 8th Ohio was crowded beyond the Roulette lane and with the 132nd Pennsylvania and 7th West Virginia, marched in good order up the hill, passed the 108th New York, which was retreating in some disorder, and as they mounted the crest, came under fire of Confederate artillery on Cemetery ridge and received the fire of Anderson's men, who were waiting for them, with guns resting on the rails in front. This fire was terrific and deadly. Colonel Oakford, commanding the 132nd Pennsylvania, was killed, many officers and men of the two regiments and the company of the 8th Ohio were struck down, the advance was checked, and the line fell back under cover of the crest and laid down. When the company of the 8th Ohio reached the crest there were some of the 4th New York still holding ground, these were relieved and joined their comrades near the Clipp house, and the veteran Ohioans crawling forward and getting such shelter as the ground afforded, opened a very cool and effective enfilading fire upon the 2nd North Carolina and right wing of the 6th Alabama, who were in that part of the Sunken Road, west of the Roulette lane and in the immediate front of the right wing of the brigade.

The Roulette lane, dividing the wings of Kimball's brigade requires a brief description. From the Hagerstown road the Sunken Road runs easterly 550 yards, then nearly southeast 450 yards, to where it makes an angle and runs nearly south. For the first hundred yards the road is level, then rises to pass over a rocky ledge, where it turns southeast. From this last rock ledge, the angle in the road, it descends 80 yards to the mouth of the Roulette lane, the descent in the 80 yards being 20 feet. From the mouth of the lane the road begins to ascend and at 150 yards reaches the plateau upon which it runs to its southerly course. It will thus be seen that the mouth of the Roulette lane is in a depression, which is the beginning of a ravine or cleft that, running northerly, bisects the ridge or high ground overlooking the Sunken Road; and in this ravine runs the narrow Roulette lane, the ground rising abruptly 30 to 40 feet on either side of it.

The conformation of the ground determined the position of the troops. Kimball's right wing was west of Roulette's lane, on a hill sloping south to the Sunken Road and east to the lane. Its right, the 14th Indiana, was about 80 yards from the angle of the Sunken Road in front, its left, the 8th Ohio rested on the Roulette lane 105 yards from its mouth. This position gave a direct fire to the front upon the right of Rodes Brigade and the 2nd North Carolina of Anderson's, and an enfilading fire upon the left of the 14th

The Roulette lane looking south toward the Sunken Road and Confederate line. The Sunken Road is on the other side of the hill and behind the trees. *Author's collection.*

North Carolina, east of the mouth of the lane, from which it suffered terribly. Immediately east of the lane the ridge was higher, sloping both west and south, and on a grassy knoll 100 yards from the mouth of the lane and overlooking it, was the company of the 8th Ohio. From this point the crest of the ridge trends southeast, gradually nearing the Sunken Road, and on it, to the rear and left of the Ohio company were the 132nd Pennsylvania and 7th West Virginia, the left of the latter about 100 yards from the road.

Rodes and Anderson, including men of Colquitt and Garland, who had rallied on the extreme left, had about 2,400 men. With these they had withstood the attack of French's 5,700 men, without yielding a foot of ground. Being well protected, save near the Roulette lane, they had not suffered greatly, but had inflicted great loss.

While all this was transpiring on his front French was with Tompkins' guns on the right of his division. After the repulse of Sedgwick, Tompkins was ordered by Sumner to hold his position until properly relieved and not to retire on any account, even to the risk of losing his guns. Soon after this French came up and expressed some solicitation at the gap between his right and the left of Greene, a gap covered only by the battery and two small regiments of Greene. While in conversation Saunders' artillery battalion went into position in front, and, soon thereafter, R. H. Anderson's infantry division was seen coming over the field toward the Hagerstown road, with the evident intention to charge the battery and attack French's right. Tompkins opened his guns on Saunders' artillery and Anderson's infantry, and French impressed upon him the great necessity of holding his position, remarking that if the guns went his division would go to.

There were now several batteries of Confederate artillery on the high ground between Reel's and the Hagerstown road, which had been gathered there under Lee's orders to form a nucleus for a new line, and among them was Branch's Battery of Walker's Division, to which Jackson rode up and asked why it was not engaged. "No orders and no supports," was the reply. "Go in at once" was the curt rejoinder, "You artillery men are too much afraid of losing your guns." The battery and another advanced but were quickly driven back.

R. H. Anderson's Division followed McLaws in crossing the Potomac and halted near Lee's headquarters. It had six brigades of infantry and an artillery battalion of four batteries. The brigades were those of Wright, commanded by General A. W. Wright; Wilcox's, commanded by Colonel Alfred Cumming; Featherston's, commanded by Colonel Carnot Posey; Pryor's, commanded by General R. A. Pryor; Mahone's, commanded by Colonel W. A. Parham, and Armistead's, commanded by General Lewis A. Armistead. Mahone's Brigade had been so badly broken [at] Crampton's Gap that it had but 82 men at Sharpsburg and was consolidated

Looking from the area near the right section of Tompkins' Battery A, 1st Rhode Island toward the Sunken Road and Piper orchard. *Author's collection.*

into a regiment and acted with Pryor's Brigade. Armistead's Brigade was detached and ordered to the support of McLaws on the left.

Saunders' artillery battalion was composed of Huger's Virginia battery of 4 guns, commanded by Captain Frank Huger; the Portsmouth Battery, 4 guns, commanded by Captain Carey F. Grimes; Moorman's Battery, 4 guns, commanded by Captain M. M. Moorman; and the Donaldsonville, Louisiana, Battery, commanded by Captain Victor Maurin. In the absence of Major John S. Saunders, the battalion was under the command of Captain Grimes. The battalion moved through Sharpsburg and up the Hagerstown road and went into position on the ridge northwest from Piper's barn. Grimes, leading his own battery, went into position on the right of the road and about 60 yards from it; Moorman on Grimes right and 50 yards west of the barn, and Huger and Maurin west of the road. This position was taken soon after Kimball had crowned the ridge overlooking the Sunken Road, and the four batteries opened fire upon him, a fire that was very effective upon the right of the 14th Indiana, but of no particular effect upon other parts of his line. Tompkins turned four guns upon them, the 14th Indiana poured in a musketry fire at from 600 to 700 yards, and the long range guns beyond the Antietam enfiladed them and they were partially silenced in less than 20 minutes. Meanwhile R. H. Anderson's infantry came up.

It was near 10 a.m. when Anderson was ordered forward. He passed to the left of Sharpsburg and halted to pile knapsacks. He then marched, left in front, Pryor's Brigade in advance, northeasterly across the open fields, under a wicked and demoralizing fire of Tompkins' guns, reached the Hagerstown road about 100 yards south of Piper's Lane, and Pryor's Brigade marched up the road to the lane, then down the lane until it passed Piper's barn, where it filed to the left and went up the hill to the left, on the left of the orchard, and was halted by a staff officer. Wilcox's Brigade followed Pryor's as far as the Hagerstown road, which it crossed and, bearing to the right, moved nearly to the crest of Cemetery ridge, south of Piper's house, then halted and threw out skirmishers in the direction of the Antietam. Featherston's Brigade followed Wilcox's and formed near it on Cemetery ridge.

Wright's Brigade did not follow Wilcox's and Featherston's to the Cemetery ridge, but, bearing to the left, under fire from Tompkins' guns, crossed the stone fence of the Hagerstown road, north of Piper's lane, passed the barn and rear of Pryor's Brigade and, facing to the left, was in rear of Piper's apple orchard. The orchard was enclosed by a close and strong oak picket fence, and in tearing it down the brigade suffered greatly from a cross fire of artillery—Tompkins in front and the guns beyond the Antietam on the flank. The 3rd Georgia was on the right and in order named on its left were the 48th Georgia, 44th Alabama, and 22nd Georgia.

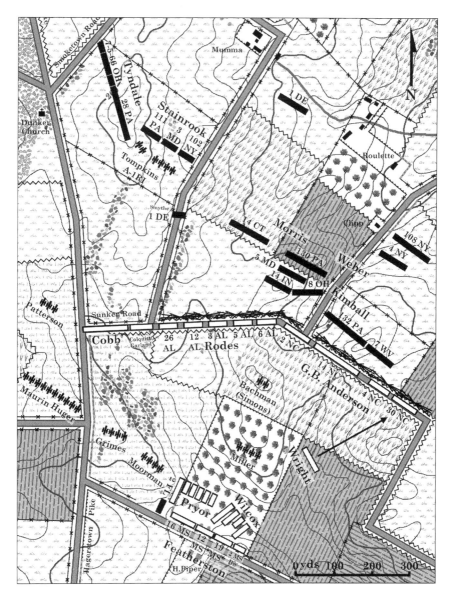

The fire from French's division begins to take its toll on the defenders in the road, thinning their ranks considerably. Wright's Brigade continues on toward the right flank of G. B. Anderson's brigade.

As soon as the fence was torn down sufficiently to admit passage, in places, the brigade moved through the orchard obliquely toward the northeast corner of the cornfield, all the time under artillery fire, and when it reached the high ground in the cornfield came under musketry fire and men fell by the score. While going through the orchard General Wright's horse was torn in pieces by a shell, and the general thrown to the ground, but disengaging himself from the fallen horse he led his brigade on foot through the cornfield, and as he approached the Sunken Road his left came up in rear of the right wing of the 30th North Carolina, receiving such a severe and unexpected fire, as it emerged from the corn, that it was driven back, but soon rallied and took ground to the right. General Wright was shot down, Colonel Robert Jones, who succeeded to the command, was wounded and disabled by a musket ball that went through his breast; the brigade, now reduced to about 250 men, reached the Sunken Road, on George B. Anderson's right, and lay down in it, Colonel William Gibson, 48th Georgia, assumed command.

In front and to the left, not over a hundred yards distant, was the 7th West Virginia which now poured in its fire and began to gain ground to the left. There was some protection in the road from musketry fire; the brigade had passed out of the line of fire of Tompkins' guns, but was subjected to a terrible enfilade fire of the guns from beyond the Antietam, which disheartened the officers and men, who were encouraged to hold on a little longer as General Pryor would soon join on the right and an advance be made. But Pryor did not come up, there was an increasing fire in front, and, by Wright's direction, who was still lying on the ground, twice wounded, unable to rise, Gibson ordered a charge upon the extended and exposed flank of the 7th West Virginia. The left and center of the brigade made little if any advance, but the 3rd Georgia, on the extreme right, led by Colonel R. B. Nisbet, leaped out of the road and making a slight left wheel, charged the 7th West Virginia, which changed front by refusing its left and advancing its right, and after a short but severe fight drove the Georgians back to the road, leaving their colonel, badly wounded, on the field, to be taken prisoner a little later.

Wright's Brigade had suffered greatly. Its commander had been wounded and disabled, Lieutenant Colonel Derby, commanding 44th Alabama, killed, Colonels Jones and Nisbet wounded and a long list of line officers killed and wounded. One regiment had one officer only, and many companies of the brigade were in command of sergeants or corporals, but all remained in the road and kept up warm fire.

It was about this time that George B. Anderson, informed that a column of the enemy was approaching his right, threatening to envelop it, rode to the rear to report to D. H. Hill. Upon returning he was wounded at the south edge of the corn, near the northeast corner of the orchard, and sent

The Sunken Road from behind its right flank and in the Piper cornfield. Wright's and Wilcox's Brigades traversed and fought in this area. The Union regiments on the heights could fire over the heads of the Confederates in the road into those moving through the cornfield. *Author's collection.*

his courier to Colonel Parker of the 30th North Carolina, with instructions that Adjutant Fred Philips be sent to Colonel Tew, 2nd North Carolina, and inform him that he was in command of the brigade. Philips made his way, under severe fire, down the line to the left of the 14th North Carolina and from that point word was passed along the line of the 2nd North Carolina. Tew, who was lying down with his men, rose from the ground, acknowledged the receipt of the message by raising his cap and was instantly killed. The command of the brigade fell to Colonel R. T. Bennett, 14th North Carolina, who reports that at this time the brigade "appeared perfectly self-possessed" and that soon thereafter word came for the command to keep a lookout on the extreme right. This was when Richardson's Division was forming for attack.

Major General Israel B. Richardson's Division was composed of three brigades commanded by Generals J. C. Caldwell, Thomas F. Meagher and Colonel John R Brooke, 53rd Pennsylvania. On the night of the 16th it was in position at the east foot of the bluff bordering the Antietam, its left on the Sharpsburg and Keedysville road. It received orders at 7:40 a.m., to march when relieved by Morell's Division of the Fifth Corps, and it was not until 9 a.m. that Morell arrived from his bivouac on the suburbs of Keedysville, a mile distant. It was bad enough that Sumner did not receive his orders to march before 7:30 a.m., it was worse that this fine division was delayed, an hour and a half later, and there was no good reason for it. The events already narrated in this chapter are good proof that had Richardson closely followed French, and joined in the advance upon the Sunken Road, D. H. Hill's men would have been driven from it before the arrival of R. H. Anderson's Division.

The division was put in motion at 9 a.m., went back a short distance on the road to Keedysville, filed to the left, descended the hill to the ford by which Sumner had crossed, which it went over about 9:30 a.m., and made a brief halt to permit the men to wring the water from their socks. The march was resumed in a direction nearly parallel to the creek and, passing Neikirk's, the division halted in a ravine through which ran a spring branch to the Antietam. Here the men piled knapsacks and blankets and the lines were then formed in a cornfield on the northeastern slope of the high ground that overlooked Roulette's house and about 450 yards east of it and 700 yards northeast of the Sunken Road. Meagher's Brigade, on the right, deployed from column into line of battle on the northeastern edge of the cornfield, marched through it 200 yards and to its southwestern edge, under a scattering fire that clipped the corn and wounded a few men. From right to left the brigade was thus formed, 69th New York, 29th Massachusetts, 63rd and 88th New York. Caldwell's Brigade advanced through the same cornfield on Meagher's left, and Brooke's Brigade followed in second line.

Major General Israel B. Richardson
Library of Congress.

The infantry strength of the division was 4,029 officers and men and it was not accompanied by its artillery, this had preceded it the evening before.

Owing to the smallness of the pioneer corps, which had become much reduced by service on the Peninsula, there was much embarrassment and delay in crossing the fence, during which many officers and men were killed and wounded. The same trouble occurred in passing a second fence, but here volunteers gave assistance, and the line went forward in fine order, ascended the rising ground overlooking the Sunken Road and to within 75 to 100 yards of it and received a murderous fire from the Confederate line in the road and the artillery beyond. Meagher says: "In coming into this close and fatal contest with the enemy, the officers and men of the brigade waved their swords and hats and gave the heartiest cheers for their general, George B. McClellan, and the Army of the Potomac. Never were men in higher spirits. Never did men with such alacrity and generosity of heart press forward and encounter the perils of the battle-field."

Meagher's Brigade was known in the army and throughout the country as "The Irish Brigade," and was even so designated in orders and reports of commanding officers. As a matter of fact the brigade at Antietam, and for some months before and after that campaign, was not strictly an Irish Brigade. Three regiments were composed mainly of Irishmen and men of Irish parentage. These regiments, recruited in New York, marched and fought under the green flag of Ireland. The 29th Massachusetts, constituting one fourth of the brigade, was not an Irish regiment. On the contrary, it was intensely American in its make up. All its field officers were lineal descendants of the early colonists, and with scarcely an exception the line officers were thoroughbred Americans, nearly all of Revolutionary stock; and so with the men—mainly genuine Americans. It is doubtful if there was a regiment from Massachusetts with a larger percentage of Americans in its ranks. Every regiment of the brigade was superb, and the 29th Massachusetts prides itself upon its service in it, "and at no time during its four years war experience," writes a prominent officer of the regiment, "was fairer or better treatment accorded the regiment, from a gentlemanly and soldierly standpoint than that received while associated with the Irishmen of Meagher's Brigade."

Notwithstanding the terrible punishment they had received from the first volley these brave Irishmen and men of Massachusetts stood steadily and bravely to their work. Meagher's orders were, that, after the first and second volleys, delivered in line of battle by the brigade, it should charge with fixed bayonets upon the enemy, and relying on the impetuosity and recklessness of Irish soldiers in a charge, he felt confident that before such a charge the enemy would give way and be dispersed. Meagher says:

Brigadier General George B. Anderson's section of the Sunken Road from the modern Observation Tower. The left flank regiments from French's division, and Richardson's entire division, fought the Confederates in the road from the slope to the right. *Scott Felsen.*

Advancing on the right and left obliquely from the center, the brigade poured an effective and fearful fire upon the column, which it was their special duty to dislodge. Despite a fire of musketry, which literally cut lanes through our approaching lines, the brigade advanced under my personal command within 30 [60] paces of the enemy, and at this point, Lieutenant Colonel James Kelly having been shot through the face and Captain Felix Duffy having fallen dead in front of his command, the regiment (69th New York) halted. At the same time Lieutenant Colonel Fowler and Major Richard Bentley, of the 63rd, on the left of our line, having been seriously wounded and compelled to retire, the charge of bayonets I had ordered on the left was arrested, and thus the brigade, instead of advancing and dispersing the column with the bayonet, stood and delivered its fire persistently and effectively, maintaining every inch of the ground they occupied.

Meagher was close to the 69th New York on the right of his brigade. This regiment in its advance marched over some troops lying on the ground, under shelter of the brow of the hill, and when it ascended the ridge its right was 80 yards from the Sunken Road its left much nearer, the whole line on the top of the ridge and much exposed. Meagher permitted the regiment to fire five or six volleys, when it was ordered to stop firing and charge and a like order was sent to the 63rd and 88th New York on the left. After an advance of about 30 yards the order to charge was counter-manded and the 69th fell back to its first position and resumed firing. The left of the line was gradually advanced to within 100 yards of the road, the right standing fast.

Beyond a slight depression in the ridge, which was held by the 29th Massachusetts, of which we shall treat later, were drawn up the 63rd and 88th New York. The 63rd was on the right and received several deadly volleys without replying, by which it was greatly thinned. The charge it was ordered to make by Meagher failed, owing to its heavy losses the first few minutes. The men began firing with round ball and buckshot, the brigade being armed with smooth bores, and an officer states that "it was give and take until ammunition ran out." The nature and severity of the contest is graphically and touchingly told in the report of Lieutenant Colonel Fowler:

> In the early part of the action Capt. P. J. Condon and Lieut. Thomas W. Cartwright, both of Company G, fell wounded while gallantly cheering on their men bravely at their post, as also Capt. M. O'Sullivan, Company F, while Lieut. P. W. Lydon, commanding Company D, Lieut. Cadwalader Smith, Company C, and Lieutenant McConnell, of Company K, bravely rallying the gallant remaining few, fell pierced by bullets, instantly fatal.

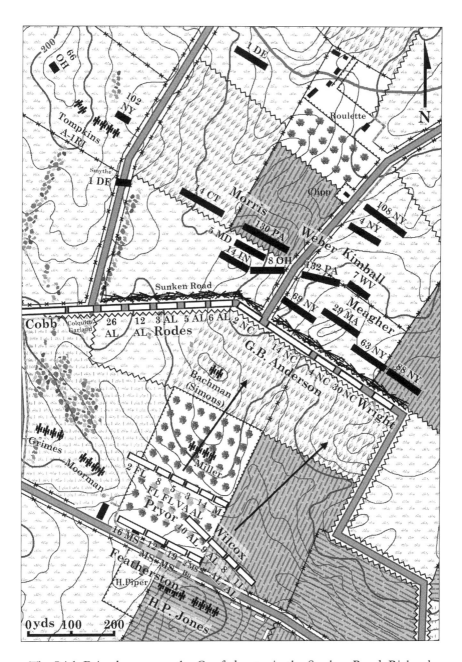

The Irish Brigade engages the Confederates in the Sunken Road. Richard H. Anderson's Division moves forward to re-inforce the Sunken Road.

As the right wing had fallen before me, I hastened to the left, where I found the major (Bentley) close upon the line, and Capt. Joseph O'Neill, Company A, whose company had all fallen around him on the right, now assisting the major on the left. Here also was the stalwart Lieutenant Gleason, Company H, raising and supporting the repeatedly falling colors, with Lieut. John Sullivan commanding and pushing forward Company K; and here lay the slender form of Captain Kavanagh, Company I, cold in death; the brave and enthusiastic Lieut. R. P. Moore, Company E, passing from right to left, boldly urging his men to stand firm, and the gallant Lieut. George Lynch, second lieutenant Company G, bravely pressing on until he too fell, mortally wounded. The killed died as brave men, sword in hand, and amid the thickest of the fight. Major Bentley was now wounded, and retired to have his wound dressed. Our number now left was less than 50 men; our colors, although in ribbons, and staff shot through, were still there, sustained at a bloody sacrifice, 16 men having fallen while carrying them. I now received a severe wound, and was compelled to retire just as the lines of the enemy were breaking.

It is now a solace to my mind, while suffering from my wound, to testify how gallantly and promptly each officer in his place and each company moved forward and delivered their fire in the face of the most destructive storm of leaden hail, that in an instant killed or wounded every officer but one and more than one-half the rank and file of the right wing. For a moment they staggered, but the scattered few quickly rallied upon the left, closing on the colors, where they nobly fought, bled, and died protecting their own loved banner and their country's flag, until the brigade was relieved.[4]

On the left of the 63rd was the 88th New York. As it came into position it received the same deadly fire as had the 63rd, and returned it. During the engagement an aide rode up and ordered it to charge with the 63rd and take the enemy's colors if possible. Lieutenant Colonel Kelly at once gave the order, and the regiment advanced about 25 or 30 yards, but seeing he had no support Kelly halted the regiment and inquired why the 63rd had not advanced. Lieutenant Colonel Fowler and Major Bently of the 63rd had been wounded. Captain O'Neill, who was on the left, said he would advance with the 88th, if he had any one to command the regiment, but not

---

[4] Pasted by Carman into the manuscript. U. S. War Department, *War of the Rebellion: A Compilation of the Official Records of the Union and Confederate Armies*, Series I, vol. 19, part I, pp. 295-296. Hereafter cited as *OR*. All references are to Series I unless otherwise noted.

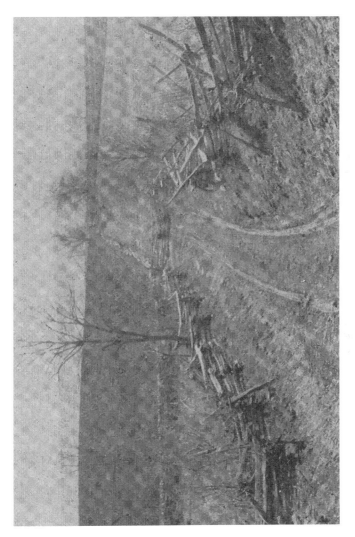

The Sunken Road from the intersection of Rodes' and George B. Anderson's Brigades looking east. The Roulette lane is to the left. *History of the Fourteenth Regiment, Connecticut Vol. Infantry.*

knowing who was in command he did not wish to do so, upon which Kelly ordered the 88th to fall back a few feet.

We have stated that the 29th Massachusetts covered a depression in the ridge between the 69th and 63rd New York. It had been under heavy infantry and artillery fire in its advance, which it returned, but on reaching its position about 100 yards from the road ceased firing for it could not see the enemy in the road, nor could the enemy see it, as it was in the depression between the higher ground on its right and left and the ridge along the Sunken Road completely sheltered it, but it had a good range on the cornfield in the rear of the road, which was on higher ground opening wide before it, its shots cutting down the green stalks of corn as would a scythe and having their effect upon the enemy, who were hiding there or who came up as support to those in the road, and from these it received a severe fire.

When Meagher's Brigade took position it was confronted by Anderson's North Carolinians and Wright's Georgians and Alabamians, but soon thereafter Anderson was reinforced by the brigades of Pryor, Featherston and Wilcox which made an effort to charge Meagher.

After Rodes had rallied his men, when repulsed in his attack upon French, he noticed troops, Wright's Brigade, going in to the support of G. B. Anderson, or to his right, and that a body of troops, instead of passing on to the front, stopped in the hollow immediately in his rear and near the orchard. As the fire between his own men and Kimball was now desultory he went to these troops and found that they belonged to Pryor's Brigade and that they had been halted there by somebody, not General Pryor.

Colonel Ballantine, commanding 2nd Florida, says Pryor's Brigade had been halted some time, his own regiment very much exposed, being near the crest of a small hill, when Rodes came from the front and asked him to what command he belonged and why not engaged, to which Ballantine replied, that he had no orders. Rodes said troops were needed at the front and ordered Ballantine to form line and go in, told him where to go, and then found Pryor to whom he stated the conduct of his brigade and the necessity for it at the front.

R. H. Anderson had been wounded very soon after coming upon the field and Pryor, who succeeded to the command, was unaware of the orders under which Anderson was acting and did not rise to the occasion, and the consequent movements of his command were disjointed and without proper direction, but, when apprized by Rodes of the condition of affairs, he ordered his own brigade forward.

Without waiting for this order Colonel Ballantine changed front forward on left company, the movement being in a measure masked by the orchard and cornfield in front and the line of the 2nd Florida was established fronting the cornfield, the right in the orchard and the left in the open

Looking from the Sunken Road northeast toward the Irish Brigade's position. *Author's collection.*

ground west of it. The other regiments executed the movement, forming double-quick on the right of the 2nd Florida, in this order from left to right, 8th Florida, Lieutenant Colonel De Coppens; 5th Florida, Colonel John C. Hately; 3rd Virginia, Colonel Joseph Mayo; 14th Alabama, Major James A. Broome, and Mahone's Brigade, Colonel W. A. Parham, now reduced to less than 50 men. Colonel Hately, 5th Florida, was in command of the brigade, and, as soon as formed he ordered it forward. It advanced through the orchard and as it entered the cornfield came under the fire of Tompkins' guns and the musketry of Kimball and Meagher, Colonel De Coppens of the 8th Florida was killed, and immediately after Captain Waller, who succeeded him in command, fell dead, with the colors of the regiment draped over his shoulders, and every regiment suffered great loss. Passing through the cornfield the left of the brigade came up in rear of the right wing of the 14th North Carolina, the right extending beyond the 14th North Carolina. When it reached the road, it met with a severe fire which checked a part of the line, a part of it went beyond the road a few yards but was quickly driven back with great loss and all lay down with Anderson's men and opened fire.

Featherston's Brigade was close on the heels of Pryor's. With Wilcox it had remained some time on the ridge south of Piper's and then was recalled and formed line in the orchard in Pryor's rear, and it was at this time that Pryor went forward. From right to left the brigade was thus formed, 2nd Mississippi Battalion, Major W. S. Wilson; 19th Mississippi, Colonel Nathaniel S. Harris; 12th Mississippi, Colonel W. H. Taylor, and 16th Mississippi, Captain A. M. Feltus. As soon as formed it followed Pryor's Brigade through the orchard and entered the cornfield under a heavy artillery fire on both flanks and a sweeping fire of musketry in front, by which it suffered greatly, and came upon Anderson's and Pryor's men lying in the Sunken Road, its left behind the center of the 14th North Carolina, its right in rear of the left of the 30th North Carolina. It did not halt in the road, but passed over those in it about 30 to 40 yards and fiercely engaged Meagher, but in about five minutes was driven back to the road with great loss. Colonel Bennett, 14th North Carolina says Featherston's men "flowed over and out of the road and many of them were killed in this overflow. The 16th Mississippi disappeared as if it had gone into the earth."

By this time the ranks of Meagher's Brigade had been greatly thinned, the 69th New York had nearly melted away and but a few heroic Irishmen were left, huddling about the two colors, when one of the enemy shouted from the Sunken Road, "Bring them colors in here"; upon which the two color bearers instantly advanced a few steps, shook their colors in the very face of the enemy and replied, "Come and take them you damned rebels."

This defiant exchange appeared to exasperate the enemy to another advance, and Lieutenant-Colonel Barnes, 29th Massachusetts, fearful that

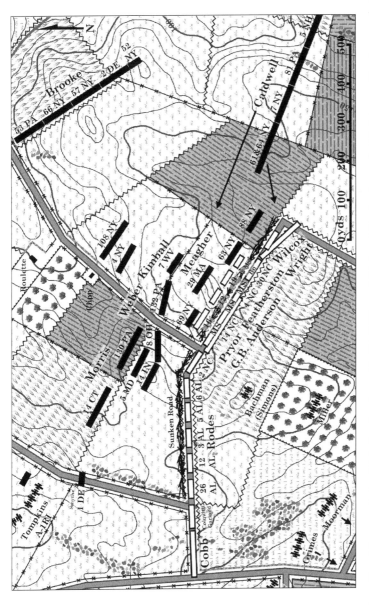

The Sunken Road is crowded with brigades from D. H. Hill's and Richard H. Anderson's Divisions. Featherston's Brigade advances over the road and briefly counterattacks the Irish Brigade. Caldwell's brigade is ordered to the right to support the Irish Brigade.

they might make a dash for the colors and possibly pierce the line and turn the right of his regiment, ordered three cheers to be given and a charge made. The historian of the 29th Massachusetts says:

> An hour had nearly elapsed since the front had been reached; several of the captains had reported that the guns of their men were getting so hot that the rammers were leaping out of the pipes at every discharge. The men had already nearly expended their ammunition. Several times during the battle the enemy had undertaken to come forward, but as often as they attempted it, they were swept back by our fire. Since General Meagher had been disabled, there had been no general officer present, each colonel acting upon his own responsibility. The enemy were well covered and determined. Up to this time neither regiment had known the fate of the others, nor the extent of their respective losses. Colonel Barnes now hastened to the right of the 29th, for the purpose of taking a careful survey of the field. To his dismay, he perceived that the 69th, though holding on bravely, had lost nearly half their number; the 63rd had fared equally hard, and the officers and men of both regiments were striving to keep up their formation. The Colonel, feeling a deep responsibility, saw at once that something must be done to prevent disaster; he knew, though he had received no orders since entering the fight, that from necessity the brigade would soon be relieved, and was every moment expecting to hear the welcome shouts of fresh troops. Hastily giving his idea to Major Charles Chipman, his brave and worthy subordinate, he called upon the regiment for three cheers. The Major took up the order to the left, and the boys gave the cheers with a will. Colonel Barnes then gave the order, "forward!" Instantly Sergeant Francis M. Kingman, the dauntless color bearer, sprang to the front, the whole regiment promptly following him. Above the noise of the battle were heard the answering shouts of the brave Irishmen of the brigade, their warlike spirit gaining fresh impulse as they started forward on the charge. The crisis was over now; the bold forward movement had saved the brigade from even one blot upon its bright record of fame. The shouts of our men, and their sudden dash toward the sunken road, so startled the enemy that their fire visibly slackened, their line wavered, and squads of two and three began leaving the road and running into the corn. Now the rush of troops was heard in the rear; now the air was rent with wild yells. It was altogether too much of a shock for the enemy; they broke, and fled for the cornfield. The next moment, Caldwell's Brigade, led by General Richardson in person, with Cross, Barlow, and all its other heroes, came sweeping up behind the sheltered lines of the Irish Brigade. The flight of the enemy was now

The 29th Massachusetts's view from the top of the hill over the Sunken Road. From here, they were partially sheltered from direct fire from the road, but could fire behind them into the Piper cornfield and any Confederate reinforcements trying to make their way forward. *Author's collection.*

complete. In a few moments Caldwell's men were in possession of the road, and driving the Confederates through the cornfield and into the orchard beyond.

When it was relieved and went to the rear Meagher's Brigade had been reduced to less than 500 men. The loss of the 29th Massachusetts was comparatively light, but the three New York regiments had suffered heavily: the 88th New York 33 8/10 per cent; the 63rd New York, 59 1/4 per cent; and the 69th New York, 61 8/10 per cent. The loss in officers was very large. With all the original officers and men of the Irish Brigade, Antietam was its great day, its crowning glory, though it brought no captured flags away. At Fredericksburg where the brigade was nearly extinguished, when charging over ground upon which the Confederate artillery officers boasted that "a chicken could not live" under the fire of their guns, the rallying cry of the officers was: "Come on boys; this is nothing to Antietam."

Before accompanying Caldwell's advance we must note the condition of affairs within the Confederate lines. Since early morning there had been heavy artillery firing along the line south of the Sunken Road; for nearly two miles, there was battery after battery, on the high ground running south, aggregating nearly 80 guns. D. H. Hill says he had 26 guns of his own command, besides that of Cutts' Battalion, temporarily under his command, and "positions were selected for as many of these guns as could be used, but all the ground in my front was completely commanded by the long range artillery of the Yankees on the other side of the Antietam, which concentrated their fire every gun that opened and soon disabled or silenced it." Hill further says that the artillery was badly handled and "could not cope with the superior weight, caliber, range, and number of the Yankee guns; hence it ought only to have been used against masses of infantry. On the contrary, our guns were made to reply to the Yankee guns, and were smashed up or withdrawn before they could be effectively turned against massive columns of attack."

Early in the morning Major H. P. Jones' artillery battalion of four Virginia batteries was on Cemetery ridge, between Piper's and the Keedysville road, under orders to prevent the crossing of the middle bridge, and was soon engaged with the batteries beyond the Antietam, but being inferior to them in weight of metal and range, and threatened by an enfilade fire on the right by Weed's and Benjamin's batteries, Jones was ordered by General Lee to withdraw under cover of the ridge to the lower ground between it and the Hagerstown road.

While Jones was on the ridge he was witness to this incident narrated by Longstreet:

128

Labelled "Group of Irish brigade as they lay on the battlefield of Antietam, 19th Sept., 1862" by photographer Alexander Gardner, the exact location of this photo has yet to be determined. Likely it is along the approach march before reaching the heights above the Sunken Road. *Library of Congress.*

During the progress of the battle General Lee and I were riding along my line and D. H. Hill's, when we received a report of movement of the enemy and started up the ridge to make a reconnaissance. General Lee and I dismounted, but Hill declined to do so. I said to him, 'If you insist on riding up there and drawing the fire, give us a little interval so that we may not be in the line of fire when they open on you.' General Lee and I stood on the top of the crest with our glasses, looking at the movements of the Federals on the rear left. After a moment I turned my glass to the right—the Federal left. As I did so, I noticed a puff of white smoke from the mouth of a cannon. 'There is a shot for you' I said to General Hill. The gunner was a mile away, and the cannon-shot came whisking through the air for three or four seconds and took off the front legs of the horse that Hill sat on and let the animal down upon its stumps. The horse's head was so low and his croup so high that Hill was in a most ludicrous position. With one foot in the stirrup he made several efforts to get the other leg over the croup, but failed. Finally we prevailed upon him to try the other end of the horse, and he got down. That shot at Hill was the second best shot I ever saw.

This incident occurred about 20 feet north of the Keedysville road and the shot was fired by Captain Stephen H. Weed, commanding Battery I, 5th United States Artillery.

After Major Jones withdrew from the ridge Peyton's Battery was withdrawn and sent to the left and Boyce's South Carolina battery passed from the Keedysville road along the ridge to the left. Later in the forenoon Jones re-occupied the ridge with three batteries, two guns of R. C. M. Page's Battery were placed close to the Keedysville road, to fire to the front, in the direction of the middle bridge and the other guns so arranged that their field of fire was off to the left, and then opened fire on Richardson's Division, firing solid shot, which struck the ground in front of the column, Jones says "with wonderful effect."

Boyce's South Carolina battery of 6 guns bivouacked on the night of the 16th in a hollow in rear of Cemetery hill. Captain Boyce reports that early on the 17th he was ordered by Colonel Walton beyond the road north of Sharpsburg to meet and check the enemy. He marched about 150 yards on the Keedysville road, then turned to the left and marched along Cemetery ridge to the vicinity he supposed he should occupy, and was placed by Colonel Stevens of Evans' Brigade, on the slope of the second hill from the road; but, finding his battery could be of no service in this position, he was posted farther down in front of another battery. Here, discovering that he was still where he could not see the enemy, he moved his battery through a cornfield immediately in front, and, on reaching the far side of this field,

A 3-inch Ordnance Rifle. Several Union batteries containing these guns, along with numerous larger 20-pdr Parrott rifles, were stationed on the east side of Antietam Creek, providing long range fire against the Confederates. If Carman is accurate about Captain Stephen H. Weed's Battery I, 5th United States firing the round from "a mile away" as described in General Longstreet's anecdote, it would have been from a gun like this. *Author's collection.*

found the whole line of battle, for at least a mile, extending before him. He placed his guns in battery in easy range of a portion of the line, but he had to wait for an opportunity to fire, as his own friends, engaging the enemy, intervened. After a protracted struggle immediately in his front the Confederate infantry abandoned the field to overwhelming numbers. Boyce says:

> My battery was at this time thrown forward into an open field 200 or 300 yards in advance of its original position. The enemy then advanced through a cornfield to the field in which my battery had taken position, showing a front of several hundred yards in extent, plainly on the right and center, but partially concealed by the corn on the left. The whole line of the enemy here was within canister range, and I opened upon him a destructive fire, cutting down two of his flags at the second or third discharge of the guns. The right and center soon gave way and retired. The battery was then turned up on the left which held its position more obstinately. This portion of the line took shelter in a ravine at the base of the hill from which I was firing, and it was only with one or two guns that they could be reached. Having no support of infantry, and no other battery assisting me in resisting this large body of the enemy, and being exposed the whole time to a galling fire of the enemy's sharpshooters, after firing 70 rounds of canister and some solid shot I was forced to retire from this hazardous position, to the cornfield from which I had advanced.

It is difficult to locate the various positions held by Boyce but he appears to have been engaged with the advance of French's Division and also with Richardson's and to have fallen back into the cornfield from the open ground east of it.

At about 9:15 a.m., Miller's Battery of 4 Napoleon guns, Washington Artillery, was ordered from its position on Cemetery hill to the left. It went through Sharpsburg, then out on the Hagerstown road and was ordered by Longstreet up the hill through Piper's orchard to a position near the center of the orchard, and about 100 yards south of the cornfield in front. In taking position a rain of bullets came showering over it from the right, left and in front, but it immediately opened fire on Richardson's advance. In a very short time two gunners and several cannoneers were wounded and Longstreet ordered the battery to cease firing and go under cover, by withdrawing a few yards down the hill.

Very early in the morning Hardaway's Alabama battery, of 3 guns, under command of Lieutenant John W. Tullis was near the southwest corner of Mumma's cornfield, the position subsequently occupied by Patterson's Georgia battery. It had rifled guns and fired to the front, until the

Miller's Battery position along the northern edge of the Piper orchard. Looking northeast toward the Sunken Road. *Author's collection.*

contestants were too close to distinguish the lines, when the guns were turned upon those beyond the Antietam, near McClellan's headquarters. About 8 a.m. it crossed the Hagerstown road and went into position opposite the mouth of the Sunken Road and 100 yards from it, and from this position opened fire upon French's Division in its advance, but was soon driven back by Tompkins (or Monroe) to a position 300 yards west of the road and 50 yards south of the large cornfield. Here it remained until R. H. Anderson's artillery came up, when it fell back to a rock ledge, with a depression in rear, where the caissons were sheltered. This position was about 150 yards southeast of Reel's house and about the same distance from what is known as the Landing road, and in this position the battery remained during the day, and with its long range guns assisted in resisting Richardson's advance.

"Thus," says Longstreet, "when Richardson's march approached its objective, the Confederate's had Boyce's Battery in the cornfield facing the march; Miller's section with the Napoleons in the center, and a single battery at McLaws' rear."

Saunders' artillery had been withdrawn. It had been engaged with Tompkins in front and had fired at French's men, but was quickly silenced, and was inactive while Pryor's, Wright's, and Featherston's brigades were advancing through the orchard and corn to the Sunken Road, and about this time Captain Grimes advanced one gun of his battery to the left and front and fired at some infantry between the Dunker Church and Mumma's. Men of the 14th Indiana saw the movement, several of them, gaining favorable position on the right, opened fire, Grimes was struck from his horse by a shot in the thigh, and his men were bearing him from the field, when a second ball struck him in the groin and gave him a mortal wound. Meanwhile the other batteries had re-opened fire but were quickly silenced and withdrawn. Moorman's Battery was badly used up and retired into park two miles from the field in the direction of Shepherdstown. Grimes' Battery followed and Huger's Battery, abandoning one gun, followed Moorman and Grimes. The withdrawal was soon followed by the retreat of Rodes' Brigade from the Sunken Road.

We left Rodes after he had ordered Pryor's Brigade to the front. After he had found Pryor and informed him of the fact and Pryor, also, had sent an order for the brigade to go forward, Rodes started back to his own brigade and met Lieutenant Colonel Lightfoot of the 6th Alabama, looking for him. Colonel Gordon had been desperately wounded and Lightfoot was in command of the regiment. Upon his telling Rodes that the right of the 6th Alabama was being subjected to a terrific enfilading fire, which the enemy were enabled to deliver by reason of their gaining somewhat on G. B. Anderson, and that he had but few men left in that wing, Rodes ordered him to hasten back, and throw his right wing back out of the road, or rather

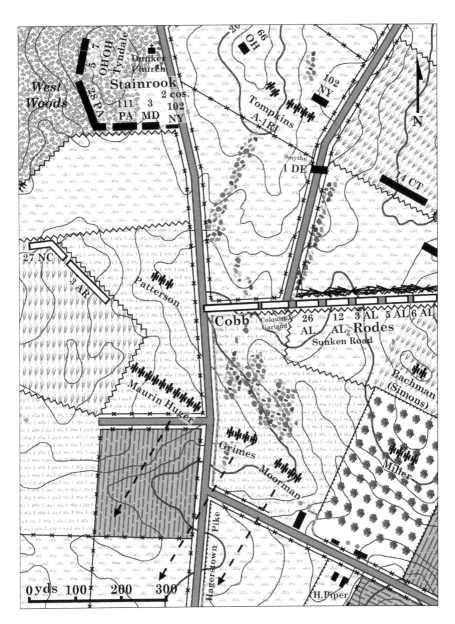

Saunder's Battalion of artillery begins withdrawing.

from its exposed position on a ledge crossing the road immediately in front of the right of the 14th Indiana. Instead of executing the order as given by Rodes, for the right wing to fall back, Lightfoot moved briskly to the rear of the regiment and gave the command, "Sixth Alabama, about face; forward march." Major Hobson, of the 5th, seeing this, asked if the order was intended for the whole brigade; he replied yes, "Yes," and thereupon the 5th, and the other troops on their left, retreated. Rodes says:

> I did not see their retrograde movement until it was too late for me to rally them, for this reason: Just as I was moving on after Lightfoot, I heard a shot strike Lieutenant Birney, who was immediately behind me. Wheeling I found him falling, and found that he had been struck in the face. He found that he could walk after I raised him, though a shot or piece of shell had penetrated his head just under the eye. I followed him a few paces, and watched him until he had reached a barn (Piper's), a short distance to the rear, where he first encountered some men to help him in case he needed it.
>
> As I turned toward the brigade, I was struck heavily by a piece of shell on my thigh. At first I thought the wound was serious, but finding upon examination, that it was slight, I again turned toward the brigade, when I discovered it, without visible cause to me, retreating in confusion. I hastened to intercept it at the Hagerstown road. I found, though, that with the exception of a few men of the 26th, 12th, and 3rd Alabama, and a few men under Major Hobson, not more than 40 men in all, the brigade had completely disappeared from this portion of the field. This small number, together with some Mississippians and North Carolinians, making in all about 150 men, I stationed behind a small ridge leading from the Hagerstown road eastward toward the orchard and about 150 (370[5]) yards in rear of my last position....After this, my time was spent mainly in directing the fire of some artillery and getting up stragglers.

Rodes testifies to the gallantry of his brigade, which "finally fell back only when, the men and officers supposed, they had been ordered to do so," and maintains the troops on his right had already given way when his own men began to retreat.

On the contrary D. H. Hill says George B. Anderson "still nobly held his ground, but the Yankees began to pour in through the gap made by the retreat of Rodes." Colonel Bennett, then in command of Anderson's Brigade, says Rodes had retreated before he fell back with the two North Carolina regiments on his immediate right. As a matter of fact Rodes fell

---

[5] Carman wrote in 370.

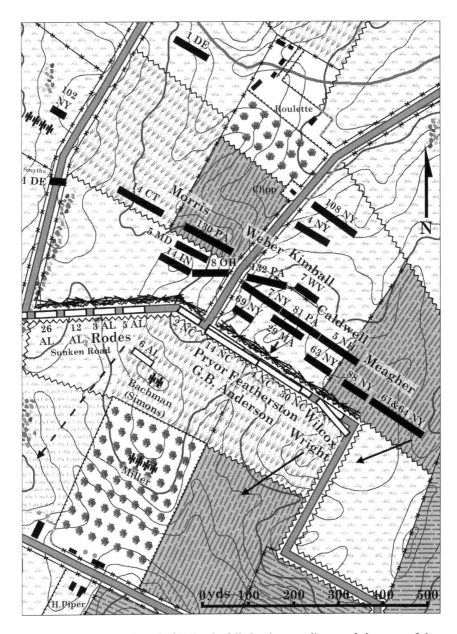

The 6th Alabama of Rodes' Brigade falls back to realign, and the rest of the brigade erroneously follows suit. Before Rodes can fix the situation, the brigade falls back without orders, leaving a huge gap in the lines. Wright's Brigade on the right leaves the Sunken Road and falls back as well. The 61st & 64th New York moves to enfilade the entire road.

137

back at the time Wright's, Pryor's and Featherston's brigades with the 4th and 30th North Carolina , of Anderson's, retreated in confusion from the Sunken Road before Caldwell's advance, to which we now return.

Caldwell's Brigade was at first on Meagher's left, but beyond the range of the immediate infantry contest and well sheltered, being on the reverse or northeast slope of the high ground where, farther to the right and front, Meagher was so much exposed. Caldwell, finding no enemy in his immediate front, began to wheel his brigade cautiously to the right, which if the movement had been energetically continued, would have taken in flank the Confederate position in the Sunken Road very soon after Meagher had became engaged, but the movement was very slow and exasperating to those on the right of the line, in plain view of the Irish Brigade, which was standing up under a galling fire, and Colonels Barlow and Miles impatiently strode along the line making the air blue, cursing the fate or want of generalship that compelled slow and halting movement when dash was required. But an order was now received from Richardson to relieve Meagher, upon which the brigade moved by the right flank in rear of Meagher, then, facing to the left, passed his line to the front, under a severe fire of musketry. The movement was not made with that precision described in the official reports, by breaking companies to the front, Meagher's regiments breaking by companies to the rear, but the brigade was running when it reached Meagher's line, and without slacking pace, dashed through his ranks, passing the line by simply pushing its way through, Meagher's men quickly conforming to the movement. Walker says the movement "was effected perfect composure, and Caldwell's Brigade became the front line, and was soon involved in a most spirited contest, in which both the gallantry of the troops and the exceptional intelligence, skill and audacity of the regimental commanders were displayed to the highest advantage."

The brigade was thus formed: on the right the 61st and 64th New York, temporarily consolidated under the command of Colonel Francis C. Barlow; 7th New York, Captain Charles Brestel; 81st Pennsylvania, Major H. Boyd McKeen; and 5th New Hampshire, Colonel E. E. Cross.

While Pryor's and Featherston's brigades, after their repulse, were lying in the road with G. B. Anderson's men, they were subjected to a severe fire of artillery and musketry. The sudden advance ordered by Colonel Barnes started some of the men to the rear and Colonel Posey, observing the crowded condition of the troops in the road, subjected to much loss, ordered his own brigade to retire. A scene of great confusion now ensued from the mingling of different brigades. Caldwell's Brigade now swept to the front and Pryor's and Featherston's men retreated carrying with them the 4th and 30th North Carolina. Colonel Bennett reports that while he was observing the right of his brigade "masses of Confederate troops in great

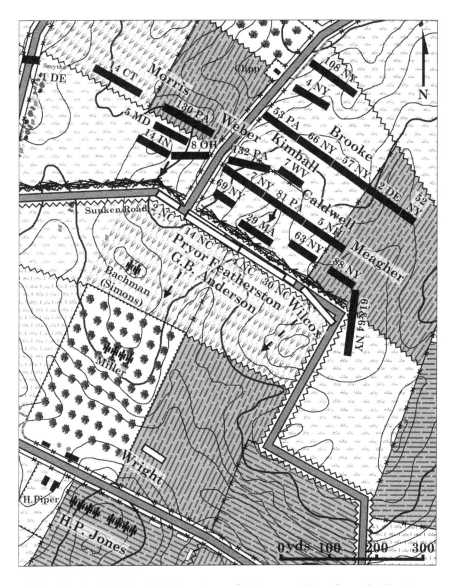

The 61st & 64th New York attains a flanking position along the Sunken Road and delivers a devastating fire along it length. Confederate units in the road begin to fall back.

confusion were seen, portions of Major General Anderson's Division, as we then knew, for the 16th Mississippi and the 2nd Florida of that command (left regiments respectively of Featherston and Pryor), coming to our succor, broke beyond the power of rallying after five minutes stay. In this stampede, if we may so term it, the 4th North Carolina State Troops and the 30th North Carolina State Troops participated." As an officer of the 4th North Carolina writes: "I think Featherston was started to the right, but instead of getting there came up behind us, where he was not needed, for we could have held our position indefinitely. He sustained great loss in killed and wounded and I have always thought was the cause of the line breaking, for when he found he was not needed there he gave an order to fall back, which was mistaken for a general order and all that could walk went back with him, which caused a general break in the line."

Wright's Brigade had fallen back before the break occurred. Colonel Gibson, who was in command, says: "Seeing a new formation of the enemy in our front of a very large force...I withdrew the brigade in order to a stone fence in the rear," the fence was on the Hagerstown road. Gibson's withdrawal was followed by that of Wilcox's Brigade. This brigade, as we have seen, had been sent to a ridge south of Piper's. After observing the advance of Pleasonton's cavalry from the middle bridge to the ridge midway to the Antietam, and that "it stopped there, the brigade recrossed the Hagerstown road, then crossed it east, north of Piper's lane, moved northwest through the orchard, to the northeast corner of the cornfield and became heavily engaged on Pryor's right, but the entire brigade did not succeed in reaching the Sunken Road. It lost heavily in its advance, and when reaching position was confronted by "a heavy compact line of infantry about 120 yards in front" and a battery of artillery on its right flank "shelled it with terrible accuracy." It remained until Pryor and Featherston gave way, when it retreated in some disorder, every man for himself, and rallied in the low ground south of the corn, near Piper's lane and a few yards east of the lower part of the orchard. A few men remained in the Sunken Road and were captured.

As we have said, when the right of Caldwell's line rushed through Meagher's skeleton line and crowned the crest of the ridge overlooking the Sunken Road the Confederates in front of the left were beginning to leave, the entire division of R. H. Anderson gave way, carrying with it the 4th and 30th North Carolina of G. B. Anderson's Brigade, and exposing the right flank of the 14th and 2nd North Carolina. Barlow had led the 61st and 64th New York up the ridge directly in front of these two regiments; as he crowned it he was met by a severe fire, upon which he quickly withdrew under cover of the ridge and moved rapidly to the left near the northeast corner of the cornfield, and was quick to see the opportunity presented by the exposed flank of the North Carolinians. Advancing his left he poured

The Sunken Road and Confederate position from the 61st and 64th New York and its flanking position. *Author's collection.*

an enfilading fire down the road just as the two regiments had been ordered to retreat. Colonel Bennett, commanding Anderson's Brigade, says:

> Anderson's Division had gone to the rear. Two regiments (4th and 30th) of our own brigade were missing. The dark lines of the enemy had swept around our right, and were gradually closing upon the ground of Rodes' Brigade. They having gone to resist the lines in front was an easy task, to contend against front and rear attacks we were totally inadequate, and the bare alternate of retreat was presented. The command was ordered to make the retreat by the right oblique with frightful loss...and reformed in the road leading to Sharpsburg.

Barlow reports that he secured over 300 prisoners in the road, and, seeing no enemy in his immediate front, halted. The 7th New York and 81st Pennsylvania and 5th New Hampshire came up in quick succession, on Barlow's left and entered the cornfield, where they were soon met by a severe fire of infantry and canister, from Miller's guns in the orchard, and shell from two guns of the Donaldsonville battery, farther to the right beyond the Hagerstown road. The 81st Pennsylvania came up in rear of the 2nd Delaware of Brooke's Brigade, which had crossed the Sunken Road farther to the right, and the 5th New Hampshire on the extreme left, advancing to a small depression, about half way through the corn, saw a body of Confederates advancing from the direction of Piper's house and lane, which was quickly driven back.

Barlow's success was shared in by Kimball's Brigade, the 132nd Pennsylvania, and parts of the 7th West Virginia and 108th New York, on his right, joining in the fire on the enemy in the road and advancing to it, where they halted, but the 2nd Delaware and 52nd New York, closely following, charged across the road, and into the cornfield driving everything out of it, the 2nd Delaware coming under a heavy fire from Piper's orchard, which threw it into confusion, but the 81st Pennsylvania coming up in its rear it soon rallied. The 52nd New York advanced to the crest of the hill in the cornfield and Colonel Frank, its commander, receiving information that two Confederate regiments were on his right, on lower ground, marched the regiment to the high ground at the west end of the cornfield and opened fire on the flank of these two regiments, the 7th New York coming up on his left and supporting him most gallantly. Here he was joined by Barlow with the 61st and 64th New York.

After describing his movement on the flank of the Confederates in the Sunken Road and their capture Barlow says:

> After these events my regiments, with the rest of our line, advanced into the cornfield through which the enemy had fled. Our troops were

Confederate dead and debris in the Sunken Road along the line of George B. Anderson's Brigade. *Library of Congress.*

joined together without much order—several regiments in front of others, and none in my neighborhood having very favorable opportunities to use their fire. Seeing quite a body of the enemy moving briskly on the right of our line, at no great distance, to attack us on the flank, my regiments changed front and moved to the crest of a hill on our right flank, occupying the only position where I found we could use our fire to advantage. This was to the right of the 52nd New York.

In this position the two regiments were behind a fence bordering Piper's cornfield on the west, the right of the 64th New York resting on the Sunken Road, where the right of Rodes men had been. At this time Kimball was resisting a flank attack on his brigade and Barlow gave him great assistance, by opening an oblique fire to the right, on the edge of Mumma's cornfield.

As stated in the preceding pages, Kimball, west of the Roulette lane, had been severely engaged. Nearly half of the men of the 14th Indiana and 8th Ohio were killed and wounded. The men complained that their guns were foul and their ammunition exhausted. The ground was covered with arms and the men were ordered to change their pieces for these, and the officers busied themselves in gathering ammunition from the cartridge boxes of the dead and wounded and carrying it in their hats and pockets to the men. It was while thus engaged that Caldwell advanced and Kimball made a charge, which was followed by the retreat of Rodes, soon followed by that of the 2nd and 14th North Carolina. Kimball says he drove the enemy "some distance into the cornfield beyond." As a line the 14th Indiana and 8th Ohio did not go beyond the Sunken Road, but Company A, 14th Indiana, and Company B, 8th Ohio, did cross close upon the heels of the 2nd and 14th North Carolina, secured some prisoners and went some 20 to 30 feet into the cornfield and were driven back, and at this moment a galling artillery fire was poured upon Kimball's right flank and lines of Confederate infantry were seen sweeping down upon it from the direction of the Dunker Church and the eastern end of the Sunken Road.

Longstreet, who was on this part of the line, perceiving the pressure on the right of R. H. Anderson's Division had ordered an attack on the flank of Kimball's brigade to relieve it. He directed the artillery west of the Hagerstown road to concentrate its fire upon Kimball; Cobb's Brigade and Colonel Cooke, commanding 27th North Carolina and 3rd Arkansas, were ordered to charge upon his flank and rear.

Cooke was then in the edge of a cornfield about 300 yards west of the Hagerstown road and 200 yards south of the West Woods, and, when the order was received, had just ordered a charge for the capture of two guns that had moved into the woods near the Dunker Church, on the left of

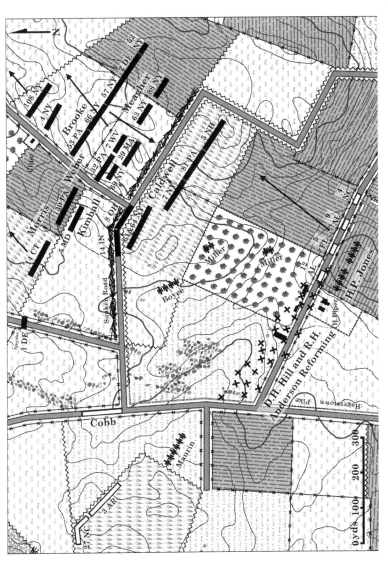

Caldwell's brigade moves across the Sunken Road into the Piper cornfield. Several regiments from Richard H. Anderson's Division rally and march back into the cornfield to counterattack.

Greene's Division. Cobb's Brigade was on Cooke's right. When this brigade fell back from the charge made in conjunction with Rodes' Brigade it was to a fence in the west end of the Sunken Road, where it remained until Rodes retreated, when, to prevent being flanked on the right, it changed front to the rear, which brought it behind a stone fence on the Hagerstown road, its left standing fast and resting on the Sunken Road. This movement had scarcely been executed when D. H. Hill rode up and ordered it forward. Lieutenant Colonel Sanders, though extremely ill, had retained command up to this time, but was now so much exhausted that he relinquished command to Lieutenant Colonel McRae, 15th North Carolina, who led the brigade, about 250 men, up the hill in front and to the right, to the board fences of Mumma's lane at a point just south of the of the cornfield. Cooke, abandoning his movement on the guns, charged across the Hagerstown road, close on the heels of Greene's Division, which had just been driven from the West Woods, swept over the plateau opposite the church and, wheeling to the right, made directly for the cornfield in the rear of Kimball's right.

Just before these movements were seen by Kimball, the 14th Connecticut, which had been in the cornfield on his right and rear, left its position, and there was now nothing to check Cooke, who was charging down on the flank and rear. Kimball promptly ordered a change of front. The colors of the 8th Ohio and 14th Indiana were run to the right and rear to the adjoining plowed field south of Clipp's house, and planted on a slight ridge that ran nearly parallel to the Roulette lane and about 60 feet from it, and the fragments of the two regiments, rallied on their colors, the 14th Indiana on the right and a part of the 132nd Pennsylvania on the left of the 8th Ohio. Barely had Kimball's men taken their new position than Cooke's 27th North Carolina and 3rd Arkansas, crossed the fences of the Mumma lane and entered the cornfield. Fire was immediately opened on both sides and Cooke was checked near the middle of the cornfield. Assistance now came to Kimball's right. Brooke's Brigade which had been in second line to Meagher had started to move forward and relieve him but Caldwell having moved by the flank and interposed, Brooke halted and ordered his men to lie down. When Cooke was seen coming over the plateau opposite the church Brooke "led the 57th and 66th New York and 53rd Pennsylvania to the right, to check any attempt the enemy might make to reach the rear." When Cooke reached the cornfield the 53rd Pennsylvania was ordered forward to check him, also to hold at all hazards the Roulette barn and orchard, the barn being used as a hospital. The regiment advanced under a shower of musketry gained the barn, reached high ground in the orchard and opened fire upon the left of the 27th North Carolina, and at almost the same moment the 7th Maine of Irwin's Brigade, Sixth Corps, approached the north fence of the cornfield and delivered a volley full upon its left

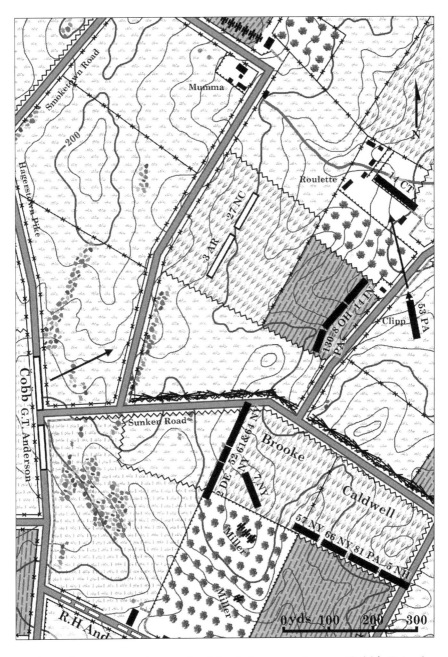

Units rush to counter the attack of Cooke's two regiments. Cobb's Brigade begins its advance.

flank. All this was more than Cooke could stand and he ordered a retreat to the position from which he had started, which was closely followed by Irwin's Brigade, Cooke not halting until he had recrossed the Hagerstown road to his old position.

Very soon after Cooke entered the Mumma cornfield, Cobb's Brigade which had moved from the mouth of the Sunken road about 100 yards up the Hagerstown road, charged up the hill on the right to the Mumma lane, just south of the corn, and was not long in this position when Barlow came up and opened fire upon it and upon Cooke in the corn, the distance being about 350 yards, and after firing about 20 rounds Cobb's men, being now unsupported by Cooke, who had retreated, fell back in disorder across the Hagerstown road and joined Cooke.

McRae commanding Cobb's Brigade, reports that he held his enemy in check, until his ammunition was exhausted, and seeing no sign of support was compelled to give the command to fall back, leaving the field with not more than 50 of the 250 men he started with.

Brooks' Vermont brigade of the Sixth Corps had been ordered to the support of French's Division; it came up after the flank attack had been repulsed and took position in the Mumma cornfield, on the line which had been held by the 14th Connecticut, and Kimball's Brigade fell back to near the Roulette buildings. Kimball had been continuously engaged for more than two hours, handling his brigade splendidly and losing 121 killed, 510 wounded, and 8 missing. The heaviest loss was sustained by the 14th Indiana and the 8th Ohio, the former losing 56 1/2 per cent, the latter 48 2/3 per cent.

Meanwhile a desultory contest continued in Piper's cornfield, where as Barlow reports "the troops were joined together without much order." Walker writes, in his *History of the Second Army Corps*: "The colonels of the regiments of Caldwell's Brigade fought the battle pretty nearly at their own discretion in the absence of direction from the brigade commanders, so that the regiments were not in continuous line much of the time. They faced in varying directions and at varying intervals from each other and sometimes were interspersed with regiments of other brigades." The like conditions, though worse, obtained on the Confederate side.

The Confederate line went back from the Sunken Road in some confusion and when Caldwell followed it to the corn the confusion was increased and disorder reigned supreme. Brigade and regimental commanders undertook to rally their broken commands, but found it impossible to do so, and the greater part of D. H. Hill's and R. H. Anderson's divisions fell back to the Piper buildings and under cover of the ridge running from the barn to the Hagerstown road; some were rallied behind the stone fences of the road, and all this at the time Longstreet was counting on their holding the Sunken Road and co-operating in the attack

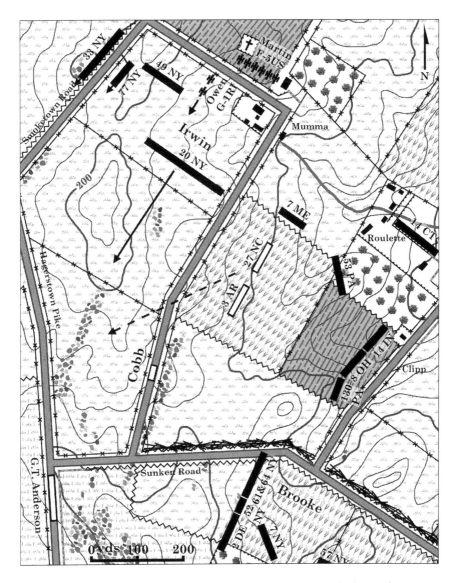

The solidifying resistance from the front, and the arrival of Irwin's Sixth Corps brigade on his flank, convince Cooke to retreat.

on Kimball's flank by a united movement on Richardson's front and flank. Cooke and Cobb had moved promptly and been repulsed, but when the time came for the assistance of Hill's and Anderson's divisions they had been driven from the Sunken Road and were in disorder. After great effort parts of each division were rallied and charged northeast through the orchard and corn to attack Richardson's left; Miller's Battery, with a small infantry support being left in the orchard to hold the right and center in check. It is impossible to say with any degree of certainty how the brigades were formed in line. There is a general agreement that regiments and brigades were intermingled one with another and considerably disorganized and demoralized by the loss of an unusually large number of officers and many men. In a general sense D. H. Hill was on the left, but when the charge had reached its limit, some of his men were on the extreme right of R. H. Anderson's.

At the time this advance was made the Union line was much extended and not continuous. The 5th New Hampshire was on the extreme left and front, somewhat detached from the 81st Pennsylvania, and Barlow with the 61st and 64th New York was still on the extreme right, where he was just repulsing Cobb's Brigade. The 52nd New York on Barlow's left after a half hours fighting saw the enemy break in his front, and, being without ammunition was falling back. Still in the corn between the 81st Pennsylvania and Barlow were the 2nd Delaware and 7th New York both in a somewhat disordered condition. The 5th New Hampshire had repulsed an attempted advance of a body of Confederates from the direction of the Piper's house and now, marching by the right flank obliquely to the rear, under a heavy fire of shell and canister, that killed and wounded many officers and men, had already reached its position on the left of the 81st Pennsylvania and opened fire on the Confederates in the orchard, when an officer of the regiment saw the Confederates moving through the corn, "cautiously attempting to outflank the entire division with a strong force concealed by a ridge" in the cornfield. They had in fact advanced within 200 yards of the left of the regiment and were preparing to charge, when Colonel Cross "instantly ordered a change of front to the rear, which was executed in time to confront the advancing line of the enemy in their center with a volley at very short range, which staggered and hurled them back." Cross says they rallied and attempted to gain his left, "but were again confronted and held, until, assistance being received, they were driven back with loss," leaving in the hands of the New Hampshire men the colors of the 4th North Carolina. In this movement Cross had gained ground to the left and rear and held the Sunken Road at the northeast corner of the cornfield. The assistance he received was from the 81st Pennsylvania, Major H. Boyd McKeen. McKeen "noticed the enemy's flags approaching from the orchard, and engaging the 5th New Hampshire," and the 5th having

Looking east from behind Cobb's Brigade across the Hagerstown Pike. Cobb's men would have marched straight forward toward the high ground in front and the Mumma lane just on the other side. *Author's collection.*

taken its position on the edge of the cornfield and in the Sunken Road, he immediately moved to the left and rear and, taking position on the right of the New Hampshire men, opened fire on the Confederates and then, says McKeen: "the 5th New Hampshire and 81st Pennsylvania completely frustrated an attempt to flank the division." While these engaged there was heard the rattle of musketry on the left and front, along the road to the middle bridge, the rattle of Pleasonton's carbines.

It was just as he had repulsed Cobb's Brigade that Barlow was attracted by the noise of the contest on the left, indicating an advance through the corn on his original front, and, as he was of no more use in his present position, he flanked to the left and filed left through the corn to the assistance of the other regiments of his brigade, until he connected on the right of the 7th New York, when he came to a front and advanced. Brooke, who had held the 57th New York, Lieutenant Colonel Philip J. Parisen, and 66th New York, Captain Julius Wehle, in hand, until the attack on the right had been repulsed, now led them forward to fill the gap in the line of Caldwell's Brigade, and swept across the Sunken Road and into the corn just as Barlow was closing in from the right. The 7th New York was crowded out of line, and the 57th New York, on the right, connected with Barlow's left and all swept forward through the corn under a very hot artillery fire and a scattering fire of musketry, by which Parisen was killed and many others struck down. Brooke's two regiments struck the Confederates that had been so signally repulsed by the 5th New Hampshire and 81st Pennsylvania, drove them in disorder and followed to the south edge of the cornfield, parts of them charged to the Piper lane, but were quickly driven back. In the advance through the corn the 57th New York captured the colors of the 12th Alabama and many prisoners, and the 66th New York captured a lieutenant of the 5th Florida, with his whole company and a stand of colors. All this was in the corn northeast of the orchard. Barlow was brought to a stand before reaching the orchard by three guns of Miller's Battery and their infantry support.

The cornfield ran east and west 560 yards along the south of the Sunken Road, and from north to south had an average depth of 210 yards, being deepest in front of the apple orchard, which lay beyond its western end. The orchard joined the corn, was 225 yards in width, east and west, and ran south 340 yards to Piper's lane. For 150 to 175 yards from the corn it was on high ground. Then the ground descended abruptly 30 feet or more to a level bottom.

Early in the engagement Miller's Battery, of 4 guns, Washington Artillery, was in position in the northern part of the orchard, on the high ground, about a 100 yards from the cornfield, but being exposed to a severe fire, which it was unable to return because of the Confederate line in its

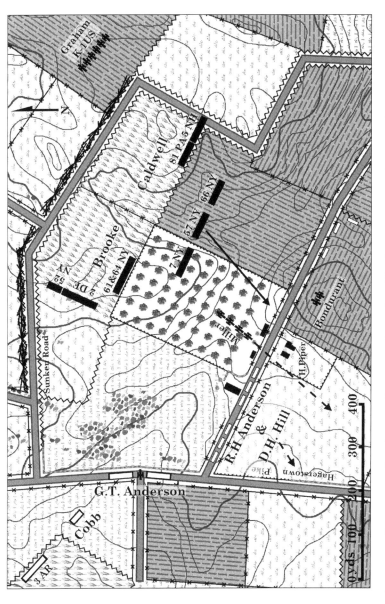

Regiments or fragments of regiments from Brooke and Caldwell move forward out of the Piper cornfield and toward the farm houses.

immediate front, Longstreet ordered it to take cover, by withdrawing a few yards down the hill. Here it remained 20 minutes,

> when, the enemy again advancing, the battery again took position. Lieutenant Hero having been wounded and Lieutenant McElroy having been left to watch the movements of the enemy on the right, Captain Miller found himself the only officer with his company, and, having barely enough men left to work a section effectively, he opened upon the enemy with his two pieces with splendid effect. After an action of half an hour he moved his section to a more advantageous position 100 yards to the front and right, placing the remaining section under Sergeant Ellis, directing him to take it completely under cover. He then continued the action until the ammunition was nearly exhausted, when Sergeant Ellis brought up one of the remaining caissons. The enemy had made two determined attempts to force our line, and had been twice signally repulsed. They were now advancing the third time, and were within canister range, when Sergeant Ellis, who had succeeded in rallying some infantry to his assistance, brought one of the guns of his section into action on Miller's left, and gave them canister, with terrible effect. The three guns succeeded in checking the enemy's advance.

Longstreet was with Miller's guns at this time, and, as Miller was short handed, by reason of his loss of cannoneers, Longstreet's staff assisted in working the guns, while their chief held the horses, and directed the fire of the guns. Longstreet writes:

> Miller was short of hands and ammunition, even for two guns...Our line was throbbing at every point, so that I dared not call on General Lee for help...As Richardson advanced through the corn he cut off the battery under Boyce, so that it was obliged to retire to save itself, and as Barlow came upon our center, the battery on our left was for a time thrown out of fire lest they might injure friend as well as foe. Barlow marched in steady good ranks, and the remnants before him rose to the emergency. They seemed to forget that they had known fatigue, the guns were played with life; and the brave spirits manning them claimed that they were there to hold or to go down with the guns. As our shots rattled against the armored ranks, Colonel Fairfax clapped his hands and ran for other charges. The mood of the gunners to a man was of quiet but unflinching resolve to stand to the last gun. Captain Miller charged and double-charged with spherical case and canister until his guns at the discharge leaped into the air from 10 to 12 inches.

Major General James Longstreet
Library of Congress.

It was against these three guns, firing double charges of spherical case and canister, and their infantry supports, that Barlow led the 61st and 64th New York. Barlow says that from these pieces, and others still farther to the right, the enemy had been pouring a destructive fire of shell, grape, and spherical-case shot during the infantry engagement, and that while moving on the guns in the orchard he was wounded in the groin by a spherical-case shot. Lieutenant Colonel Nelson A. Miles then assumed command of the regiments and "immediately deployed skirmishers forward through the field to the orchard." Richardson now suspended the further advance of his division, partly that it had become somewhat dislocated, but more particularly because it was exposed to a heavy fire that he could not silence, as he had no artillery.

At this time the Confederate left center under D. H. Hill was thoroughly broken up. But a few scattered handfuls of Hill's men were left and R. H. Anderson's Division was hopelessly confused and broken. The Confederate artillery, however, kept up a vigorous fire upon the right, left and center of the Federals, and Hill, seeing that the center of Lee's position was in danger of being carried, exerted himself to the utmost, and successfully, to stop further progress. He brought up Boyce's Battery and made it open vigorously, though itself exposed to a furious direct, and reverse fire.

Hill says: "Affairs looked very critical. I found a battery concealed in a cornfield and ordered it to move out and open fire upon the Yankee columns. This proved to be Boyce's South Carolina battery. It moved out most gallantly...and with grape and canister drove the enemy back."

It was this fire of Boyce's Battery in connection with Miller's guns in the orchard, and from some batteries west of the Hagerstown road and on the ridge south of Piper's that caused Richardson to withdraw. Brooke's two regiments at the south edge of the corn were specially annoyed by this fire and Brooke: "finding that the enemy made no attempt to regain the field, sought for and obtained the permission of General Richardson to withdraw from the now untenable position, being exposed to a cross fire of the enemy's batteries."

We have stated that parts of the 57th and 66th New York advanced to the Piper lane. Just before this advance was made George T. Anderson's Brigade, which had been engaged in the West Woods, earlier in the day, was behind the stone fence of the Hagerstown road a short distance south of the Sunken Road. An enfilade fire of long range artillery compelled Anderson to change position down the road toward Sharpsburg, under the crest of a hill and at the end of the Piper lane. "At this point," says Anderson, "I found a 6-pounder gun, and, getting a few men to assist putting it in position, a lieutenant of infantry, whose name or regiment I do not know, served it most handsomely until the ammunition was exhausted."

Colonel Francis C. Barlow, commander of the 61st & 64th New York.
Photographed later in the war as a Major General.
Library of Congress.

The gun belonged to Huger's Battery and was abandoned when its battery left position west of the road and nearly opposite the Piper lane, because its horses had been killed, and the officer who served it was Lieutenant William A. Chamberlaine of the 6th Virginia, Mahone's Brigade. The gun was abandoned at a gate, on the west side of the road, a few yards south of Piper's lane. Chamberlaine, with others of the brigade and division who had been driven back, was assisting in rallying men in the Hagerstown road, when he noticed the abandoned gun and with the aid of a few men, mostly of G. T. Anderson's Brigade, but some of the 6th Virginia, ran it up the road about 100 yards, nearly to the top of the ridge, where it opened fire upon Richardson's men, moving through the cornfield, but the exposure here was so great that, after two or three shots, it was run back to the mouth of the Piper lane, and its first shot in this position was by Major J. W. Fairfax of Longstreet's staff, and was down the lane at the skirmishers of the 57th and 66th New York, who were crossing the lane to the Piper house. Two or three shots were fired in that direction, the New York men fell back, and the gun was then moved back, up the road, about 50 yards and turned upon Brooke's men, with case shot, as they were seen at the edge of the corn. Here several shots were fired and the gun continued in action until Richardson's line fell back.

It was after Boyce's Battery "with grape and canister drove the Yankees back" that Hill records: "I was satisfied that the Yankees were so demoralized that a single regiment of fresh men could drive the whole of them in our front across the Antietam. I got up about 200 men, who said they were willing to advance to the attack if I would lead them. We met, however, with a warm reception, and the little command was broken up and dispersed." Rodes reports that about 150 of the 200 men were of his brigade and that they were led by Hill through the orchard, "the general himself handling a musket in the fight."

There was now no body of Confederate infantry that could have resisted a serious advance of Richardson's Division, but the artillery fire rendered his position untenable and the entire line was withdrawn across the Sunken Road and formed under cover of the ridge upon which Meagher had fought.

The serious infantry firing on this part of the field ended with the withdrawal of Richardson's Division about 1 p.m., at which time the Confederates re-occupied the Piper house and the adjoining buildings and advanced their skirmishers into the orchard, and their artillery "from the south end of the West Woods round to Boonsboro turnpike swept the country in Richardson's front with their fire." Richardson's men suffered severely from this artillery fire in taking up their new position, and it could not be replied to, for, up to this time, the division was without artillery, but now a section of Robertson's Battery of horse artillery, commanded by

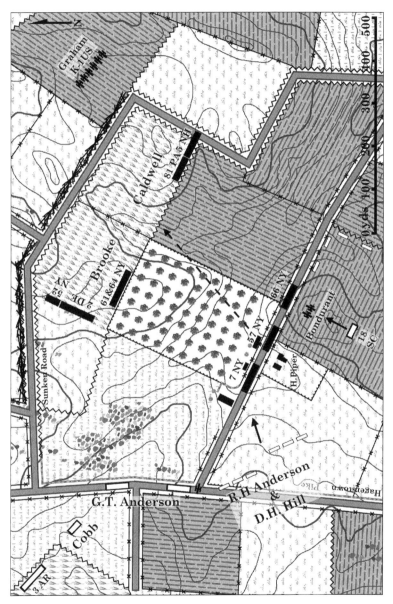

Pressure from several sides force the Union regiments at the Piper farm to retreat.

Lieutenant Albert O. Vincent, 2nd U. S. Artillery, arrived on the ground, and, taking position on Richardson's left, opened fire upon the Confederate batteries in its front and beyond the Hagerstown road. Its fire was directly, principally, upon Miller's Battery, in Piper's apple orchard, which was temporarily silenced. Vincent's section was relieved by Graham's Battery (K, 1st United States) 6 brass guns. A rifled battery had been asked for; there was none available on the right, and General Hunt, chief of artillery, was requested to furnish one. Hunt had none at his disposal; all were actively engaged or had been detached to other points, but Graham's light 12's were sent instead.

Graham moved from his bivouac near Porterstown about noon, passed up behind the heavy batteries on the high ridge east of the Antietam, crossed the stream at Pry's Ford, went through the Neikirk place, and, following the ravines, under cover, ascended the high ground, where Meagher had been engaged and, relieving Vincent's guns, which retired at once, took position about 80 yards north of the Sunken Road, and on the left of Richardson's infantry, and engaged a section of Confederate artillery about 700 yards southwest, behind a group of three hay stacks, in a field to the right of an orchard, which he silenced in about ten minutes. A very sharp fire of shot, spherical-case, and shell were opened on Graham by several batteries, two of which had rifled guns, and one of these, probably (Hardaway's), situated on a rocky ledge, beyond the Hagerstown road, enfiladed his guns. Graham returned the fire as rapidly as possible, but after firing for some 20 minutes found that they were beyond the range of his smooth bore guns, his solid shot falling short several hundred yards, and having called Richardson's attention to the fact, was told by him that he wished to save the battery as much as possible, in order that it might advance with his division at a signal then expected from Sumner. While communicating this to Graham, Richardson was mortally wounded by a ball of a spherical case from the battery enfilading Graham. After this Graham continued his fire some five minutes and then, after losing 4 men killed, 5 severely wounded, 17 horses killed and 6 severely wounded, withdrew 200 yards under cover of the ridge. Graham's action was in plain view from McClellan's headquarters and is described by Colonel Strother of the staff:

> About this time, one of the handsomest exhibitions of gallantry which occurred during the day. A battery of ours was seen entering the field in the vicinity of Richardson's Division. Moving at a walk and taking position apparently in advance of our line, it opened fire at short range, and maintained its ground for half an hour under the concentrated fire of at least 40 guns of the enemy. As they moved in with the greatest deliberation I saw a number of shells overthrow men and horses, and during the combat the battery sometimes

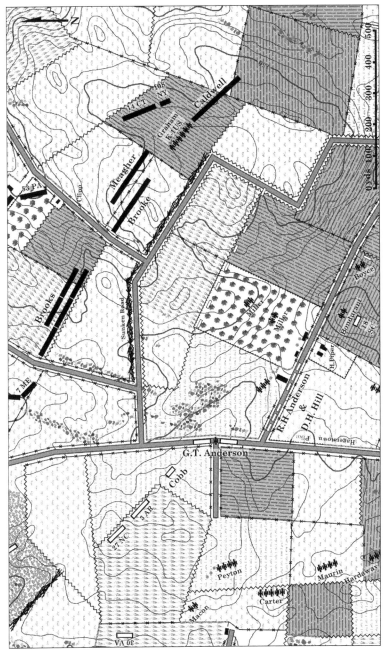

The Union and Confederate lines face off against each other at approximate 1 o'clock.

appeared covered with the dust and smoke of the enemy's bursting shells. Unable to sustain the unequal contest they at length withdrew to shelter, and then we saw parties returning to the ground to bring off the wounded in blankets, and to remove the limbers of two guns, the horses of which had been killed…The affair was observed from headquarters with the greatest interest, and elicited the warmest commendation.

The Confederate batteries engaging Graham were those of Miller in the orchard, the Donaldsonville artillery, near the hay stacks beyond the Hagerstown road, Hardaway's, and Carter's Battery and others, of D. H. Hill's Division, and Cutts' Battalion. Captain Carter says:

I now received an order from General Rodes to plant my battery on the left of the Hagerstown road near the Donaldsonville Artillery. With the consent of General Lee, I at once moved my battery to this point. In reaching it I found several batteries engaged in driving off a Yankee battery (Graham's) posted near the spot occupied in the morning by my two howitzers. My battery at once took part in this fire, and continued firing until the battery was withdrawn. There was at this time a pause in the engagement.

Soon after the withdrawal of Graham's Battery, D. H. Hill advanced his skirmishers to the upper part of the orchard and into the cornfield on the right and left.

Although Richardson's Division had been withdrawn to the cover of the crest, upon which it had begun its engagement, the center of the Confederate line, held by D. H. Hill and Longstreet, was still menaced by Franklin's Sixth Corps. Brooks' Vermont brigade had relieved French's Division and was fresh, strong and intact, and on Brooks' right was Irwin's Brigade. Both were in good condition and liable at any moment to be launched upon the Confederates, very much disorganized, partially demoralized, some of them out of ammunition, and not able to resist a serious onset of infantry. Part of Hill's and R. H. Anderson's divisions were under cover of the ridge from Piper's barn to the Hagerstown road, and along the stone fences of the road, while on their left, filling thinly the space to the south edge of the West Woods, was Colonel Cooke with the 27th North Carolina, 3rd Arkansas and the small remnant of Cobb's Brigade. Cooke was confronting Irwin's Brigade and out of ammunition, and to repeated requests for it Longstreet replied that he had none to give him and that he must hold his position with the bayonet. Longstreet says: "Cooke stood with his empty guns, and waved his colors to show that his troops were in position."

The Sunken Road after the battle. Looking east along Rodes' line. *Library of Congress.*

The Union troops engaged in the struggle for the Sunken Road numbered about 10,000 men; French's Division of 5,700 and Richardson's of 4,300. The Confederates opposing these were G. B. Anderson's Brigade of 1,174 men; Rodes' of 550, remnants of Colquitt about 200, G. T. Anderson's Brigade of about 500, Cobb's Brigade of 398, the 27th North Carolina, 325, the 3rd Arkansas 350, and R. H. Anderson's Division, with its artillery, excluding Armistead's Brigade, 3,400—in all, with artillery, about 7,200 men, not including the artillery belonging to other organizations than D. H. Hill and R. H. Anderson.

The Union Loss in French's Division was 1,750; in Richardson's Division 1,161, in all 2,911 for the two divisions, to which must be added the loss in Graham's Battery of 4 killed and 5 wounded, making an aggregate of 2,920, 29 per cent of the number engaged.

The Confederate loss was 1,243 in the five brigades and artillery of R. H. Anderson's Division, 156 in Cobb's Brigade, 217 in the 3rd Arkansas, about 150 in the 27th North Carolina, 50 in G. T. Anderson's Brigade; 203 in Rodes' Brigade; 475 in G. B. Anderson's Brigade and about 50 in the remnant of Colquitt's Brigade. The batteries in D. H. Hill's Division lost about 30 men. The aggregate is 2,574 or about 30 1/2 per cent of those engaged. Some of R. H. Anderson's regiments suffered a loss of over 50 per cent, the 16th Mississippi over 63 per cent, and the 3rd Arkansas of Manning's Brigade, Walker's Division, lost 62 per cent.

Chapter 19

The Dunker Church
(11 a.m. to 1 p.m.)

Once more we return to the Dunker Church, which we left at 11 a.m. At that hour the divisions of the First Corps and Sedgwick's Division of the Second were rallying in support of the artillery on the Poffenberger hill. Hofmann's Brigade which, with two guns of Cooper's Battery, had advanced to the crossroad leading to the Potomac, and assisted greatly in checking McLaws' pursuit, remained in this position about half an hour "when a large cavalry force was seen passing in rear of a narrow strip of woods" evidently intending to attack the brigade in flank; on the right a heavy body of infantry much larger than his brigade followed, upon which Hofmann retired to the small cornfield across the Hagerstown road, where he could command the open field west of the road. He was soon ordered to the left, where he remained until late in the afternoon, when Sumner ordered him to join his division, "just below the crest of a hill" and immediately "in rear of a long line of artillery."

Williams' Division of the Twelfth Corps was holding the East Woods and supporting the batteries of Woodruff, Cothran, Knap, Bruen and Frank, which were in the open fields in front of the woods, and Greene's five regiments were in the West Woods to the rear and left of the church. Soon after 11 o'clock the 13th New Jersey, moving from the East Woods through the batteries and over the open ground south of the cornfield, entered the West Woods at the church, and relieved the 5th and 7th Ohio; these two small, gallant regiments, much reduced in numbers and entirely out of ammunition, retiring to the plateau east of the road, where they rejoined the 66th Ohio, which, with the 102nd New York, had been left near Tompkins' guns. Soon after this the Purnell Legion, 200 strong, of Goodrich's Brigade, which had been supporting the 124th Pennsylvania, near the Hagerstown road, entered the West Woods and formed line to the right of the church and about 90 yards beyond it, but not as far advanced as, nor forming close connection with, the 13th New Jersey. These regiments were sent Greene in response to his urgent request for more men to hold his important position; he had asked a much larger force, but Williams could not spare it, and an appeal to Sumner was not successful, nor could he succeed in recalling Goodrich's Brigade for the purpose.

It will be remembered that when Manning's Brigade made its charge against Greene's position, it moved in such a way as to be almost entirely covered from the fire of Woodruff's Battery by the peculiar conformation of the ground, Woodruff found it impracticable to change front for want of time and the fact that, while protecting one flank he should expose the other, and being without infantry support, his only course was to fall back about 240 yards to the edge of the East Woods, his left gun sweeping the Smoketown road. Here he was supported on the right and could protect his left. After firing from this position of few rounds down the road, in the direction of the church, and, observing that Manning's attack had been repulsed, Woodruff retired and was relieved by Battery A, 4th U. S. Artillery, commanded by Lieutenant Evan Thomas. Thomas, who had been halted in the East Woods, ran his right section to the front and out it in position, then advanced his other guns, the left close to the Smoketown road, and the entire battery remained some time without firing a shot. About the time Woodruff retired Cothran moved his battery back a few yards and Thomas formed on his left but not closely connecting. The 107th New York, supporting Cothran, fell back to the edge of the woods. For a short time Knap's Battery remained in the southeast corner of the corn on Cothran's right and rear.

As it neared 12 o'clock Tompkins' Battery, running out of ammunition, was relieved by Battery G, 1st Rhode Island, Captain Charles C. Owens, and withdrew to the position from which it had advanced early in the morning. It is doubtful that any battery on the field did more solid and effective work than Tompkins. It took position on the plateau, opposite the church, at a most critical moment, contributed largely to the repulse of Kershaw and Manning; aided in the repulse of Rodes' attack on French; opened an effective and demoralizing fire upon R. H. Anderson's infantry as it approached the field, swept the Piper cornfield with terrible effect as it went through it, and silenced some of its artillery. During a great part of the time engaged it had very little infantry support and was exposed on the right to an enfilading fire from the Confederate infantry. It expended 83 rounds of canister, 68 rounds of solid shot; 427 rounds of shell and 454

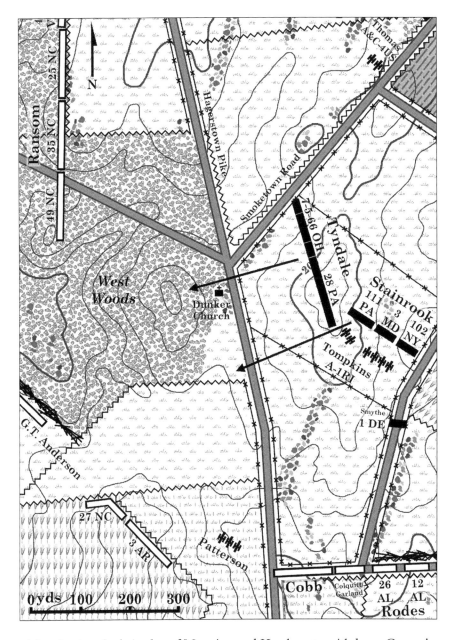

After forcing the brigades of Manning and Kershaw to withdraw, Greene's division advances into the West Woods.

rounds of case- shot—1,032 rounds in all. With the exceptions of the shots fired at a battery on its right, which was hidden by a ridge, every shot was fired at a visible enemy, the guns pointed with care, and the accuracy of aim and length of fuse noted. It loss was 4 killed and 15 wounded.

On the night of the 16th Owen's Battery bivouacked a short distance east of the Smoketown road, near Mansfield's Corps, and about a mile and a quarter north of the East Woods; in the morning of the 17th it moved to the left and front in search of some position where it could be used to advantage and about 9.30 a.m. passed through the East Woods and was about to take position in the field south of the Smoketown road when the 125th Pennsylvania and 34th New York came retreating from the Dunker Church, upon which Owens took position behind the burning Mumma buildings and reported to Major Clarke, Sumner's chief of artillery, for orders. Clarke had already more batteries than could be used and directed Owens to get his battery under cover, and it was moved to the open ground behind the Mumma's orchard, where it remained until ordered to relieve Tompkins. It went forward and immediately engaged a battery a mile distant, in the direction of Sharpsburg, which was pouring in a heavy fire. In about twenty minutes the Confederate was silenced and Owens ceased firing.

About 11:30 a.m., the advance of the 6th Corps arrived. We left the 6th Corps and Couch's Division in Pleasant Valley, where they remained on the 15th and 16th. During the night of the 16th Franklin received orders to move toward Keedysville in the morning with his two divisions, and to leave Couch to occupy Maryland Heights. Leaving the 121st New York to guard Crampton's Gap, bury the dead and care for the wounded, Franklin started at 6 a.m. of the 17th, Smith's Division in advance. Smith marched through Rohrersville to the old Sharpsburg road, thence to the nose of Elk Ridge, where he was met by an order of McClellan to mass his division near army headquarters, upon which he left the road on which he had been marching, struck across the fields and massed his command alongside of the Keedysville and Sharpsburg road not far from headquarters, ready to support the attack on the right or the left as required. McClellan says: "It was first intended to keep this corps in reserve on the east side of the Antietam, to operate on either flank or on the center, as circumstances might require, but on nearing Keedysville the strong opposition on the right, developed by the attacks of Hooker and Sumner, rendered it necessary at once to send this corps to the assistance of the right wing." Smith massed his division at the road about 10 a.m. In a short time he was ordered to form his division to command the ford by which Sumner had crossed the Antietam, and shortly after was ordered to cross the creek and occupy a point in rear of where it was supposed the Union right was engaged.

Brigadier General William F. Smith
Photographed as a Major General
Library of Congress.

Smith went down the hill to the right of the Pry house, crossed the Antietam by the ford and came up in rear of Sumner's right about 11 a.m., and was ordered to form his division in rear of the batteries on the extreme right. The division was then behind and to the right of the East Woods.

Before forming his division Smith was informed by Lieutenant Colonel Taylor of Sumner's staff, that a battery on the right center was unsupported, and ordered two regiments of Hancock's Brigade to its support. Shortly after, on visiting the ground, he ordered the remaining regiments and two batteries forward to the threatened point. The two batteries here referred to were the 1st New York, Captain Andrew Cowan and Battery B, Maryland Light Artillery, Lieutenant Theodore J. Vanneman. Cowan went through the East Woods and took position in the grass field east of D. R. Miller's and north of the cornfield, the same field occupied earlier in the day by the batteries of Stewart, Ransom, Thompson and Matthews. Vanneman's Battery relieved Knap's, which was moving to the left; two guns going up the Smoketown road to the Dunker Church, where we shall soon follow them. Hancock's disposition of his troops is shown in his official report:

> Arriving on the ground, the regiments of my brigade were placed in position supporting three batteries—Cowan's, of Smith's division, on the right (3-inch guns); Frank's, of French's division, in the center (12-pounder brass guns), and Cothran's battery, of Banks' corps (rifled guns), on the left, the regiments being placed in the following order: The Forty-ninth Pennsylvania Volunteers, under Lieut. Col. William Brisbane, on the right of Cowan's battery; the Forty-third New York Volunteers, under command of Maj. John Wilson and the One hundred and thirty-seventh Regiment Pennsylvania Volunteers, under Col. Henry N. Bossert, between Cowan's and Frank's batteries; the Sixth Maine Volunteers, under Col. Hiram Burnham, and the Fifth Wisconsin Volunteers, under Col. Amasa Cobb, between Frank's and Cothran's batteries, the whole line being parallel to the woods in front, then occupied in force by the enemy, and at canister distance therefrom.[6]

Skirmishers were immediately thrown forward into the corn, who came under fire of those of the enemy, lying behind the fences of the Hagerstown road, and the D. R. Miller house and enclosures were occupied by detachments from the command. Very soon the Confederate placed two batteries in front of the West Woods, their infantry in the edge of it in support, and opened a heavy fire with shell, round shot, shrapnel, and grape, and Hancock called upon Sumner for another regiment to place in

---

[6] *OR*, vol. 19, part I, p. 406.

This field would have been filled with Union artillery batteries at the time of the battle. Looking north roughly along the wartime edge of the East Woods. Several Union batteries switched places along this position facing to the left, or west, during the course of the afternoon. *Author's collection.*

the woods on his extreme right. The 20th Massachusetts was given him by Howard and posted in the west edge of the north part of the East Woods in support to a battery in its front. After a severe cannonade, the skirmishers assisting, the two batteries were silenced by Cowan's, Frank's, Vanneman's and Cothran's guns, and withdrawn from that part of the field. Hancock's loss, in infantry, was very slight, but the batteries met some losses in men and horses.

To the left of Hancock's line was Evan Thomas's Battery of the Second Corps; Knap was taking position with four guns on Thomas's right, between him and Cothran; Ayers' Battery (F, 5th U. S.) , under command of Lieutenant Leonard Martin, was going forward to position on Thomas's left, and Smith was forming Irwin's Brigade to support these batteries and extend Hancock's left, when circumstances demanded more active duty, and, leaving Smith for a moment, we return to Greene at the Dunker Church.

The left of Greene's line, held by two small companies of the 102nd New York, the 3rd Maryland and 111th Pennsylvania, was at the south fence of the West Woods, 168 yards to the left of the church, all facing south and all engaged in sharp skirmishing with the 27th North Carolina and 3rd Arkansas. On the right of the 111th was the 28th Pennsylvania, now 300 strong, a part of its left facing south, but the greater part of the regiment facing southwest, and firing into the corn and upon skirmishers who made their appearance in the woods in its front and to the right. On the right of the 28th Pennsylvania was the 13th New Jersey, facing west, and firing obliquely to the left, into the corn, and to the front and right upon some skirmishers in the woods; its center was opposite to and about 190 yards west of the church. To the right and about 80 yards in rear of the 13th New Jersey was the Purnell Legion of about 200 men. The left of this regiment rested to the right of the church and about 90 yards beyond it, and faced a little north of west. In all Greene had about 1,350 men from four different brigades of the Twelfth Corps.

When he entered the woods at 10:30 a.m., Greene supposed that Sedgwick was still in the woods to his right and front, and knew not to the contrary, nearly the whole time he was in them, but he knew there was a wide interval on his right and it was to fill this interval that he had called urgently for reinforcements, a call partially answered by sending him the 13th New Jersey and Purnell Legion. Soon after taking position on Greene's right the colonel of the 13th New Jersey, finding his flank in air and knowing from his experience and that of the 2nd Massachusetts, on the Hagerstown road, about an hour before, that the enemy were near his right, sent a message to Greene, who was on the extreme left, that his flank was exposed to the enemy, who were not far from his right. When this message was communicated to Greene, he replied: "Tell your colonel not to be

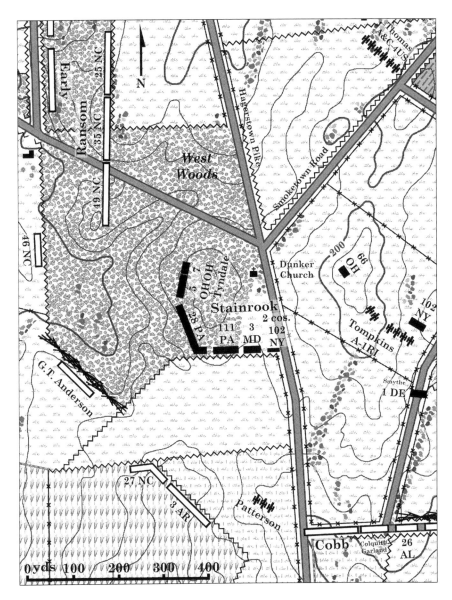

Greene's position in the West Woods.

uneasy about his flank, the whole of Sedgwick's Division is in the woods on his right." And Greene had good reason for his belief; he had not been informed of Sedgwick's repulse; he, himself, had repulsed two brigades of McLaws' right; he had seen Barksdale's Brigade, the 3rd South Carolina, and a stream of stragglers going through the woods to seek shelter beyond them; there was a cessation of infantry fire on the right, and he concluded that the whole Confederate line had been repulsed.

Men were now seen moving off toward the right, recognized as Confederates, and the adjutant of the 13th New Jersey was sent to Greene with the information and with the further information that the colonel of the regiment was thoroughly convinced, absolutely sure, that the identical position supposed to be held by Sedgwick, was, in fact, held by the enemy. This brought Greene to the right; he made a hurried examination of the position, insisted that Sedgwick was on the right, told the colonel that he was surely mistaken in the idea that the enemy were in the woods, on the right, and gave stringent orders that the men should under no circumstances be permitted to fire to the right. After informing the colonel that the greatest danger was on the left, and directing him to keep up an oblique fire in that direction, into the corn, and upon anything seen directly in front. Greene rode to the left, when an officer of the corps staff came up, to whom he stated that the officers on his right were laboring under the delusion that Sedgwick had been driven from the woods. "Why, yes, General," was the reply "didn't you know it." Greene's response was more picturesquely sulfurous than polite. As Greene says: "The position of the division in the advanced woods was very critical. We were in advance of our lines. Guns were sent for...and I sought reinforcements from General Williams. None were at the time available." He was separated from French, on the left, by an interval of nearly 600 yards, filled only by Tompkins' Battery, supported by about 300 infantry, most of whom had expended their ammunition, and the nearest troops on his right were those of Williams' Division, the nearest of whom, were a half mile in his rear.

Meanwhile Confederate skirmishers were advancing, a company each of the 30th Virginia and 46th North Carolina, on the front and on the right, up a ravine. These were driven back by the 28th Pennsylvania and 13th New Jersey, and immediately thereafter the commanding officer of the Purnell Legion, sent some skirmishers to the right, who, going but a few yards, saw a regiment—the 49th North Carolina—lying down in the woods, well concealed, very near the right and front, beyond a ravine, and where it had lain the entire time that Greene was in the woods; and other troops were seen moving steadily and closing up on the left of this regiment. It was about this time that the two guns Greene had just sent for were being placed in position in the woods near the church.

The West Woods from the 13th New Jersey's right flank looking toward the approach of the 49th North Carolina. The trees would have been taller with little underbrush present. *Author's collection.*

It was little after half past eleven that Lieutenant C. T. Greene, son and aide to the general, rode up to Knap with orders to advance two guns towards the church to assist in holding the woods. Lieutenant James C. McGill was sent with the right section. He passed from the cornfield and along the west edge of the East Woods to and across the Smoketown road, taking position on the high open ground opposite the church, when Lieutenant Colonel Tyndale came up and ordered him into the woods beyond the church, to dislodge the 27th North Carolina and 3rd Arkansas from the cornfield, to which order McGill made an earnest protest, stating, among other reasons, that the guns could be easily captured if a charge should be made and any of the horses shot. Tyndale insisted; McGill replied that the woods was no place for artillery in the face of concealed infantry, but that he would obey orders. As the high post and rail fences of the Hagerstown road were obstacles to an advance directly to the front, McGill moved back into the Smoketown road and down it to the church, and thence about 100 yards down the Hagerstown road. One gun went into the woods a short distance and halted; the other remaining on the road, while McGill awaited more specific orders as to where his fire should be directed. At this time the limbs and branches were falling off the trees from the fire of the Confederate artillery and to the left was the cornfield, bounded by a fence skirted with trees, and concealed by this fence and the tall corn were the 27th North Carolina and 3rd Arkansas, who were annoying the infantry in the woods.

Tyndale called McGill's attention to a group of horsemen and some dismounted officers gathered on a slight elevation southwest of the church, and remarked, "just take my glass lieutenant and you can see them." McGill looked a moment, returned the glass, went to his advanced gun, moved it a short distance to rising ground in the woods and ordered it to unlimber, when the 27th North Carolina and 3rd Arkansas, rose up from behind the cornfield fence and with a yell, poured a volley at the gun, two horses were shot, one cannoneer was killed and another wounded, a cannon shot cut the limb of a tree, which, falling on the pole team, pinned the horses to the ground, several infantrymen rushed to assist in extricating the gun, when on the extreme right there was a crash of musketry and a wild yell; and at the same moment Colonel Cooke, with his two regiments, charged on the left and the gun was abandoned and lost, the only gun ever lost by the Twelfth Corps in action. Fortunately the second gun was still in the road and not yet unlimbered. It fired as it fell back, at the pursuing enemy, and quickly made its way by the Smoketown road and rejoined its battery.

This simultaneous charge of Ransom and Cooke, on either flank of Greene's line was not a concerted one, directed to be made at the same moment. Ransom, without orders charged to capture the guns, and Cooke, when he saw the guns coming into position had just received orders from

Looking west from the area occupied by Greene's division toward the West Woods. The 5th, 7th, and 66th Ohio held this area alone while the rest of the division occupied the West Woods. McGill's section of Knap's Battery E, Pennsylvania Light deployed in this area across the Hagerstown Pike before being overrun and forced back. *Author's collection.*

Longstreet, who was engaged at the Sunken Road, to charge in conjunction with Cobb's Brigade on his right, on the flank of French's Division. These two movements on Greene's flanks require separate treatment.

There are always two sides to a fight, and we must now look into the Confederate lines as they appeared immediately preceding the events above recited, and at the hour Greene was attacked on both flanks, which was about quarter past twelve. Kershaw's and Barksdale's brigades, which had fallen back, were still in the fields beyond the West Woods, under cover of rock-ledges, stone and rail fences, and Semmes was near them, and, on their left, in the same open ground, were the 30th Virginia, 46th and 48th North Carolina of Manning's Brigade, the 46th North Carolina being at the west fence of the woods. The 27th North Carolina and 3rd Arkansas were in line south of the woods opposing Greene, and Cobb's Brigade was on their right, opposite the mouth of the Sunken Road. Three regiments of Ransom's Brigade were under cover of the long rock ledge at the edge of the middle body of the West Woods, nearly parallel to and about 225 yards from the Hagerstown road, which they faced. Early's Brigade was to their left, and Armistead was to the left and rear of Early. Armistead's Brigade belonged to R. H. Anderson's Division; acted as a rear guard to the infantry, and was last of the command to cross the Potomac, and not in the attack made by McLaws, although it had been detached from its division to join him. As it approached Hauser's it came under heavy artillery fire, by which Captain W. G. Pollard, commanding 53rd Virginia, was killed and a few men wounded. It formed line east of Hauser's and moved into the West Woods, in the rear of Ransom's Brigade. The adjutant of the 35th North Carolina was sent to pilot it into position, and as it entered the woods Armistead was wounded in the foot by a rolling ball: "He saw the ball as it came rolling down the hill, and could have moved out of its course with all care, but, probably thinking it a shell and likely to explode, stood as one transfixed and did not move his foot or a muscle." There was a severe artillery fire at the time and some confusion in the ranks, Colonel J. G. Hodges, 14th Virginia, assumed command and led the Brigade to the left, where it took the position held by Early, who moved to the right on the edge of the plateau facing the Harper's Ferry road, and on Ransom's left. Armistead came up very soon after McLaws had fallen back, did not become engaged, but suffered some from artillery fire. Stuart, with cavalry, artillery, and the 13th Virginia and 24th North Carolina, was on the extreme left, where he had been checked, awaiting reinforcements that Jackson had promised to renew the battle. Hood's Division and Hays' Brigade, having replenished ammunition and partaken of some food, were approaching the West Woods to take position in them about midway west of the church.

But before Hood arrived there was no Confederate line in the woods immediately west of the church and there was a wide gap, which was now

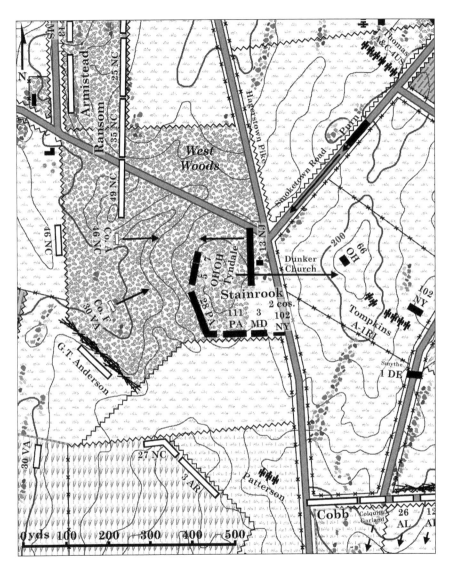

The 13th New Jersey relieves the 5th and 7th Ohio. Confederate skirmishers advance to confront the Federals.

sought to be filled by the 46th North Carolina and a company of the 30th Virginia. It will be remembered that when Greene crossed the Hagerstown road the 46th North Carolina was driven clear out of the woods. Here Colonel Hall was met by General Jackson, who ordered him to report to McLaws, by whom he was ordered to endeavor to hold the woods at all hazards. He then "advanced in line of battle to the edge of the woods, which was by this time filled with the enemy, and placed the regiment behind a ledge of rocks, throwing out company A and the company from the 30th Virginia as skirmishers."

The company from the 30th Virginia was commanded by Captain Hudgins and was not with the regiment in its disastrous charge across the Hagerstown road, at the church, having been left on picket near Snavely's Ford. When relieved and rejoining its regiment it was assigned as a support to a battery, and then ordered into the West Woods, deployed as sharpshooters, with orders if pressed by heavy line to fall back on the 46th North Carolina. Hudgins with his company and the one of the 46th North Carolina advanced and were met by such a severe fire from the 28th Pennsylvania and 13th New Jersey, by which many of their men were killed and wounded, that they fell back on the 46th North Carolina, "sheltered under a ledge of rock along the rear slope of the hill in the woods and at the west edge of them."

Just before these men went back Colonel M. W. Ransom, 35th North Carolina, saw McGill with his two guns go from the Smoketown road into the Hagerstown road at the church, and came to the quick conclusion to capture them. At this time General Ransom, in command of the brigade, had gone to the left to recall the 24th North Carolina, which was with Stuart, and Colonel Ransom was in temporary command of the brigade— the 25th, 35th and 49th North Carolina. The two regiments on the left of the brigade were behind the ledge in the edge of the middle woods and looking over the open ground west of the Hagerstown road, across which Barksdale's Brigade and the 3rd South Carolina had charged, the 49th North Carolina, on the right, was in the woods on a sloping hill side, well protected by the rock ledge and concealed by the foliage of the woods. Ransom ordered the 49th North Carolina to file down to the ravine, then change front forward on first company, and charge for the church, the two regiments on the left to close in on the 49th and follow its movements; all of which was instantly done.

On level ground everything could be seen through the woods, but on the side hills and in the ravine the foliage of the tree tops was so dense that nothing could be seen beyond the ravine, so that the 49th North Carolina was not seen by the 13th New Jersey and Purnell Legion until its right was nearly at the lowest depression of the ravine, and its entire line was changing front forward on first company. When this was seen the three

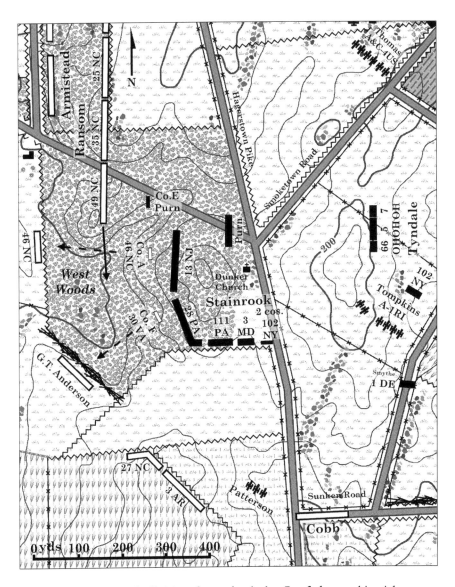

Fire from Greene's division forces back the Confederate skirmishers.
Ransom's Brigade, commanded by his brother Colonel Matt W. Ransom at
the moment, begins moving south to confront Greene.

right companies of the 13th New Jersey were swung back at nearly a right angle to their former position but, even now, so impressed were the officers of the regiment by Greene's warning, and he had not cautioned them otherwise, that the adjutant, immediately followed by an officer of the Purnell Legion, went forward to get a closer view and determine whether they were friends or enemies, for their uniforms could not be distinguished.

The same uncertainty possessed the Confederates. When Ransom ordered the movement it was for the purpose of capturing McGill's guns at the church, and he appears not to have been aware that there was any infantry between him and the church, although he must have seen the 13th New Jersey and Purnell Legion enter the woods at the church. Be this as it may, when the right of the 49th North Carolina came to a halt, and began to change front to make a charge for the guns, they were surprised to see infantry in their front, and at the same time that the officers of the Union line were going forward to determine who the 49th North Carolina were, two officers of the 49th were sent out to ascertain who the Purnell Legion and the Jersey men were, but before any of them returned a simultaneous fire was opened on both sides, as though done by one order. The 49th North Carolina without waiting to complete its change of front, after the right had fired two volleys, charged, not directly for the church, as at first intended, but, descending into the ravine, where it was under partial cover, made directly for the right and flank of the Purnell Legion, which fired three or four volleys and retreated out of the woods and across the Hagerstown road. Lieutenant Colonel Simpson reports: "the enemy appeared in overwhelming numbers and compelled it to retire." The 13th New Jersey followed the Purnell Legion. It fired two or three volleys; its right was pressed by the right of the 49th North Carolina, the left of that regiment was gaining its rear, and it retreated from the woods and across the road; the commanding officer reports: "Being flanked on the right the whole brigade was obliged to retire." The 28th Pennsylvania came under the fire of this flank attack, but, perceiving the retreat of the troops on its right and hearing the Confederate yell in its rear and to the right, and feeling the pressure on its left, also, fell back out of the woods, followed by everything on its left. Major Raphael, commanding the regiment, reports that "the overwhelming force of the enemy, advancing in three columns on our right, left, and center, threatening annihilation to the small force in that position" compelled him to retire, and General Greene, referring to his whole command, reports: "the enemy advancing in large force, threatening to engulf the small command, they were forced to retire."

The 49th North Carolina, closely supported by a part of the 35th on its left, following closely the left of the retreating troops, reached the Hagerstown road about 130 yards north of the church and continued fire on the retreating troops as they went over the plateau opposite the church,

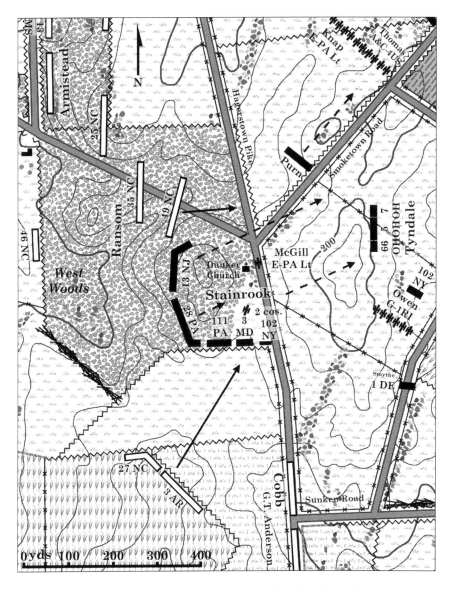

The attack of the 49th North Carolina causes first the Purnell Legion to fall back, and then the 13th New Jersey. The 27th North Carolina and 3rd Arkansas commanded by Colonel John R. Cooke attack from the south. The combined efforts lead Greene to abandon the West Woods and retreat.

and upon McGill, who, driven from position south of the church, was retiring with one gun and two caissons down the Smoketown road. Some of the North Carolina men had crossed the road, but the main body had halted at a barricade at the edge of the woods, when Cothran's and Knap's guns, ten in all, opened upon them with a most savage fire, the heaviest artillery fire the regiment ever experienced, which ploughed up the ground around them, killing and wounding many officers and men, and it fell back into the woods and to the left.

Some of Greene's men retreated across the road north of the church; the greater part of them crossed south of the church, and officers of every grade made efforts to check the retreat on the plateau, where Greene had so successfully repulsed Kershaw and Manning, but effort availed nothing, the retreat was continued to the East Woods. Colonel Cooke with his two regiments, supported on the right by Cobb's Brigade, pursuing closely on the left flank and in the rear, the left of his line as far as the Mumma place. Owens' Rhode Island battery, which, twenty minutes before had relieved Tompkins, had just ceased firing in the direction of Sharpsburg and the Sunken Road, was involved in the retreat. Owens was about to proceed toward the brow of the hill to engage the enemy's infantry, then in plain sight from that position, beyond the Sunken Road and around the Piper barn, when, he says: "A noise from my right attracted my attention, and I saw our infantry retreating in disorder toward me, and then about 150 yards off, and closely pursued by the rebels. I limbered up quickly and started on a trot into the road leading direct from the ruins (Mumma's), and when the last caisson left the ground the enemy were close upon us."

When the 27th North Carolina and 3rd Arkansas first took position south of the Dunker Church woods, they were on line of fence parallel to the woods; after skirmishing with Greene some time, all, save a few sharpshooters on the left, were drawn back about 20 paces in the corn and the right thrown back on a line with Cobb's Brigade and the end of the Sunken Road. The sharpshooters on the left kept up a lively fire upon Greene's men in the woods and the right engaged Tompkins' Battery, which replied with an annoying fire of canister and shell. The regiments had been in this position about half an hour when Tyndale ordered the two guns of Knap's Battery into the woods south of the church.

Colonel Cooke, who was observing the movement, ordered the four left companies up to the fence and directed them to fire at the two guns, both plainly seen, and particularly at the advanced gun and the horses. At the first fire the horses and some of the men were seen to fall, and the infantry which had been moved to support the gun, showed signs of wavering, and at this moment came Longstreet's order to charge, in connection with Cobb's Brigade and D. H. Hill's command, upon the flank of French's Division. Cooke ordered the charge and the 27th North Carolina and 3rd

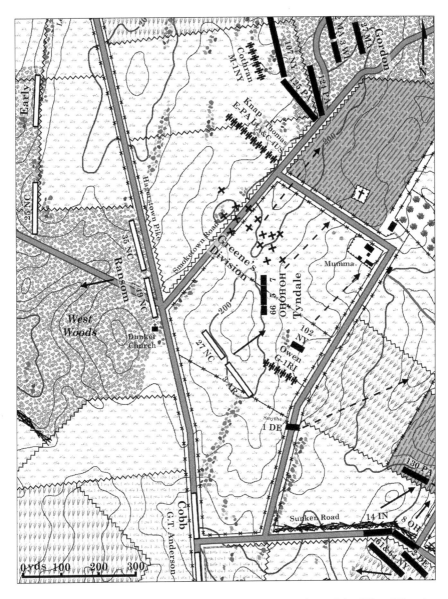

Colonel Ransom's two regiments remain near the edge of the West Woods briefly, but fall back under artillery fire. Cooke's two regiments continue in their pursuit of Greene's division, pushing back the rest of Tyndale's brigade and Owen's battery. They then turn east toward the flank and rear of French and Richardson's divisions at the Sunken Road.

Arkansas leaped the fence and made for the guns; McGill, who had one gun in the road, unlimbered, fired as it fell back, past the church, and narrowly escaped capture by the 49th North Carolina, as it turned into the Smoketown road. The charging line had not proceeded over 50 yards when it was seen that one gun had escaped and that Greene's men were crossing the road and retreating over the plateau, upon which Cooke, leaving the abandoned gun to his left, changed direction slightly, to the right, and pursued Greene, keeping up a running fire and taking some prisoners. In the pursuit the color bearers of the two regiments forged ahead of the line some distance and Cooke cautioned the bearer of his own colors to go slower as the regiment could not keep up with him, which brought the happy response: "Colonel, I can't let that Arkansas fellow got ahead of me." It was in such rapid pursuit as this that Cooke reached the crest of the plateau; saw that Greene's men had reached the cover of artillery, which now opened upon him, and that he, himself, had gone entirely too far to the left, upon which he wheeled to the right, crossed the fences of Mumma's lane and entered the cornfield in rear of where French's right had been but was now fronting him. Just before the line reached the lane Captains Adams and Graham, commanding the left companies of the 27th North Carolina, observed some officers and men behind the hay or grain stacks near Mumma's and double-quicking to the left and captured them; ordering them to the rear, they double-quicked back to their commands, which had then reached the middle of the cornfield and been checked. Immediately in front, behind a ledge, were Kimball's men, who had changed front; on their left front were three regiments of Brooke's Brigade; Barlow, with the 61st and 64th New York, was coming into position on their right front and some of Irwin's Brigade skirmishers appeared and opened fire on the left flank. The two regiments fell back, at a double-quick, Irwin's Brigade at their heels and on their flank, firing into them, killing and wounding many. They went back over nearly the same ground of their advance, to the position from which they had advanced and, with the few cartridges remaining, assisted in checking Irwin's pursuit, which did not reach the Hagerstown road. One half of the officers and men of the two regiments had fallen.

Cobb's Brigade supported Colonel Cooke's right. By its action earlier in the day it had been reduced to about 250 men. It had been advanced from the mouth of the Sunken Road to the board fences of Mumma's Lane, striking the fences just south of the cornfield and came under the fire of the 61st and 64th New York. Its loss was heavy; when the 27th North Carolina and 3rd Arkansas fell back it was left without support, and was ordered back. Colonel McRae, commanding the brigade, reports that it left the field with not more than 50 of the 250 men. It fell back across the Hagerstown

The field south of the Roulette farm where Cooke's two Confederate regiments were brought to a halt. The photograph is looking west from the Roulette lane and the Union line put together to halt the advance. The 7th Maine approached Cooke's flank from the right of the photo. *Author's collection.*

road and joined the right of Cooke's command, remaining with it, until relieved about 3 p.m.

As Greene's men retreated to the East Woods, General Smith was about to form Irwin's Brigade on Hancock's left, when it was observed that the enemy was advancing and that Evan Thomas had turned his guns to the left upon the 27th North Carolina and 3rd Arkansas, opening with spherical case upon them as they crossed the crest of the plateau, and then with canister upon the two left companies of the 27th North Carolina as they approached the grain stacks, but, as we have seen, these two companies quickly fell back and joined their regiment in the Mumma cornfield. The 7th Maine, 20th and 49th New York were in line of battle with the 33rd and 77th New York as skirmishers on the right. The 20th New York was the largest regiment in the brigade and led the advance, the 49th New York in echelon, on its right, and the 7th Maine, in echelon, on its left. The 20th New York cleared the East Woods and went forward, south of the Smoketown road, in fine line, General Smith, Colonel Vegesack and his field officers, riding close behind and pushing it on in the most spirited manner, the Confederate skirmishers falling rapidly back. Under Smith's order the regiment was to halt under cover of the crest that had sheltered Greene earlier in the day, but, in the ardor of pursuit, the men passed the crest and immediately came under fire of Cooke's infantry and a 4 gun battery south of the church, which opened with canister inflicting much loss. The regiment was quickly recalled and ordered to lie down under cover, and the 49th New York came up and lay down on its right. The 7th Maine, moving in echelon, on the left, charged a body of Confederates at the Roulette buildings, drove it out with the loss of 12 men, and double-quicked to the left of the 20th New York, joining it just as it halted, and lay down on its left.

Irwin had ordered the 33rd and 77th New York to advance on the right as skirmishers; from some misunderstanding, they both went forward by the right flank, passed through Thomas' Battery, and, as they neared the church, the 33rd on the right of the Smoketown road and the 77th on its left. The 49th North Carolina, supported by the 35th, which had fallen to the left and rear out of range of the batteries, seeing them coming, re-occupied the rail barricade from which it had been driven, and poured a volley upon both regiments which "staggered them and threw both into momentary confusion." Irwin says it was, "a severe and unexpected volley from the woods on the right, struck full on the 77th and 33rd New York, which staggered them for a moment, but they closed up and faced by the rear rank, and poured in a close and scorching fire driving back the enemy." Lieutenant Colonel Corning, commanding 33rd New York, reports that he "received orders from the commanding divisional general to support the right, and was ordered to march near the woods in front." His regiment was

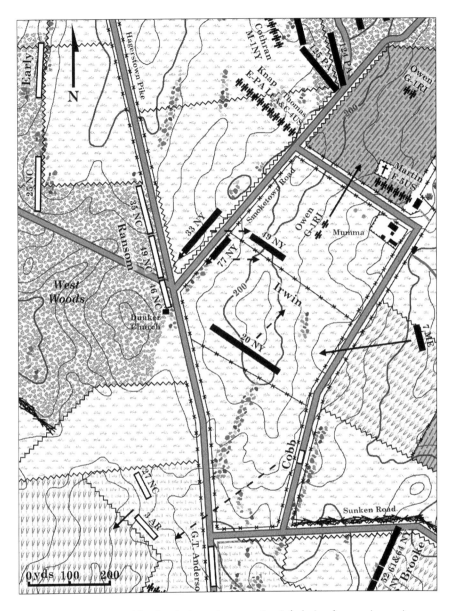

After pushing aside Cooke's regiments, Irwin's brigade continues its advance. The 20th New York crests the plateau but is driven back by Confederate fire. The 33rd and 77th New York advance in column by the flank too close to the West Woods, and are likewise disrupted and forced to retire when they are fired upon from the woods.

in column, marching by the right flank and: "when near the woods the enemy suddenly and unexpectedly opened a heavy fire from their infantry who were in the woods. This sudden and unexpected attack caused a momentary unsteadiness in the ranks, which was quickly rectified. The battalion faced by the rear rank and returned the fire, when, by order of the commanding general, the regiment retired a short distance, under cover of a ridge." Captain Babcock, 77th New York, was at first ordered to support the 33rd New York, but while advancing, was ordered to the front "for the purpose of cutting off the flying enemy, already routed by the left of your columns; and it was while endeavoring to execute this order that our position became critical, and in which most of the casualties occurred. A large force of the enemy had advanced on our right under cover of the woods, and were about to cut us off from the rest of the command,"[7] when the danger was discovered and the regiment ordered to fall back to the cover of a hill about 50 yards. Babcock says his men "only wavered a moment" and then retired and reformed in good order, "after delivering two well directed volleys" into nearly if not quite a brigade of the enemy, so near the right of the regiment that "you could see the white of their eyes at the time of retiring." The two regiments had come up a hill to the right of the church, and Smith says:

> At this point a severe flank fire from the woods was received...which threw both regiments slightly into confusion. They were immediately rallied by their officers and faced by the rear rank, and ordered to lie down behind the crest of a slope facing towards the woods. The rest of the brigade was ordered to form behind a crest at right angles to the other, facing to their proper front.

A section of Owens' Rhode Island battery accompanied the advance of Irwin's Brigade. The battery when swept from position by Greene's men, halted a few hundred yards in rear and, after replenishing ammunition, Owens "took the pieces alone of the right section and proceeded up behind the advance that retook the field, but the infantry was quite unsteady on the right and broke a second time" and not deeming it prudent to risk his guns under such circumstances, he withdrew and reported to Sumner.

It was the impression, if not the understanding, among the officers of Irwin's Brigade that they were to retake the woods at the church, and this view was shared by General Franklin, who in his testimony before the committee on the Conduct of the War, said: "General Smith made a charge with this brigade on the advancing enemy, and after a severe musketry fire

---

[7] Carman mangled the quote from Babcock's report, leaving out words and using incorrect quotation marks. I have corrected it for the sake of clarity.

The view west of the 20th New York's monument. Here the regiment crested the plateau and was met by a heavy fire from the Confederates stationed in the woods. The New Yorkers then fell back behind the crest. *Author's collection.*

of fifteen or twenty minutes drove them back into the woods. He attempted to follow them into the woods, but was met by a fire from a superior force in the woods, and halted just this side of the crest of the hill, where his troops were screened from that fire."

On the contrary, General Smith says, in a letter written December 15, 1897, that he never contemplated a movement into the woods, that when he had cleared the front of the enemy's skirmishers, and put the 20th and 49th New York under cover of the crest of the hill, near the church, he had done and without orders all he had set out to do; that he did not see Irwin and the other three regiments of the brigade and supposed he had intimated to a staff officer, that, when Irwin came up, he was to take position behind the crest to the left of the two regiments he had put into position. In view of this statement and the fact that "Baldy" Smith was too good a soldier to put any part of his command in close action by the flank, we must conclude that the responsibility rests upon Irwin, who, as events proved later in the day, should not have been entrusted with any responsibility.

As soon as Irwin's Brigade was formed and ordered to lie down, skirmishers were thrown out to the crest of the hill along its front. A Confederate battery advanced and played with severity along the flank of the brigade and through the line of the 20th New York, which from the nature of the ground was compelled to refuse its left, and thus received the fire along its entire front. Irwin says: "Sharpshooters from the woods to the right and to the extreme left also opened upon us. Shell and canister swept from left to right. The practice of the enemy was rapid and very accurate, and in a short time the loss was very heavy and the ranks encumbered with dead and wounded."

Before the entire brigade had been established on the line held by Greene in the morning Smith sent for Brooks' Brigade to act as a support, but, without his knowledge or consent, it had been ordered by Sumner to support French. At first it was ordered to the support of Sedgwick on the extreme right but, before getting into position, French reported his ammunition exhausted and Brooks was ordered by Sumner to reinforce him, but, on gaining French's right, he found the enemy had been checked and repulsed, and the brigade took position in the south edge of Mumma's cornfield 170 yards from and parallel to the Sunken Road. This brought it on Irwin's left and the position was maintained until the close of the battle, the men lying on their arms and subjected to quite a galling fire of both artillery and sharpshooters, causing numerous casualties.

Meanwhile Ayres' Battery (F, 5th U. S.), Lieutenant Leonard Martin, went into position 110 yards south of the Smoketown road, and near the small grave-yard, where it remained, substantially in the same position until the close of the battle, firing at intervals during the afternoon of the 17th, upon the enemy's artillery in the woods around the church and in the field

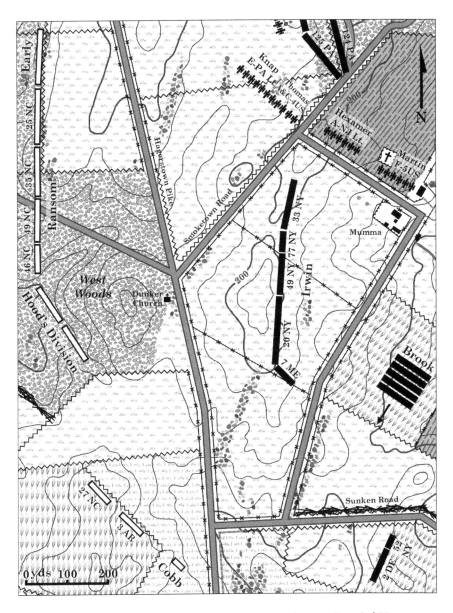

Irwin's brigade settles into position behind the plateau. Brooks' Vermont brigade advances and takes a supporting position on his left. The Confederates reform in the West Woods.

south of it. Irwin records that to the excellent service of this battery the safety of his brigade "may be largely imputed," and that "had it not checked the heavy fire from the batteries of the enemy, they would have destroyed the greater part of my command."

Soon after Martin had taken this position Slocum's Division arrived and its artillery was put in position. Lieutenant E. B. Williston's Battery (D, 2nd U. S.) on Martin's right, with its right gun about 12 yards from the Smoketown road and 75 yards from Mumma's Lane and opened fire at the Dunker church and the woods surrounding it, to drive therefrom the Confederate sharpshooters, that were annoying Irwin. Battery A, Massachusetts Light Artillery, Captain Josiah Porter, relieved Thomas' and Knap's batteries, which, after the advance of Irwin's Brigade, had opened fire upon the woods north of the church, and, upon Slocum's arrival, had retired beyond the East Woods. Porter took position on Williston's right, north of the Smoketown road and about 100 yards in front of the East Woods. Cothran's Battery, with its support, the 107th New York, was relieved by Battery A, Maryland Light Artillery, 8 guns, Captain John W. Wolcott, and retired to the fields beyond the East Woods. From the field east of D. R. Miller's to Mumma's house, there were now seven batteries— Cowan's, Frank's, Vanneman's, Wolcott's, Porter's, Williston's and Martin's—aggregating 44 guns so closely placed, that there was no room for more, and Hexamer's New Jersey battery was held in reserve, in a depression in the East Woods, near the Smoketown road.

Slocum had marched through Keedysville, crossed the Antietam by the upper bridge and it was about 12 o'clock, noon, when his advance reached the field. While the batteries were being put in position Franklin, Slocum, and Smith were considering a charge upon the woods at the church. Newton's and Torbett's[8] (i.e., Torbert's) brigades had come up and been formed beyond the woods and Bartlett's arrival was awaited to form a reserve, when it was found that Sumner had retained Bartlett to strengthen his own right, in place of Brooks', whom he had sent to Franklin. General Franklin says:

> Immediately after its (Slocum's) arrival two of his brigades (Newton's and Torbert's) were formed in column, to carry the wood in the immediate vicinity of the white church. The other brigade (Bartlett's) had been ordered by General Sumner to keep near his right. As this brigade was to form the reserve for the column of attack, I waited until it came up. About the same time General Sumner arrived on the spot, and directed the attack to be postponed.... Shortly afterward the

---

[8] Carman misspells Torbert's name twice in the initial manuscript, but corrects himself.

Major General William B. Franklin
Library of Congress.

commanding general came to the position and decided that it would not be prudent to make the attack, our position on the right then being considerably in advance of what it had been in the morning.

In the *Battles and Leaders of the Civil War* (Vol. II, p. 597) Franklin writes:

> While awaiting the arrival of Slocum, I went to the right, held by Sumner. I found him at the head of his troops, but much depressed. He told me that his whole corps was exhausted and could do nothing more that day.... About 300 yards in its front, across an open field, was a wood...strongly held by the enemy. The corps had been driven back from an attack on this wood with great loss. When General Slocum arrived I placed two brigades of his division on General Sumner's left and was awaiting the arrival of his third brigade, which was to be in reserve. With the two brigades I intended to make an attack on the woods referred to, and General Sumner was informed of my intention. The two brigades were ready to move. Just as the third brigade arrived, General Sumner rode up and directed me not to make the attack, giving as a reason for his order, that if I were defeated the right would be entirely routed, mine being the only troops left on the right that had any life in them. Major Hammerstein, of McClellan's staff, was near, and I requested him to inform General McClellan of the state of affairs, and that I thought the attack ought to be made. Shortly afterward McClellan rode up, and, after hearing the statements of Sumner and myself, decided that as the day had gone so well on the other parts of the line it would be unsafe to risk anything on the right. Of course, no advance was made by the division.

Palfrey says: "Wisely or unwisely, Sumner paralyzed the action of Franklin's Corps, first detaching from Smith and then from Slocum." But the responsibility rested upon McClellan for staying Franklin's advance. There was yet time to make it when he came upon this part of the field. He says:

> Toward the middle of the afternoon, proceeding to the right, I found that Sumner's, Hooker's and Mansfield's Corps had met with serious losses. Several general officers had been carried from the field severely wounded, and the aspect of affairs was anything but promising. At the risk of greatly exposing our center, I ordered two brigades from Porter's Corps to reinforce the right. General Sumner expressed the most decided opinion against another attempt during that day to assault the enemy's position in front, as portions of our troops were so scattered and demoralized. In view of these circumstances, after

Major General George B. McClellan
Library of Congress.

making changes in position of some of the troops, I directed the different commanders to hold their positions, and, being satisfied that this could be done without the assistance of the two brigades from the center, I countermanded the order, which was in course of execution.

After the abandonment of aggressive movement, Williams' Division of the Twelfth Corps fell back into the East Woods and acted as a support to Franklin's Corps. Smith's Division retained its position, Newton's Brigade of Slocum's Division, formed on Hancock's left and supported the two Maryland batteries, Torbert's New Jersey brigade formed on Newton's left and on either side of the Smoketown road, supporting the batteries of Porter, Hexamer, Williston, and Martin, and Bartlett's Brigade was, for the present, held in reserve.

The remainder of the day was employed in collecting stragglers, straightening the line, filling the gaps in it and relieving batteries that had been long in action by fresh men. "The troops lay," writes Walker, "with the bodies of the Union and Confederate slain all around, in momentary readiness to move forward;...now and then the bustle of the staff presaged new combinations, or the movement of troops to fill the gaps in the line of battle was taken to mean that hot work was at once to begin; at intervals the artillery broke out in furious cannonading all along the line, or here and there two ambitious battery commanders tested the range of their guns and the skill of their cannoneers in a duel across the crouching lines of infantry."

Soon after Irwin had taken position under the crest of the plateau, nearly opposite the Dunker Church, a Confederate battery, south of the church, became very active in throwing shot and shell at the two regular batteries, south of the Smoketown road, and into the ranks of the New Jersey brigade supporting them, causing some casualties and much annoyance. The two batteries seemed unable to reach or silence it and Hexamer's Battery was sent for and soon appeared. As he came up at a gallop, Hexamer said: "I'll silence that battery or cut down every tree in the woods." The other batteries ceased firing, Hexamer passed them a few yards and opened fire. For fifteen or twenty minutes he rained shot and shell into and around that battery and it ceased to respond. He gave a few more shots and then withdrew amid the cheers of all who witnessed his fine practice.

Soon after this artillery duel, about 3 p.m., the 5th Maine and 16th New York of Bartlett's Brigade, then in second line in the edge of the East Woods, were ordered to the left as a support to Irwin and to fill an interval between him and Brooks. When in position their left rested on the Mumma lane and a little to the rear of Brooks' right. For the next hour there was comparative quiet on this part of the field, when about 4:30 p.m., quiet was broken by the rapid roar of artillery on the extreme right, bringing every

Panoramic view of the David R. Miller farm just days after the battle. Taken just south of the Smoketown Road looking north toward the infamous Miller Cornfield, and the North Woods in the far distance. Knap's Battery E, Pennsylvania Light is the focus of the photograph. *Library of Congress.*

infantryman to his feet and the cannoneers to their guns in anticipation of a Confederate advance. For the cause of this we must go inside the Confederate lines.

At the hour when McClellan and Sumner came to the conclusion that further offensive movements were inadvisable and that the right wing of the army should remain on the defensive, Lee had ordered an attack by Jackson on McClellan's right, in order to relieve his center from the pressure of Richardson's attack and the threatening movement of Pleasonton on the Boonsboro and Sharpsburg road, and Stuart was then massing cavalry, artillery and infantry for the purpose.

McLaws says that the enemy having abandoned their attempt to advance, he had an opportunity to examine the relative position of his own line and that of the enemy and soon "became convinced that we had nothing to gain by an advance of our troops." But Lee, Longstreet and Jackson had come to a different conclusion. Longstreet does not refer to the matter in his official report, but elsewhere says:

> At one or two points near our center were dead angles into which I rode from time to time for closer observation of the enemy when his active aggression was suspended. General Burnside was busy at his crossing, but no report of progress had been sent me. One of my rides towards the Dunker chapel revealed efforts of the enemy to renew his work on that part of the field. Our troops were ordered to be ready to receive it. Its non-aggression suggested an opportunity for the Confederates, and I ordered McLaws and Walker to prepare to assault. Hood was back in position with his brigades, and Jackson was reported on his way, all in full supply of ammunition. It seemed probable that by concealing our movements under cover of the wood from the massed batteries of Doubleday's artillery on the north, and the batteries of position on the east, we could draw our columns so near to the enemy in front before our move could be known that we would have but a few rods to march before we could mingle our ranks with those of the enemy; that our columns massed and in goodly numbers, pressing severely upon a single point, would give the enemy much trouble, and might cut him in two, and break up his battle arrangements at the lower bridge; but just then General Jackson reported, with authority from General Lee, that he with the cavalry was ordered to march around and turn the entire position of the enemy by his right flank, and strike at his rear. He found that the

Looking east from the edge of the West Woods along the Hagerstown Pike. Irwin's brigade was stationed on the reverse slope of the high ground now occupied by the National Park Visitor's Center. This was also the view from Kershaw's and Manning's Brigades as they battled Greene's division earlier in the morning. *Author's collection.*

march would be long and extremely hazardous, and abandoned his orders.[9]

Walker was with Ransom's Brigade when the order was brought from Longstreet, directing Ransom to advance and capture the Union battery in his front. Having been previously instructed by Jackson to hold his position in the woods until Stuart could turn the Union right and then advance, Walker directed Ransom to delay the execution of Longstreet's order until he could see Longstreet. Walker's action was approved. This was about 3 o'clock.

Ransom says:

> About noon, General Longstreet sent me word to take the battery in our front, and the order to advance was given, when General McLaws arrived and ordered me to postpone the attempt. Again, about 2 or 3 o'clock, I received instructions to advance and take the batteries. Just at this time the enemy was observed to have massed a strong force about the batteries, and General Walker, having arrived, forbade the movement until he could communicate with General Longstreet, in person. Shortly afterward, orders came to defer any attempt upon the enemy's position until General Jackson should have attacked him upon his right flank.

It appears from an incident given by the adjutant of the 35th North Carolina that Jackson, in person, came to Ransom's Brigade and gave orders to be in readiness to join in an attack upon the Union right.

> About 2 o'clock Stonewall Jackson came along our lines.... He remarked to Colonel Ransom, as he did to other colonels along the line, that with Stuart's cavalry and some infantry he was going around the Federal right and get in their rear, and added 'When you hear the rattle of my small arms, this whole line must advance.' He wished to ascertain the force opposed, and a man of our regiment named Hood was sent up a large tree, which he climbed carefully to avoid observation by the enemy. Stonewall called out to know how many Yankees he could see over the hill and beyond the East Woods. Hood replied: 'Whew! There are oceans of them, General.' 'Count their flags,' said Jackson. This Hood proceeded to do until he had counted 39, when the general told him that would do and to come down.

---

[9]James Longstreet, *From Manassas to Appomattox* (Philadelphia, PA: J. B. Lippincott Co., 1896) p. 256-257.

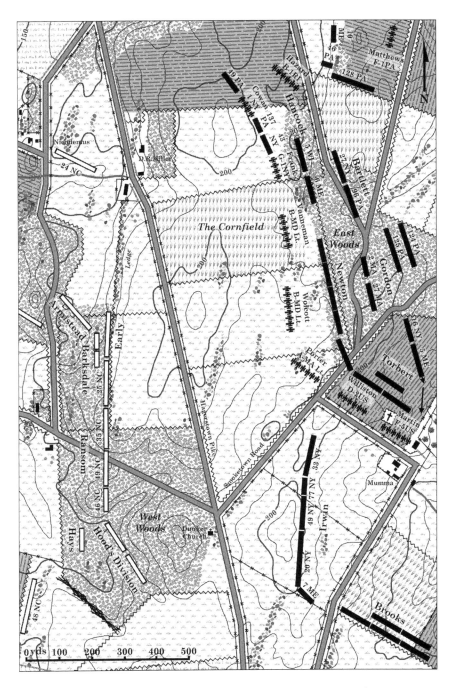

The position of the opposing lines at approximately 3 o'clock.

Longstreet's idea was an attack directly to the front. Lee sought to relieve the pressure upon the center and right by turning McClellan's right. Jackson contemplated both the turning movement and an attack in front.

As elsewhere stated Jackson was disappointed at the partial success of McLaws' attack and directed Stuart, who, with his cavalry, 13th Virginia and 24th North Carolina, had been checked, well to the left and front, "to hold this advance position, and that he would send all the infantry he could get in order to follow up the success." These reinforcements were, says Stuart, however, "directed to other parts of the field." But Jackson was not discouraged; he believed the enemy had done their worst, were sorely punished, and there was still the chance of an opportunity to sweep the Union right from the field and gain a decisive victory.

General John G. Walker says:

> The Federal infantry assaults having ceased, about half-past twelve I sought Jackson to report that from the front of my position in the wood I thought I had observed a movement of the enemy, as if to pass through the gap where I had posted Colonel Cooke's two regiments. I found Jackson in rear of Barksdale's brigade, under an apple-tree, sitting on his horse, with one leg thrown carelessly over the pommel of his saddle, plucking and eating the fruit. Without making any reply to my report, he asked me abruptly: 'Can you spare me a regiment and a battery?' I replied that Colonel Hill's 49th North Carolina, a very strong regiment, was in reserve, and could be spared, and that I could also give him both French's and Branch's batteries, but that they were with-out long-range ammunition, which had been exhausted at Harper's Ferry. Jackson then went on to say that, owing to the nature of the ground, General Stuart's cavalry could take no part in the battle and were in the rear, but that Stuart himself had reported for such duty as he could perform.
>
> Jackson added that he wished to make up, from the different commands on our left, a force of four or five thousand men, and give them to Stuart, with orders to turn the enemy's right, and attack him in the rear; that I must give orders to my division to advance to the front, and attack the enemy as soon as I should hear Stuart's guns and that our whole left wing would move to the attack at the same time. Then, replacing his foot in the stirrup, he said with great emphasis: 'We'll drive McClellan into the Potomac.'
>
> After giving orders for the regiment and batteries to report to Stuart, I galloped down the line where I had posted Cooke...Soon returning to my command, I repeated General Jackson's order to my brigade commanders and directed them to listen for the sound of Stuart's guns. We all confidently expected to hear the welcome sound

First Lieutenant Job Dillingham Barnard of Co. K, 25th North Carolina
Infantry Regiment. *Library of Congress.*

by 2 o'clock, at least, and as that hour approached every ear was on the alert. Napoleon at Waterloo did not listen more intently for the sound of Grouchy's fire than did we for Stuart's. Two o'clock came, but nothing was heard of Stuart. Half-past two and then three, and still Stuart made no sign.

About half -past three a staff-officer of General Longstreet brought me an order from that general to advance and attack the enemy in my front. As 'the execution of this order would materially interfere with Jackson's plans, I thought it my duty before beginning the movement to communicate with General Longstreet personally. I found him in rear of the position in which I had posted Cooke in the morning, and upon informing him of Jackson's intentions, he withdrew his order.'[10]

As soon as the order was given by Lee for the movement, Stuart massed his cavalry to lead in its execution. Fitz Hugh Lee's Brigade was then in rear of Jackson's left and near it was the 7th Virginia Cavalry of Munford's Brigade; and Wade Hampton's Brigade was brought from the right. Hampton had acted as rear-guard to McLaws in the march from Harper's Ferry and crossing the Potomac, partly by Knott's Ford, at the mouth of the Antietam, and partly at Shepherdstown Ford, reached the vicinity of Lee's headquarters about the middle of the forenoon, and remained until about 1 p.m., when he moved rapidly to the left, where Fitz Hugh Lee had already massed three of his regiments at the Cox place, on the river road. Hampton formed on Lee's right, under cover of the Nicodemus hill, upon which were several batteries of artillery, slightly withdrawn from the crest of the hill.

In all Stuart had seven regiments of cavalry and nine guns from various batteries, one of which was from Poague, two from Raine's, and three from Brockenbrough's, under Captain John Pelham, and, in addition, the batteries of French and Branch, supported by the 48th North Carolina Infantry of Walker's Division. The advance was made about 3 p.m., the 4th Virginia Cavalry leading. The column, starting from Cox's, passed up the road, under cover of the high ground on its right, until the advance reached New Industry, where it halted, while the guns under Pelham turning to the right and moving a short distance on the road, leading to the Hagerstown road at the toll-gate, turned to the left and went into position on the high ground 900 yards from and directly west of Doubleday's guns on the Poffenberger hill. Stuart's guns were greeted with such a heavy fire as they took position that they were quickly used up and forced to withdraw. Poague, who commanded one gun, says, "Along with 6 or 8 other guns,

---

[10] *Battles & Leaders of the Civil War* (New York, NY: The Century Co., 1887) Vol. II, pp. 679-680.

Major General James E. B. Stuart's attempt to flank the Union line. Overwhelming artillery fire from the massed batteries near the Joseph Poffenberger farm forced Stuart to recall his artillery and retreat back into the Confederate lines.

under the command of Major Pelham, an attempt was made to dislodge the enemy's batteries but failed completely, being silenced in 15 or 20 minutes by a most terrific fire."

Hampton's Brigade moved but a short distance to the left before the head of column was halted. Branch's and French's guns went into position on Nicodemus hill about the time Pelham's guns were driven off, and were almost instantly silenced, losing many killed and wounded, by Doubleday's guns, which turned savagely upon them. The 48th North Carolina which had moved double-quick to the left to support these guns was not engaged. Stuart, after halting his head of column an hour or more, withdrew and gave up the intended movement on McClellan's right, and the entire force fell back.

Stuart reports: "In this movement I was honored with the advance. In endeavoring to pass up along the river bank, however, I found that the river made such an abrupt bend that the enemy's batteries were within 800 yards of the brink of the stream, which would have made it impossible to have succeeded in the movement proposed, and it was accordingly abandoned." Jackson says: "In the afternoon, in obedience to instructions from the commanding general, I moved to the left with a view of turning the Federal right, but I found his numerous artillery so judiciously established in their front and extending so near the Potomac, which here makes a remarkable bend, as to render it inexpedient to hazard the attempt."

When Jackson returned to near the Dunker Church he met General Walker and told him of Stuart's failure, for the reason that he had found the Union right "securely posted on the Potomac." Upon Walker's expressing surprise at this statement, Jackson replied that he also had been surprised, as he had supposed the Potomac much farther away; but he remarked that Stuart had an excellent eye for topography, and it must be as he represented. He added: "It is a great pity. We should have driven McClellan into the Potomac."

Considering the fact Stuart had been two whole days on the left, within a half mile of the Potomac and the great bend in it, one wonders that he had not informed himself of the situation on that flank. A single horseman could have gone, unopposed, a half mile and viewed the ground at the bend, which was to be plainly seen from Nicodemus hill, where he had his batteries.

As Stuart's unsuccessful movement ended Confederate operations on this part of the field and we shall have no occasion to return to it, we may as well briefly note such changes of position as were made during the afternoon. At half past twelve Hood's Division, now reduced to less than 800 men, returned to the West Woods and occupied them about 300 yards west of the church. Hays' small brigade formed in Hood's rear. The 49th North Carolina and part of the 35th after the encounter with Irwin fell back

Major General James E. B. Stuart
Library of Congress.

to the position from which they had charged Greene's flank, and the 46th North Carolina advanced from the west edge of the woods and filled an interval between the 49th and Hood. Captain Hudgins' company of the 30th Virginia and other skirmishers were ordered to the east edge of the woods to pick off the Union cannoneers, who were tearing the tree tops with shot and shell, but there was such a shower of canister poured upon them and the range being too great for their arms they fell back into the woods under shelter. J. R. Johnson's Virginia battery, which had fallen back with Trimble's Brigade, early in the morning, returned to the field about 2 p.m. and took position 300 yards to the right of and in advance of Reel's barn, a cornfield in its immediate front. It relieved Fry's Battery of H. P. Jones' battalion and immediately became severely engaged with Union artillery and poured an incessant and annoying fire upon Irwin's and Brooks brigades and upon Richardson's division, all efforts to silence it were unavailing. For some time Johnson was alone but was afterwards joined by D'Aquin's battery, which took position on his right. Both batteries were engaged until dark, with very little infantry for support. The batteries were on a point of a hill, the grass was burning around them, and when the engagement became very hot the caissons were moved to the foot of the hill to the left, near several haystacks. They retired at 8 o'clock.

Kershaw's and Barksdale's brigades, which, since their repulse, had been lying under cover of the fences and ledges beyond the woods, moved to the left, Barksdale forming on Early's right and Kershaw in the northern body of the woods on the left of Armistead. Late in the day Major Lowe, commanding Lawton's Brigade, came up with about 100 men and joined Early. Jackson's Division and Semmes' Brigade were in reserve. Between 3 and 4 p.m., Cooke's 27th North Carolina and 3rd Arkansas, and Cobb's Brigade, all out of ammunition, were relieved by Ripley's Brigade and fell back for food and ammunition. A little after 4 p.m., Hood and Hays moved from the West Woods and took position in the open ground opposite the mouth of the Sunken Road, and supporting D. H. Hill, who was lying along the fences of the Hagerstown road. About 5 p.m. the 27th North Carolina, 3rd Arkansas and Cobb's Brigade returned to the field. Cobb's Brigade went to the left and joined Kershaw, and Cooke's two regiments remained until sunset, near the southwest corner of the West Woods, and the 48th North Carolina, returning from its participation in Stuart's movement, formed along the fence on their left. At sunset Ransom's Brigade moved from its position behind the rocky ledge to the right and bivouacked for the night beyond Reel's. Barksdale gained ground to the right and occupied the position vacated by Ransom; and Van Manning's Brigade entered the woods and formed on Barksdale's right. As completed, from right to left, this was the disposition of the Confederate left for the night: Hood's Division and Hays' Brigade held the open ground opposite the Sunken

Brigadier General Jubal A. Early's view at the end of the battle from his position at the northern end of the West Woods. Outcroppings on the rock ledge featured prominently in the mornings action can be seen along the slope of the hill. The Hagerstown Pike is just at the top of the hill along the power lines. *Author's collection.*

Road; Ripley's Brigade held from Hood's left to the West Woods at a point about 100 yards west of the Hagerstown road, Manning's Brigade held the woods west of the church; Barksdale and Early were behind the ledge that ran from Miller's barn, and faced the Hagerstown road; Armistead was in the north part of the middle woods, facing nearly north, his right in rear of Early's left; Kershaw was in the north body of the woods, on the left of Armistead, facing northeast, and Cobb's Brigade was on Kershaw's left, facing north. Semmes' Brigade was in reserve near the A. Poffenberger place, and Ransom was in reserve in Hood's rear. Jackson's Division was supporting the artillery, which was under cover of the Hauser ridge ready to run onto it, at a moment's notice, and Stuart's cavalry covered the interval between the left of the infantry and the Potomac.

After Stuart's brief affair on the left there was quiet on this part of the field, with the exception of cannonading on the right and a movement of a regiment of Irwin's Brigade, connected with operations on the line of the Sunken Road to which we now return.

Early in the afternoon, after General Richardson had been grievously wounded, and [sic] Hancock was directed by McClellan, in person, to take command of his division. Having received his orders from McClellan, and some instructions from Sumner, he proceeded to the ground. Walker presents a graphic account of his ride:

> Among the galloping staffs which cross that bloody field in the early afternoon, arousing the momentary expectations of renewed attack, is one of especially notable bearing, at which men gaze long as it passes down the jagged line of troops from right to left. At its head rides a general officer whose magnificent physique, bold air, and splendid horsemanship are well calculated to impress the beholder. Behind him ride a group of as dashing aides-de-camp as the army knew. It is Hancock, sent for in haste, from his brigade of the Sixth Corps, to take command of the division at whose head the gallant Richardson had fallen, never to mount horse or draw sword more. It is not amid the pomp of review, with bands playing and well- ordered lines, but on the trampled battlefield, strewn with bloody stretchers and the wreck of caissons and ambulances, the dead and dying thick around, the wounded still limping and crawling to the rear, with shells shrieking through the air, that Hancock meets and greets the good regiments he is to lead in a score of battles. The lines are ragged from shot and shell; the uniforms are rent and soiled from hedge, fence, and ditch; the bands are engaged in carrying off the wounded, or assisting the regimental surgeons at their improvised hospitals; scarcely 2,100 men remain with the colors of this fine, strong division.

Brigadier General Winfield S. Hancock
Photographed as a Major General
Library of Congress.

Hancock's instructions were to hold the position. He formed the troops occupying one line of battle in close proximity to the enemy, who were then again in position near Piper's house. The 14th Connecticut and a detachment from the 108th New York, both under command of Colonel Dwight Morris, were in reserve, the whole command numbering about 2,100 men, with no artillery. Finding a considerable interval at a dangerous point between Meagher's and Caldwell's brigades, the 14th Connecticut was placed there, and the detachment of the 108th on the extreme left. Application was made for two batteries of artillery to the different commanders within reach, and to the chief of artillery, but none could be spared at that time. He was confident, however, of holding the position as he had been instructed, notwithstanding the absence of artillery and that the men were already suffering severely from the shells of the enemy, for he had a firm reliance upon the good qualities of the troops, but was too weak to make an attack, unless an advance was made on the right, as he had no reserves, and his line was already enfiladed by the enemy's artillery in front of the right wing, which was screened from the fire of the Union guns on the right, by the West Woods, then in Confederate possession. Soon after arriving on the ground a command of the enemy, probably George T. Anderson's, was seen in line of battle, proceeded by skirmishers advancing across his front, beyond Piper's house, and toward Pleasonton's batteries and the regular infantry, that had been thrown across the Antietam. He immediately sent a pressing message to Franklin for a battery and Hexamer's Battery of Slocum's Division was ordered to report to him.

Hexamer was then in the East Woods, to which he had retired after his affair with the battery near the church. He quickly passed to the rear, went through the low ground around Roulette's and then up and onto the open ridge, where most of the infantry were lying just behind its crest. The enemy had been sweeping the ridge with artillery and Hexamer took position near its top, very near the spot where Graham's Battery had been driven, and opened fire. At each discharge of the guns the rebound sent them down the hill and they were rolled up again with the cheerful assistance of the infantry, more than willing to give a helping hand to the "Jersey Dutchman." In a very short time the enemy's infantry disappeared from view.

While Hexamer was thus engaged, perhaps a few minutes earlier, Captain Emory Upton, Slocum's chief of artillery, rode to Irwin's Brigade and saw Hood's Division and Hays' Brigade marching towards the Sunken Road from the woods beyond the church. He suggested to Irwin that a battery should be placed in front of the left of his brigade, and Irwin, after examining the ground attentively, acquiesced, and not a moment could be lost, as "the enemy were moving in front with the evident design of throwing a powerful column against his left, and they could not be seen,

Later in the afternoon the 14th Connecticut moved into position to support Graham's Battery K, 1st United States. Here is their view looking uphill toward rear of the battery. Major General Israel B. Richardson was mortally wounded in this location near Graham's battery. *History of the Fourteenth Regiment, Connecticut Vol. Infantry.*

except from that part of the line." General Smith approved and Upton ordered up a battery which opened with three rifled guns, "playing on the masses of the enemy with great effect for half an hour," when the pieces were withdrawn. These guns were relieved by Williston's Battery of Napoleon guns, the fire of which Irwin reports as "terribly destructive."

When Williston's Battery was in full play, Piper's orchard on the left and front was occupied by D. H. Hill's skirmishers, whom, for the protection of the battery, Irwin says, it was necessary to dislodge, and ordered Major Thomas W. Hyde, commanding 7th Maine to send a company and drive them away. Hyde acted promptly and had scarcely detached the company from the regiment when Irwin rode up and exclaimed in near these words, "That is not enough, sir; go yourself; take your regiment and drive them from those trees and buildings," pointing to the orchard and the Piper buildings. Hyde was perfectly astounded at an order to do, with his 181 officers and men, what Richardson's and French's Divisions had failed to accomplish, and asked Irwin to repeat his order and point out the ground again. He did so, quite emphatically, in near the same words, and added with an oath, "Those are your orders, sir." Irwin repeated the order several times.

To the nearest point of the orchard was about 600 yards, to the nearest of the Piper buildings, the barn, it was a half mile. Hyde faced his regiment to the left and led it obliquely across the front of the skirmishers of Brooks' Vermont brigade on his left, then, coming to a front, sent out skirmishers from the edge of the cornfield and the hollow lying west of and near the orchard he was ordered to clear. The regiment closely followed the skirmishers and crossed the Sunken Road, which was so filled with dead and wounded that the mounted officers had difficulty in crossing without permitting their horses to step on them. Hyde says his horse "had to step on them to get over." As soon as the road was crossed, the regiment was halted in the trampled corn to straighten the line, and, being now under fire from the front and left, Hyde gave the order to charge, directing the regiment on a point to the right of Piper's barn. The line dashed forward with a cheer, at a double quick, down into the cup shaped hollow. D. H. Hill's men in the orchard, on the left, being flanked and in danger of being cut off, broke and ran, and those directly in front, at the straw stacks and Piper's barn retreated, and at this moment a line of Confederates rose up from the stone fences of the Hagerstown road, which were to the right and front, and poured in a volley, which, however, did not do much damage. At this Hyde ordered the regiment to oblique to the left which brought it behind the ridge running from the barn to the Hagerstown road, and somewhat protected from the fire from the stone fences, and then forward and onto the ridge at the right of the barn. Hyde was riding a few feet in front of his regiment and as he neared the crest of the ridge he saw a line

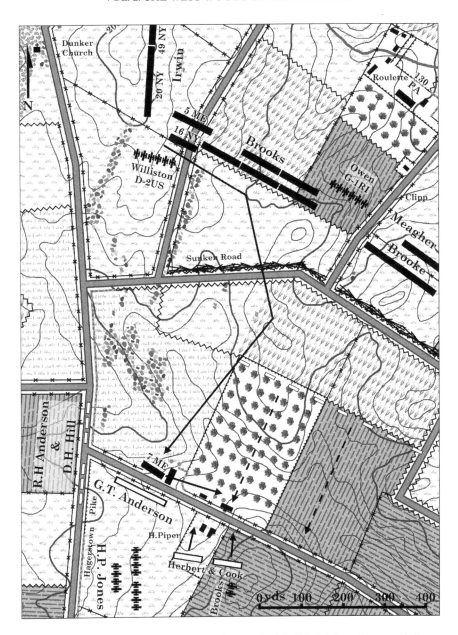

Irwin orders Major Thomas W. Hyde to take his 7th Maine alone and clear
Confederate skirmishers from the orchard and Piper buildings. The 7th
Maine clears the orchard, but diverts to the left and into the orchard to
avoid Confederate units converging upon them.

lying down, waiting for him at the ready and another body double quicking down Piper's lane and making for his left to cut off retreat.

It was but a short time before this that George T. Anderson had led his brigade back from the ridge beyond Piper's farm, out of the range of Hexamer's guns, and put it under cover of the ridge that Hyde was now mounting, and around him were the broken divisions of D. H. Hill and R. H. Anderson, some fragments with him were under cover of the ridge and others on the Hagerstown road and in the Piper lane, all in more or less disorder. Hill was walking up and down, giving words of encouragement to his already twice beaten command, when he heard the fire of the skirmishers, and going to the crest of the ridge, saw his own skirmishers running in and Hyde advancing, and called Anderson's attention to it, and Anderson ordered his men to lie down and await orders, Hill sending some men down the lane to gain Hyde's left.

All this Hyde saw at a glance as his men were breasting the ridge. As he was greatly outnumbered and saw no support coming, to avoid being surrounded, he ordered his regiment to move by the left flank before any of it had come in sight of Hill's men, and, moving double-quick, passed Piper's barn, went through an opening in the fence, into the orchard and very close to the lane. Here a new danger confronted him. After Hill's fight, at noon, Major H. A. Herbert, commanding Wilcox's Brigade, and Lieutenant Colonel Phil Cook of the 4th Georgia, who had some of Ripley's men with him and some of A. R. Wright's, came to the conclusion that they could be of some service on the right, near the Boonsboro road, and went in that direction, but did not become engaged; on returning along the ridge they saw Hill's skirmishers retreating from the orchard, and reached Piper's lane, east of the house and opposite the southeast corner of the orchard, just as Hyde passed through the fence and into the southwest corner, and immediately opened fire. Hyde returned the fire, then faced about and retreated up the hill into the orchard and formed on a small crest, where he poured another volley into Herbert's men, who were hanging on his left, and faced George T. Anderson, who had now charged from the ridge behind which he had been secreted.

Hyde was now exposed to a severe fire from three directions and the enemy advancing upon him in force. He saw four battle-flags, and a battery opened upon him with grape. Although somewhat shielded by the apple trees, he lost here quite heavily. Hexamer's and Williston's batteries shelled the orchard, which aided him some, but, having expended most of his ammunition, he ordered a retreat; gave the enemy another volley as they attempted to follow, got through the strong picket fences with difficulty and, closing up on the colors, the regiment went back through the corn and across the Sunken Road; received the hearty cheers of the Vermont brigade,

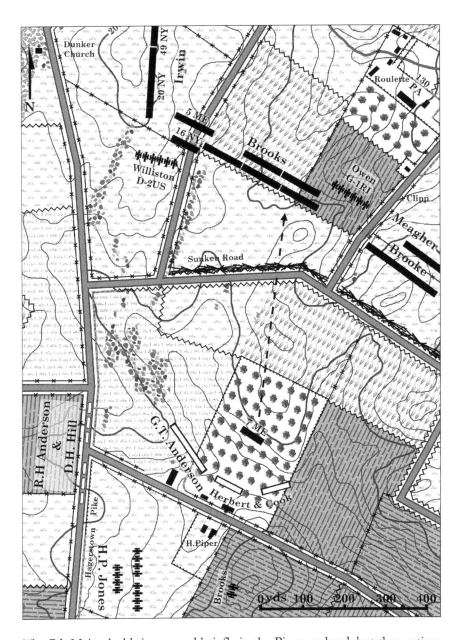

The 7th Maine holds its ground briefly in the Piper orchard, but then retires over the Sunken Road and back into Union lines.

and resumed the position from which it had advanced. It had been gone about 30 minutes and lost 88 in killed, wounded and missing.

When Irwin saw to what a serious engagement he had committed the Maine men, he was very anxious to support them, but his orders were positive not to advance his line, so he rode forward and requested the colonel of the right regiment of Brooks' Brigade to support them, which he declined to do without orders from Brooks. He then returned to his own line to ask for a support from the rear, but in a few minutes "had the extreme pleasure of seeing the shattered but brave remnant of the 7th Maine in good order return to my lines." He adds: "No words of mine can do justice to the firmness, intelligence, and heroic courage with which this regiment performed its dangerous task. Their killed and wounded and their colors riddled by balls are the proud, yet melancholy, witness of their valor."

In his *Following the Greek Cross*, Hyde writes: "When we knew our efforts were resultant from no plan or design from headquarters, but were from an imposition of John Barleycorn in our brigade commander alone, I wished I had been old enough, or distinguished enough, to have dared to disobey orders."

The Confederate reports of this affair are meager. D. H. Hill says:

A movement of a rather farcical character now took place. General Pryor had collected quite a respectable force behind a stone wall on the Hagerstown road, and Colonel G. T. Anderson had about a regiment behind a hill immediately to the right of this road. A Maine regiment came down to this hill wholly unconscious that there were any Confederate troops near it. A shout and a volley informed them of their dangerous neighborhood. The Yankee apprehension is acute; the idea was soon taken in, and was followed by the most rapid running I ever saw.

George T. Anderson says:

General Hill...called my attention to a line of the enemy advancing apparently to attack us. Suffering them to come near us, I ordered my command to charge them, which they did in splendid style and good order, killing and wounding many of the enemy, taking several prisoners, and routing the remainder. We could not pursue them as far as I wished, because of the severe fire of artillery directed against us from long range guns that we could not reach. In this charge parts of Wilcox's, Featherston's, and Pryor's brigades participated with mine.

The scene of the 7th Maine's charge. The Piper cornfield is to the left. The Piper farm buildings are in the low ground at center. *Author's collection.*

The artillery fire referred to by Anderson and which checked his pursuit of the 7th Maine came from the batteries of Hexamer and Williston in front and from Hains' Battery, just in advance of the middle bridge. Williston opened upon Anderson as he charged from the ridge and followed him into the orchard, firing over the heads of the Maine men when they rallied in the orchard. Hexamer saw the preparations made to meet Hyde and opened upon Herbert as he approached Piper's lane from the south and continued it when he pursued Hyde through the orchard. The fire of both Williston and Hexamer inflicted some casualties upon Hyde, but it did much to enable him to rally and make an orderly retreat.

Hexamer was now out of ammunition and, being relieved by Woodruff's Battery, went back to the East Woods. Williston remained in position until dark and then went back to Mumma's orchard. When Woodruff took position it was on the right of Hancock's left brigade, with orders not to fire except in reply to a Confederate battery or in case of an attack by them. Late in the evening Lieutenant A C. M. Pennington, with a section of Tidball's Battery of horse artillery, took position on an elevated ridge on Hancock's left and engaged a Confederate battery near some stacks beyond the Hagerstown road, doing material service by precision of fire in concealing the weakness of the position. Pickets were thrown out as far as possible, a very short distance, for D. H. Hill's skirmishers were again advanced to the northern part of the orchard.

French's Division, which had opened the fight in the forenoon, on this part of the field, had gone by detachments to the rear and, with the exception of the 14th Connecticut and 108th New York, was in the vicinity of the Roulette place, as a reserve and Owens' Rhode Island battery, which from the vicinity of the Clipp house had been directed late in the day to fire a few shots toward the corner of the woods near the church, was advanced beyond Brooks' left and took position on the knoll where the right of Kimball's Brigade had done its fighting.

On the extreme right Sumner made dispositions to support the powerful line of artillery on the Poffenberger hill, two guns of Hampton's Battery were moved from the barn farther to the right and front and Captain John A. Hazard's Rhode Island battery went into position at the northwest corner of the East Woods. When Williston's Battery was sent to the front and left to strengthen Irwin, Wolcott's Maryland Battery was moved from its position north of the Smoketown road and took the ground vacated by Williston. Late in the day Wolcott sent four guns of his battery a little to the left to break up a cross fire of the enemy upon him by which several of his horses had been lost. About 5:30 p.m. Greene's Division and Gordon's Brigade of the Twelfth Corps were ordered by McClellan to the support of the left of Franklin's Corps, south of the Smoketown road. These movements completed the dispositions for the night from the extreme right

Famous photograph of the Confederate dead near the Dunker Church, likely from Colonel Stephen D. Lee's artillery battalion. *Library of Congress.*

of the Union line to its center and the troops lay upon their arms, amid the dead and wounded, of the most bloody contest in history.

Hooker, with the First Corps, numbering 8,619 infantry, opened the battle at daybreak and was repulsed with a loss of 399 killed 1,978 wounded, an aggregate of 2,377, or 27 1/2 per cent of those engaged. Mansfield followed with the Twelfth Corps, numbering 7,239 infantry, and drove the enemy with a loss of 274 killed and 1,371 wounded, an aggregate of 1,645, or 22 772/100 per cent of the number engaged. Sedgwick, with his division of 5,437 infantry, was then engaged and repulsed with a loss of 369 killed and 1,572 wounded, an aggregate of 1,941 or 35 1/4 per cent. All those losses were incurred in four hours, at, north, and east of the Dunker Church, and mostly within a half mile of it.

French's Division went into action at the Sunken Road, with 5,740 infantry, and had 299 killed and 1,315 wounded, an aggregate of 1,614, or a trifle over 28 percent of the numbers engaged. Richardson's Division followed French's with 4,039 infantry, and had 209 killed and 936 wounded, an aggregate of 1,145, or over 28 per cent.

In these successive attacks the Union troops, not including Irwin's Brigade, numbered 31,000 infantry, of whom 1,550 were killed and 7,172 wounded, an aggregate of 8,722 killed and wounded, being a little over 28 per cent of the number engaged.

The Confederate forces meeting these successive attacks, and attacking in return, were Jackson's Division of 1,784 infantry; Ewell's Division of 3,904; Hood's Division of 2,000; G. T. Anderson's Brigade of 590; McLaws' Division of 2,823; Walker's Division of 3,764; R. H. Anderson's Division of 3,672; and D. H. Hill's Division of 5,449, an aggregate of 23,986 infantry.

The losses in these commands were: Jackson's Division 597 killed and wounded, or 33 1/2 per cent; Ewell's Division 1,296 or 32 1/5 per cent; Hood's Division 915 or 40 and 3/4 per cent; McLaws' Division 1,068 or 37 83/100 per cent; Walker's Division 1,006 or 26 73/100 per cent; R. H. Anderson's Division, 1,110 or 30 22/100 per cent; D. H. Hill's Division 1,716 or 31 1/2 per cent; and G. T. Anderson Brigade 85 or 14 1/2 per cent. Of these 1,304 were killed and 6,489 wounded, an aggregate of 7,793 killed and wounded, being 32 49/100 per cent of the 23,986 engaged. Some regiments lost as low as 10 percent, others exceeded 50, and at least two reached 85 per cent.

In all, on both sides 55,950 infantry were engaged on this part of the field, with a loss 2,854 killed and 13,661 wounded, an aggregate of 16,515, or 30 per cent of the number engaged. Including the loss in the artillery and in Irwin's Brigade, the killed and wounded numbered about 17,200. More than three-fourths of this loss occurred in the less than four and a half hours fighting from 6 a.m. to nearly 10.30 a.m., and within 1,100 yards of the Dunker Church; all of it occurred by 1 o'clock in the afternoon and within 1,200 yards of the church. Referring to the action, closing about half past ten, and of the field over which Hooker, Mansfield and Sedgwick had fought, which was about 1,500 yards in length, with an average width of about 900 yards, an area of about 300 acres; upon which over 13,500 had fallen, General Tidball truly says: "No other equal area on the American continent has been so drenched in human blood."

Appendix[11]

Order of Battle

Union

Army of the Potomac 55,956[12]
Major General George B. McClellan

General Headquarters

Escort
Independent Company Oneida (New York) Cavalry
4th United States Cavalry, Companies A and E

Provost Guard
Major William F. Hood
2nd United States Cavalry, Companies E, F, H, and K
8th United States, Companies A, D, F, and G
19th United States, Companies G and H

Headquarters Guard
93rd New York

---

[11] Carman published an order of battle and unit strength calculations as separate appendices. However, since I have modified it slightly to include only those units engaged in battle or on the field by September 17th, this chapter is not as Carman published it, but a new representation.

[12] Unit strengths listed as Carman presented them in his manuscript and appendixes with little clarification except using the *Official Records* to separate the strengths of attached artillery batteries from their infantry brigades where necessary. Carman calculated engaged strengths and not present for duty. Still, he's just as likely to be as accurate as other sources.

First Army Corps 9,438
Major General Joseph Hooker

1st Division 3,425
Brigadier General Abner Doubleday

<u>1st Brigade</u> 425
Colonel Walter
Phelps Jr.
22nd New York
24th New York
30th New York
84th New York*
2nd United States
Sharpshooters
*Also known as the
14th Brooklyn

<u>2nd Brigade</u> 750
Lt. Colonel J.
William Hofmann
7th Indiana
76th New York
95th New York
56th Pennsylvania

<u>3rd Brigade</u> 829
Brigadier General
Marsena R. Patrick
21st New York
23rd New York
35th New York
80th New York

<u>4th Brigade</u> 971
Brigadier General John Gibbon
19th Indiana
2nd Wisconsin
6th Wisconsin
7th Wisconsin

<u>Artillery</u> 450
1st New Hampshire Battery
Battery D, 1st Rhode Island
Battery L, 1st New York
Battery B, 4th United States

2d Division 3,158
Brigadier General James B. Ricketts

<u>1st Brigade</u> 1,100
Brigadier General
Abram Duryée
97th New York
104th New York
105th New York
107th Pennsylvania

<u>2nd Brigade</u> 937
Colonel William A.
Christian
26th New York
94th New York
88th Pennsylvania
90th Pennsylvania

<u>3rd Brigade</u> 1,000
Brigadier General
George L. Hartsuff
12th Massachusetts
13th Massachusetts
83rd New York
11th Pennsylvania

<u>Artillery</u> 121
Battery F, 1st Pennsylvania
Battery C, Pennsylvania Light

3rd Division 2,855
Brigadier General George G. Meade

<u>1st Brigade</u>
Brigadier General Truman Seymour
1st Pennsylvania Reserves
2nd Pennsylvania Reserves
5th Pennsylvania Reserves
6th Pennsylvania Reserves
13th Pennsylvania Reserves

<u>2nd Brigade</u>
Colonel Albert L. Magilton
3rd Pennsylvania Reserves
4th Pennsylvania Reserves
7th Pennsylvania Reserves
8th Pennsylvania Reserves

<u>3rd Brigade</u>
Lt. Colonel Robert Anderson
9th Pennsylvania Reserves
10th Pennsylvania Reserves
11th Pennsylvania Reserves
12th Pennsylvania Reserves

<u>Artillery</u> 248
Battery A, 1st Pennsylvania Light
Battery B, 1st Pennsylvania Light
Battery C, 5th United States

Second Army Corps 16,065
Major General Edwin V. Sumner

1st Division 4,275
Major General Israel B. Richardson

<u>1st Brigade</u> 1,339
Brigadier General John
C. Caldwell
5th New Hampshire
7th New York
61st & 64th New York
81st Pennsylvania

<u>2nd Brigade</u> 1,340
Brigadier General
Thomas F. Meagher
29th Massachusetts
63rd New York
69th New York
88th New York

<u>3rd Brigade</u> 1,336
Colonel John R.
Brooke
2nd Delaware
52nd New York
57th New York
66th New York
53rd Pennsylvania

<u>Artillery</u> 246
Battery B, 1st New York
Batteries A & C, 4th United States

2nd Division 5,681
Major General John Sedgwick

1st Brigade 1,691
Brigadier General
Willis A. Gorman
15th Massachusetts
1st Minnesota
34th New York
82nd New York
Massachusetts
Sharpshooters, 1st
Company
Minnesota
Sharpshooters, 2nd
Company

2nd Brigade 1,800
Brigadier General
Oliver O. Howard
69th Pennsylvania
71st Pennsylvania
72nd Pennsylvania
106th Pennsylvania

3rd Brigade 1,946
Brigadier General
Napoleon J. T. Dana
19th Massachusetts
20th Massachusetts
7th Michigan
42nd New York
59th New York

Artillery 244
Battery A, 1st Rhode Island
Battery I, 1st United States

3rd Division 5,740
Brigadier General William H. French

1st Brigade 1,751
Brigadier General
Nathan Kimball
14th Indiana
8th Ohio
132nd Pennsylvania
7th West Virginia

2nd Brigade 2,191
Colonel Dwight
Morris
14th Connecticut
108th New York
130th Pennsylvania

3rd Brigade 1,798
Brigadier General
Max Weber
1st Delaware
5th Maryland
4th New York

Unattached Artillery 369
Battery G, 1st New York
Battery B, 1st Rhode Island
Battery G, 1st Rhode Island

Fifth Army Corps 12,930[13]
Major General Fitz John Porter

1st Division
Major General George W. Morell

1st Brigade	2nd Brigade	3rd Brigade
Colonel James Barnes	Brigadier General Charles Griffin	Colonel Thomas B. W. Stockton
2nd Maine	2nd District of Columbia	20th Maine
18th Massachusetts	9th Massachusetts	16th Michigan
22nd Massachusetts	32nd Massachusetts	12th New York
1st Michigan	4th Michigan	17th New York
13th New York	14th New York	44th New York
25th New York	62nd Pennsylvania	83rd Pennsylvania
118th Pennsylvania		Michigan Sharpshooters, Brady's Company
Massachusetts Sharpshooters, 2nd Company		

Unassigned
1st United States Sharpshooters

Artillery
Battery C, Massachusetts Light
Battery C, 1st Rhode Island
Battery D, 5th United States

2nd Division
Brigadier General George Sykes

1st Brigade	2nd Brigade
Lt. Colonel Robert C. Buchanan	Major Charles S. Lovell
3rd United States	1st & 6th United States
4th United States	2nd & 10th United States
12th United States, 1st Battalion	11th United States
12th United States, 2nd Battalion	17th United States
14th United States, 1st Battalion	
14th United States, 2nd Battalion	

---

[13] *O.R.*, Series I, vol. 19, part I, p. 67.

3rd Brigade
Colonel Gouverneur K. Warren
5th New York
10th New York

Artillery
Batteries E & G, 1st United States
Battery I, 5th United States
Battery K, 5th United States

Artillery Reserve 950
Battery A, 1st Battalion New York
Battery B, 1st Battalion New York
Battery C, 1st Battalion New York
Battery D, 1st Battalion New York
5th New York Battery
Battery K, 1st United States
Battery G, 4th United States

Sixth Army Corps 12,300[14]
Major General William B. Franklin

1st Division
Major General Henry W. Slocum

1st Brigade	2nd Brigade	3rd Brigade
Colonel Alfred T. A. Torbert	Colonel Joseph J. Bartlett	Brigadier General John Newton
1st New Jersey	5th Maine	18th New York
2nd New Jersey	16th New York	31st New York
3rd New Jersey	27th New York	32nd New York
4th New Jersey	96th Pennsylvania	95th Pennsylvania

Artillery
Battery A, Maryland Light
Battery A, Massachusetts Light
Battery A, New Jersey Light
Battery D, 2nd United States

---

[14] *O.R.*, Series I, vol. 19, part I, p. 67.

2nd Division
Major General William F. Smith

<u>1st Brigade</u>
Brigadier General
Winfield S. Hancock
6th Maine
43rd New York
49th Pennsylvania
137th Pennsylvania
5th Wisconsin

<u>2nd Brigade</u>
Brigadier General
William T. H. Brooks
2nd Vermont
3rd Vermont
4th Vermont
5th Vermont
6th Vermont

<u>3rd Brigade</u> 1,684
Colonel William H.
Irwin
7th Maine
20th New York
33rd New York
49th New York
77th New York

<u>Artillery</u>
Battery B, Maryland Light
1st New York Light Battery
Battery F, 5th United States

Ninth Army Corps 12,765
Major General Ambrose E. Burnside
Brigadier General Jacob D. Cox

1st Division 3,248
Brigadier General Orlando B. Willcox

<u>1st Brigade</u> 1,395
Colonel Benjamin C.
Christ
28th Massachusetts
17th Michigan
79th New York
50th Pennsylvania

<u>2nd Brigade</u> 1,623
Colonel Thomas
Welsh
8th Michigan
46th New York
45th Pennsylvania
100th Pennsylvania

<u>Artillery</u> 246
8th Battery Massachusetts
Light
Battery E, 2nd United
States

2nd Division 3,254
Brigadier General Samuel D. Sturgis

<u>1st Brigade</u> 1,412
Brigadier General
James Nagle
2nd Maryland
6th New Hampshire
9th New Hampshire
48th Pennsylvania

<u>2nd Brigade</u> 1,601
Brigadier General
Edward Ferrero
21st Massachusetts
35th Massachusetts
51st New York
51st Pennsylvania

<u>Artillery</u> 241
Battery D, Pennsylvania
Light
Battery E, 4th United
States

3rd Division 2,914
Brigadier General Isaac P. Rodman

1st Brigade 943
Colonel Harrison S.
Fairchild
9th New York
89th New York
103rd New York
Co. K, 9th New York
Infantry (Battery)

2nd Brigade 1,848
Colonel Edward
Harland
8th Connecticut
11th Connecticut
16th Connecticut

4th Rhode Island

Artillery 123
Battery A, 5th United
States

Kanawha Division 3,154
Colonel Eliakim P. Scammon

1st Brigade 1,026
Colonel Hugh B. Ewing
12th Ohio
23rd Ohio
30th Ohio
Gilmore's Company West Virginia
Cavalry
Harrison's Company West Virginia
Cavalry
1st Battery Ohio Light Artillery

2nd Brigade 2,128
Colonel George Crook
11th Ohio
28th Ohio
36th Ohio
Schambeck's Company Chicago
Dragoons

Kentucky Light Artillery

Unattached
6th New York Cavalry
Ohio Cavalry, 3d Independent Co.

Unattached Artillery 195[15]
Batteries L & M 3rd United States
Battery L, 2nd New York

---

[15] Clemens, 582.

Twelfth Army Corps 7,631
Brigadier General Joseph K. Mansfield

1st Division 4,735
Brigadier General Alpheus S. Williams

<u>1st Brigade</u> 2,525
Brigadier General
Samuel W. Crawford
10th Maine
28th New York
46th Pennsylvania
124th Pennsylvania
125th Pennsylvania
128th Pennsylvania

<u>3rd Brigade</u> 2,210
Brigadier General George H.
Gordon
27th Indiana
2nd Massachusetts
13th New Jersey
107th New York
3rd Wisconsin

2nd Division 2,504
Brigadier General George S. Greene

<u>1st Brigade</u> 1,191
Lt. Colonel Hector
Tyndale
5th Ohio
7th Ohio
66th Ohio
28th Pennsylvania

<u>2nd Brigade</u> 536
Colonel Henry J.
Stainrook
3rd Maryland
102nd New York
111th Pennsylvania

<u>3rd Brigade</u> 777
Colonel William B.
Goodrich
3rd Delaware
Purnell Legion
60th New York
78th New York

<u>Artillery Battalion</u> 392
4th Maine Battery
6th Maine Battery
Battery M, 1st New York
10th New York Battery
Battery E, Pennsylvania Light
Battery F, Pennsylvania Light
Battery F, 4th United States

Cavalry Division 4,320
Brigadier General Alfred Pleasonton

1st Brigade
Major Charles J. Whiting
5th United States Cavalry
6th United States Cavalry

2nd Brigade
Colonel John F. Farnsworth
8th Illinois Cavalry
3rd Indiana Cavalry
1st Massachusetts Cavalry
8th Pennsylvania Cavalry

3rd Brigade
Colonel Richard H. Rush
4th Pennsylvania Cavalry
6th Pennsylvania Cavalry

4th Brigade
Colonel Andrew T. McReynolds
1st New York Cavalry
12th Pennsylvania Cavalry

5th Brigade
Colonel Benjamin F. Davis
8th New York Cavalry
3rd Pennsylvania Cavalry

Artillery Battalion
Battery A, 2nd United States
Batteries B & L, 2nd United States
Battery M, 2nd United States
Batteries C & G, 3rd United States

Army of Northern Virginia 37,351
General Robert E. Lee

Longstreet's Command 17,646
Major General James Longstreet

McLaw's Division 2,961
Major General Lafayette McLaws

Kershaw's Brigade 858	Barksdale's Brigade 858	Semmes' Brigade 709
Brigadier General	Brigadier General	Brigadier General
Joseph B. Kershaw	William Barksdale	Paul J. Semmes
2nd South Carolina	13th Mississippi	10th Georgia
3rd South Carolina	17th Mississippi	53rd Georgia
7th South Carolina	18th Mississippi	15th Virginia
8th South Carolina	21st Mississippi	32nd Virginia

Cobb's Brigade 398
Lt. Colonel Christopher C. Sanders
16th Georgia
24th Georgia
Cobb's Legion
15th North Carolina

Cabell's Battalion
Manly's North Carolina Battery
Pulaski Georgia Battery
Richmond Fayette Artillery
1st Richmond Howitzers
Troup Georgia Battery

Anderson's Division 4,000
Major General Richard H. Anderson

Wilcox's Brigade	Mahone's Brigade	Featherston's Brigade
Colonel Alfred Cumming	Colonel William A. Parham	Colonel Carnot Posey
8th Alabama	6th Virginia	12th Mississippi
9th Alabama	12th Virginia	16th Mississippi
10th Alabama	16th Virginia	19th Mississippi
11th Alabama	41st Virginia	2nd Mississippi Bn.

Armistead's Brigade	Pryor's Brigade	Wright's Brigade
Brigadier General Lewis A. Armistead	Brigadier General Roger A. Pryor	Brigadier General Ambrose R. Wright
9th Virginia	14th Alabama	44th Alabama
14th Virginia	2nd Florida	3rd Georgia
38th Virginia	5th Florida	22nd Georgia
53rd Virginia	8th Florida	48th Georgia
57th Virginia	3rd Virginia	

Saunders' Battalion
Donaldsonville Louisiana Battery
Norfolk Virginia Battery
Lynchburg Virginia Battery
Grimes's Virginia Battery

Jones' Division 1,540
Brigadier General David R. Jones

Garnett's Brigade 261	Jenkins' Brigade 755	Kemper's Brigade 443
Brigadier General Richard B. Garnett	Colonel Joseph Walker	Brigadier General James L. Kemper
8th Virginia	1st South Carolina	1st Virginia
18th Virginia	2nd South Carolina	7th Virginia
19th Virginia	5th South Carolina	11th Virginia
28th Virginia	6th South Carolina	17th Virginia
56th Virginia	4th South Carolina Bn.	24th Virginia
	Palmetto Sharpshooters	

Artillery 81
Wise Virginia Battery

237

Toomb's Division (temporary)* 1,852
Brigadier General Robert Toombs

Toombs' Brigade 638	Drayton's Brigade 465	Anderson's Brigade 749
Colonel Henry	Brigadier General	Brigadier General
L. Benning	Thomas F. Drayton	George T. Anderson
2nd Georgia	50th Georgia	1st Georgia Regulars
15th Georgia	51st Georgia	7th Georgia
17th Georgia	15th South Carolina	8th Georgia
20th Georgia	3rd South Carolina Bn.	9th Georgia
	Phillip's Legion	11th Georgia

*This temporary division, split from D. R. Jones', was created at the onset of the campaign at Leesburg, Virginia.

Walker's Division
Brigadier General John G. Walker

Walker's Brigade 2,279	Ransom's Brigade 1,715
Colonel Van H. Manning	Brigadier General Robert Ransom Jr.
3rd Arkansas	24th North Carolina
27th North Carolina	25th North Carolina
46th North Carolina	35th North Carolina
48th North Carolina	49th North Carolina
30th Virginia	Branch's Virginia Battery
French's Virginia Battery	

Hood's Division 2,304
Brigadier General John B. Hood

Hood's Brigade 854	Law's Brigade 1,146
Colonel William T. Wofford	Colonel Evander M. Law
18th Georgia	4th Alabama
Hampton Legion	2nd Mississippi
1st Texas	11th Mississippi
4th Texas	6th North Carolina
5th Texas	

Artillery Battalion 304
German South Carolina Battery
Palmetto South Carolina Battery
Rowan North Carolina Battery

Evans's Brigade 399
Brigadier General Nathan G. Evans*
Colonel Peter. F. Stevens
17th South Carolina
18th South Carolina
22nd South Carolina
23rd South Carolina
Holcombe Legion
Macbeth South Carolina Battery

*Believed he was a division commander and had Col. Stevens command the brigade.

Corps Artillery

Lee's Battalion 318
Ashland Virginia Battery
Bedford Virginia Battery
Brook's South Carolina Battery
Eubanks' Virginia Battery
Madison Louisiana Battery
Parker's Virginia Battery

Washington Artillery Bn. 278
1st Company
2nd Company
3rd Company
4th Company

Jackson's Command 14,584
Major General Thomas J. Jackson

Ewell's Division 4,127
Brigadier General Alexander R. Lawton

Lawton's Brigade 1,250
Colonel Marcellus
Douglass
13th Georgia
26th Georgia
31st Georgia
38th Georgia
60th Georgia
61st Georgia

Early's Brigade 1,331
Brigadier General
Jubal A. Early
13th Virginia
25th Virginia
31st Virginia
44th Virginia
49th Virginia
52nd Virginia
58th Virginia

Trimble's Brigade 761
Colonel James
A. Walker
15th Alabama
12th Georgia
21st Georgia
21st North Carolina

Hay's Brigade 598
Brigadier General Harry T. Hays
5th Louisiana
6th Louisiana
7th Louisiana
8th Louisiana
14th Louisiana

Artillery 223
Johnson's Virginia Battery
Louisiana Guard Artillery
First Maryland Battery
Staunton Virginia Battery

A. P. Hill's Light Division 2,568*
Major General Ambrose P. Hill

Branch's Brigade
Brigadier General
Lawrence O. Branch
7th North Carolina
18th North Carolina
28th North Carolina
33rd North Carolina
37th North Carolina

Gregg's Brigade
Brigadier General
Maxcy Gregg
1st South Carolina Prov. Army
1st South Carolina Rifles
12th South Carolina
13th South Carolina
14th South Carolina

Field's Brigade
Colonel John M.
Brockenbrough
40th Virginia
47th Virginia
55th Virginia
22nd Virginia Bn.

Archer's Brigade
Brigadier General James
J. Archer
5th Alabama Battalion
19th Georgia
1st Tennessee Provisional Army
7th Tennessee
14th Tennessee

Pender's Brigade
Brigadier General William
D. Pender
16th North Carolina
22nd North Carolina
34th North Carolina
38th North Carolina

Artillery Battalion 337
Crenshaw's Virginia Battery
Fredericksburg Virginia Battery
Pee Dee South Carolina Battery
Purcell Virginia Battery

*Does not include Field's or Pender's Brigades, as they were not actively engaged.

Jones' Division 2,094
Brigadier General John R. Jones

Stonewall Brigade 489
Colonel Andrew
J. Grigsby
4th Virginia
5th Virginia
27th Virginia
33rd Virginia

Taliaferro's Brigade 543
Colonel James
W. Jackson
47th Alabama
48th Alabama
23rd Virginia
37th Virginia

Jones' Brigade
Cpt. John E. Penn
21st Virginia
42nd Virginia
48th Virginia
1st Virginia Bn.

Starke's Brigade 706
Brigadier General
William E. Starke
1st Louisiana
2nd Louisiana
9th Louisiana
10th Louisiana
15th Louisiana
Coppens' Battalion

Andrew's Battalion 310
Alleghany Virginia Battery
Brockenbrough's Maryland Battery
Danville Virginia Battery
Lee Virginia Battery
Rockbridge Virginia Battery

D. H. Hill's Division 5,795
Major General Daniel H. Hill

Ripley's Brigade 1,349
Brigadier General
Roswell S. Ripley
4th Georgia
44th Georgia
1st North Carolina
3rd North Carolina

Garland's Brigade 756
Colonel Duncan
K. McRae
5th North Carolina
12th North Carolina
13th North Carolina
20th North Carolina
23rd North Carolina

Anderson's Brigade 1,174
Brigadier General
George B. Anderson
2nd North Carolina
4th North Carolina
14th North Carolina
30th North Carolina

Rodes' Brigade 850
Brigadier General Robert E. Rodes
3rd Alabama
5th Alabama
6th Alabama
12th Alabama
26th Alabama

Colquitt's Brigade 1,320
Colonel Alfred H. Colquitt
13th Alabama
6th Georgia
23rd Georgia
27th Georgia
28th Georgia

Artillery Battalion 346
Hardaway's Alabama Battery
Jefferson Davis Alabama Battery
Jones' Virginia Battery
King William Virginia Battery

Artillery Reserve 621
Brigadier General William N. Pendleton

Cutts's Artillery Battalion 319[16]
Blackshear's Georgia Battery
Irwin's Georgia Battery
Patterson's Georgia Battery
Ross' Georgia Battery

Jones' Artillery Battalion 302[17]
Morris Virginia Battery
Orange Virginia Battery
Turner's Virginia Battery
Wimbish's Virginia Battery

Miscellaneous Artillery
Cutshaw's Virginia Battery
Dixie Virginia Battery
Magruder Virginia Battery
Rice's Virginia Battery

Cavalry 4,500
Major General J .E. B. Stuart

Hampton's Brigade
Brigadier General Wade Hampton
1st North Carolina Cavalry
2nd South Carolina Cavalry
Cobb's Georgia Legion
Jeff Davis Legion

Robertson's Brigade
Colonel Thomas T. Munford
2nd Virginia Cavalry
7th Virginia Cavalry
12th Virginia Cavalry

Fitz-Hugh Lee's Brigade
Brigadier General Fitz-Hugh Lee
1st Virginia Cavalry
3rd Virginia Cavalry
4th Virginia Cavalry
5th Virginia Cavalry
9th Virginia Cavalry

Horse Artillery
Chew's Virginia Battery
Hart's South Carolina Battery
Pelham's Virginia Battery

---

[16] Clemens, 599.
[17] Ibid.

Bibliography

Armstrong Jr. Marion V. *Opposing the Second Corps at Antietam: The Fight for the Confederates Left & Center on America's Bloodiest Day*. Tuscaloosa: The University of Alabama Press, 2016.

Armstrong Jr. Marion V. *Unfurl Those Colors! McClellan, Sumner, & the Second Army Corps in the Antietam Campaign*. Tuscaloosa: The University of Alabama Press, 2008.

Brown, Edmund Randolph. *The Twenty-Seventh Indiana Volunteer Infantry in the War of the Rebellion, 1861 to 1865, First Division 12th and 20th Corps*. Monticello, 1899.

Bryant, Edwin E. *History of the Third Regiment of Wisconsin Veteran Volunteer Infantry 1861-1865*. Cleveland: The Arthur H. Clark Company, 1891.

Carman, Ezra A. *The Maryland Campaign of September 1862: Vol. II: Antietam*. Edited by Thomas G. Clemens. El Dorado Hills: Savas Beatie LLC, 2012.

Carman, Ezra A. and Emmor B. Cope. "Atlas of the Battlefield of Antietam, prepared under the direction of the Antietam Battlefield Board, Lieut. Col. Geo. W. Davis, U. S. A., president, Gen. E.A. Carman, U. S. V., Gen. H Heth, C. S. A. Surveyed by Lieut. Col. E. B. Cope, engineer, H. W. Mattern, assistant engineer, of the Gettysburg National Park. Drawn by Charles H. Ourand, 1899. Position of troops by Gen. E. A. Carman.

Published by authority of the Secretary of War, under the direction of the Chief of Engineers, U.S. Army, 1908.", 1904, Revised Edition 1908, Library of Congress.

Chapin, L. N. *A Brief History of the Thirty-Fourth Regiment N. Y. S. V. Embracing a Complete Roster of All Officers and Men and A Full Account of the Dedication of the Monument on the Battlefield of Antietam September 17, 1862 With Numerous Illustrations.* New York, 1903.

Crowell, Joseph E. *The Young Volunteer; The Everyday Experiences of a Soldier Boy in the Civil War.* Paterson: The Call, 1906.

Cunningham, D. and W. W. Miller. *Antietam: Report of the Ohio Antietam Battlefield Commission.* Springfield: Springfield Publishing Company, State Printer, 1904.

Dickert, Augustus D. *History of Kershaw's Brigade with Complete Roll of Companies, Biographical Sketches, Incidents, Anecdotes, etc.* Newberry: Elbert H. Aull Company, 1899.

Frassanito, William A. *Antietam: The Photographic Legacy of America's Bloodiest Day.* Gettysburg: Thomas Publications, 1978.

Gottfried, Bradley M. *The Maps of Antietam: An Atlas of the Antietam (Sharpsburg) Campaign, Including the Battle of South Mountain, September 2-20, 1862.* El Dorado Hills: Savas Beatie LLC, 2012.

Hinkley, Julian Wisner. *A Narrative of Service With the Third Wisconsin Infantry.* Democrat Printing Co., State Printer, 1912.

Hood, J. B. *Advance and Retreat: Personal Experiences in the United States and Confederate Armies.* Philadelphia: Burk & M'Fetridge, 1880.

Hyde, Thomas W. *Following the Greek Cross or, Memories of the Sixth Army Corps.* Cambridge: The Riverside Press, 1894.

Johnson, Curt and Richard C. Anderson Jr. *Artillery Hell: The Employment of Artillery at Antietam.* College Station: Texas A&M University Press, 1995.

Page, Charles, D. *History of the Fourteenth Regiment, Connecticut Vol. Infantry.* Meridan: The Boston Printing Co. 1906.

Pickerill, W. N. ed. *Indiana at Antietam: Report of the Indiana Antietam Monument Commission and Ceremonies at the Dedication of the Monument.* Indianapolis: The Aetna Press, 1911.

Pierro, Joseph, Ed. *The Maryland Campaign of September 1862: Ezra A. Carman's Definitive Study of the Union and Confederate Armies at Antietam.* New York: Taylor & Francis Group, LLC, 2008.

Quint, Alonzo H. *The Record of the Second Massachusetts Infantry, 1861-65.* Boston: James P. Walker, 1867.

Sid Meier's Antietam!. Firaxis Games, 1999.

United States, Army. *History of the One Hundredth and Twenty-Fifth Regiment Pennsylvania Volunteers 1862-1863.* Philadelphia: J. B. Lippincott Company, 1906.

U. S. War Department. *The War of the Rebellion: A Compilation of the Official Records of the Union and Confederate Armies.* 128 vols. Washington D. C.: Government Printing Office, 1880-1901.

Index

26, 28, 30, 34, 46, 48, 60, 70, 74, 80,
89, 90, 96, 134, 144, 165, 168, 170,
172, 184, 198, 208, 224
Duryée, Abram, 226
Early, Jubal A., 12, 14, 22, 40, 42, 68, 237
East Woods, 4, 8, 30, 32, 40, 54, 74, 76,
78, 92, 94, 96, 102, 165, 166, 168, 170,
172, 176, 184, 188, 194, 198, 202, 214,
222
Evans, Nathan G., 237
Ewing, Hugh B., 232
Fairchild, Harrison S., 232
Fairfax, J. W., 158
Farnsworth, John F., 234
Feltus, Abram A., 124
Ferrero, Edward, 231
Fowler, Henry, 118, 120
Frank, Paul, 142
Franklin, William B., 168, 190, 194, 230
French, William H., 6, 24, 92, 94, 96,
108, 192, 228
Gaillard, Franklin, 22
Garnett, Richard B., 235
Gibbon, John, 226
Gibson, J. C., 22
Gibson, William, 112, 140
Goodrich, William B., 233
Gordon, George H., 74, 78, 233
Gordon, John B., 90, 134
Gorman, Willis A., 26, 52, 228
Graham, William M., 160
Greene, Charles T., 176
Greene, George S., 166, 172, 174, 182,
233
Gregg, Maxcy, 238
Griffin, Charles, 229
Grigsby, Andrew J., 12, 68, 239
Grimes, Cary F., 110, 134
Hagerstown Turnpike, 1, 4, 8, 10, 12, 24,
30, 32, 34, 40, 42, 44, 46, 48, 52, 54,
60, 62, 64, 66, 68, 70, 72, 74, 80, 89,
90, 96, 106, 108, 110, 128, 132, 134,
136, 140, 142, 144, 146, 148, 156, 158,
160, 162, 165, 166, 170, 172, 176, 178,
180, 182, 186, 188, 206, 210, 216, 220,
222

Hall, Edward C., 180
Halltown, VA (WV), 16
Hampton, Wade, 206, 240
Hancock, Winfield S., 170, 212, 231
Harland, Edward, 232
Harper's Ferry Road, 178
Harper's Ferry, VA (WV), 16, 204, 206
Harris, Nathaniel S., 124
Hartsuff, George L., 226
Hately, John C., 124
Hauser Farm, 22, 36, 80, 178
Hauser Ridge, 30, 38, 60, 80, 212
Hays, Harry T., 238
Hazard, John A., 222
Herbert, Hilary A., 218
Hexamer, William, 198, 214, 220
Higgins, Jacob, 12
Hill, Ambrose P., 238
Hill, Daniel H., 90, 92, 112, 128, 130,
136, 146, 156, 158, 216, 239
Hinks, Edward W., 50
Hobson, E. L., 90
Hodges, James G., 178
Hoffman, H. C., 62
Hoffman, J. William, 226
Hofmann, J. William, 62
Hood, John B., 10, 14, 16, 20, 202, 236
Hood, William F., 225
Hooker, Joseph, 2, 8, 226
Hopkinson, Oliver, 98
Howard, Oliver O., 32, 46, 48, 52, 62,
64, 172, 228
Huger, Frank, 110
Hunt, Henry J., 160
Hyde, Thomas W., 214, 216, 218, 220
Irish, H. C., 74
Irwin, William H., 188, 192, 198, 214,
216, 218, 231
Jackson, James W., 239
Jackson, Thomas J., 12, 22, 70, 80, 180,
200, 202, 204, 208, 237
Johnston, Robert D., 90
Jones, David R., 235
Jones, Hilary P., 128
Jones, John R., 239
Jones, Robert H., 112

ABOUT THE AUTHORS

Ezra A. Carman was born in 1839 and served as colonel of the 13th New Jersey Infantry regiment from 1862 to 1864, moving on to brigade command during Sherman's March to the Sea. After the war, he served as chief clerk of the United States Department of Agriculture, historical expert for the Antietam National Battlefield, and Chairman of the Chickamauga-Chattanooga National Battlefield Commission. He passed away in 1909.

Brad Butkovich has a Bachelor of Arts degree in history from Georgia Southern University. He has published several books on the American Civil War including studies on the Battle of Pickett's Mill and Allatoona Pass. He has always had a keen interest in Civil War history, photography and cartography, all of which have come together in his current projects.

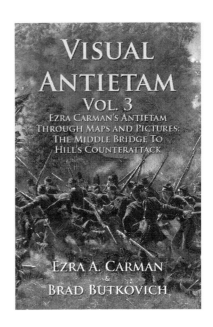

Available Now   4th Quarter 2019

Made in the USA
Columbia, SC
18 January 2022

54267735R00152